T0311729

Valuing the Environment

Six Case Studies

Edited by
Jean-Philippe Barde
and David W. Pearce

earthscan
from Routledge

First published by Earthscan in the UK and USA in 1991

For a full list of publications please contact:
Earthscan
2 Park Square, Milton Park, Abingdon, Oxon OX14 4RN
711 Third Avenue, New York, NY 10017

Earthscan is an imprint of the Taylor & Francis Group, an informa business

Copyright © Organisation for Economic
Co-operation and Development, 1991
Published by Taylor & Francis.

British Library Cataloguing in Publication Data
Valuing the Environment: six case studies
  1. Environment. Pollution. Control
  measures. Economic aspects
  I. Barde, Jean-Philippe   II. Pearce, D.W.
  (David William) 1941–   III. Organisation for
  Economic Cooperation and Development
  338.476285

ISBN 978-1-85383-074-7 (pbk)

Cover design by David King
Typeset by Selectmove, London

Contents

Werner Schulz   Scientific Adviser, German
Environmental Protection Agency,
Berlin, Germany

Kerry Turner   London Environmental Economics
Centre

Notes on the Contributors

Jean-Philippe Barde Principal Administrator, Environment Directorate, OECD, Paris, France

Maryann Froelich Division Director, Office of Policy Analysis, Environmental Protection Agency, Washington DC, USA

Nancy H. Hammet Principal, Industrial Economics Inc., Cambridge, Massachusetts, USA

Drusilla J.C. Hufford Division Chief, Office of Policy Analysis, Environmental Protection Agency, Washington DC, USA

Huib Jansen Institute for Environmental Studies, Free University of Amsterdam, The Netherlands

Onno Kuik Institute for Environmental Studies, Free University of Amsterdam, The Netherlands

Anil Markandya London Environmental Economics Centre

Ståle Navrud Researcher, Dept of Forest Economics, Agricultural University of Norway

Johannes Opschoor Professor, Director of Institute for Environmental Studies, Free University of Amsterdam, The Netherlands

Giorgio Panella Professor, Universities of Pavia and Bari, Italy

David Pearce London Environmental Economics Centre

Erika Schulz Researcher, German Institute of Economic Research, Berlin, Germany

Tables

Preface

As environmental policies are gaining more and more importance and sophistication, there is a growing need to base these policies on firm economic grounds. In particular, setting priorities and objectives requires, wihin a cost-benefit framework, a monetary assessment of the benefits expected from environmental protection measures. Over the past decade, significant progress has been achieved in the development of methodologies for the economic valuation of environmental damage and benefits. The Organisation for Economic Co-operation and Development (OECD) recently completed a survey of existing methodologies and data (David Pearce and Anil Markandya, *Environmental Policy Benefits: Monetary Valuation*, OECD, Paris, 1989) which showed, *inter alia*, that despite the existence of reliable methods, benefits assessments are rarely used in decision making.

This is why the OECD launched a study to identify and analyse the obstacles to a wider and more consistent use of benefit estimates in environmental decision making. Case studies in six OECD countries – the Federal Republic of Germany, Italy, The Netherlands, Norway, the United Kingdom and the United States – were carried out by independent experts making an in-depth analysis of the actual use and non-use of benefit estimates, and of the favourable factors and obstacles thereon. This book presents these six case studies. In order to put the issue in perspective, an introductory chapter has been added by the two editors.

Each chapter represents the opinion of its authors and does not necessarily reflect the views of the OECD.

We are indebted to Sue Pearce for editorial assistance.

J-P B
D W P

1 Introduction

Jean-Philippe Barde and David Pearce

The Problem of Valuation

In March 1990 the United Kingdom government announced that it had approved the construction of the remaining part of a major motorway in the south of England. The motorway, the M3, links London to the ports of Southampton and Portsmouth and to the popular holiday resorts of the south-west. The public inquiry into the motorway had, as with many motorway inquiries, been contentious. The decision to be made concerned the final "missing link" in the motorway. It was the last part to be considered, precisely because the joining up of the existing parts of the motorway threatened an area of great natural beauty. The only option which would minimize the environmental damage was to put the road through a tunnel. The inquiry reported that the tunnel would cost £92 million more than the other options. The government decided it was not worth it and accepted, clearly with some reluctance, the option of cutting the motorway through the area of aesthetic beauty.

In reaching their decision the UK government made no attempt to seek the monetary value of the environmental damage done. Had they, or anyone else, done so, one wonders if the conservation of an area of outstanding beauty would have been found to be worth more or less than £92 million. For this is the decision that was made: by accepting the non-tunnel option, the government had effectively said the view was *not* worth £92 million. This, presumably, was a judgement made on behalf of the people of Britain. The decision reveals some fundamental features of decision making:

(1) *Any* decision *implies* a monetary valuation. In this case, the implied valuation was that the area of great beauty was not worth £92 million. If it was worth more than £92 million, the tunnel option would have been chosen.

(2) The decision to go ahead with the non-tunnel option will, if it is finally implemented, result in an *irreversible* loss of environmental assets. Once destroyed, the area cannot, effectively anyway, be recreated. We can treat the £92 million as a "present value". Essentially, this means that the decision amounted to saying that the natural beauty of the area was not worth the equivalent of £92 million expressed as an annual value. Suppose it was possible to restore the area after 50 years, then the £92 million amounts to a value of around £7.5 million per annum (i.e. £7.5 million per annum for 50 years discounted back at 8 per cent is £92 million). The implied money valuation of the environment was therefore less than £7.5 million per annum.

(3) This implicit valuation was not made explicit. That is, the government was probably unaware that its decision implied this valuation.

(4) The valuation, implicit or otherwise, was made *without* consulting people about their valuations. Had they been asked, they might have said their values exceeded £92 million.

We shall probably never know what value the people affected by the motorway placed on the environmental damage that now seems destined to be done. Yet the techniques exist for deriving a valuation, albeit imperfectly and subject to great difficulties. The logical oddity is that it was not tried and because it was not tried we do not know whether the decision was a sound one or not in terms of economic efficiency. The example demonstrates the importance of valuation. In this case, the valuation would have been part of a *cost-benefit analysis* (CBA), comparing the costs and benefits of the motorway link-up. To add to the irony, the UK Department of Transport, responsible for building the road, *do* place money values on the time the motorway will save and on the changes in risk to life and limb arising from the motorway.

No one suggests CBA should dictate decisions. At best, it aids decision making precisely by showing up the kind of illogicality revealed by the M3 decision. Yet CBA is criticized vehemently in many quarters, not least by environmentalists who see it as placing a money value on something that cannot be valued. The logic of implied values escapes these critics.

Types of Values

What values would be relevant to a CBA? The basic rule for guiding decisions on developments such as road building is that the benefits of the development should exceed the costs. On its own this is an insufficient rule, since we really require that the net benefits from the development be higher than the net benefits obtained by any alternative use of the funds in question. But let us assume we face only a single choice, to develop or not to develop. The costs of development must be defined carefully. They consist of the resources needed for the development *and* the environmental damage done. That is, we require that

$$(Bd - Cd - NBc) > 0$$

where
Bd = money value of benefits of development (saved travel time, for example);
Cd = money value of resource costs of development (labour, land, machinery, etc.);
NBc = net benefits of conservation = Bc − Cc = benefits of conservation minus costs of conservation. The forgone benefits will include all recreational uses and other values obtained from conservation.

The NBc item is of interest since it is this which is the primary focus of this volume. We are interested in knowing about the value of conservation. The basic idea is to find the "total economic value" of the conservation (i.e. "non-development" option). *Total economic value* (TEV) is expressed as follows:
TEV = use values + indirect values + option value + existence value.

Use values arise from uses actually made of the conserved area: hill walking, rambling, picnicking, etc:

• Indirect value arises from the ecological functions that the conserved area might serve, e.g. drainage.
• Option value refers to the value that we might put on the area for future use, even though we make no use of it currently.
• Existence value refers to the value of the area in its conserved state to people who do not make use of the area, and do not expect to make use of it: they simply want it to exist. Existence

value figures prominently in decisions to donate to causes such as protecting endangered species or rainforests.

So, for the development – e.g. the motorway – to pass an economic efficiency test, we must have:

$$(Bd - Cd - TEV - Cc) > 0$$

Time complicates the decision-aid rule further. Typically, costs and benefits that are further into the future are regarded by people as having less importance than costs or benefits now. Future costs and benefits are *discounted*. To avoid complicating the equation we do not show the equation with discounting, but it is important to remember it is there.

The Rationality of Valuation

Finding the component parts of the previous inequality defines a rational economic approach to decision making. What is being measured is *people's values* in much the same way as we would ask people to vote for a political party or express their wants in the supermarket. The valuations are based on *willingness to pay* and willingness to pay depends on the existing income distribution. This distributional bias upsets some of the critics of CBA.

But, just as any decision implies a valuation, so any rule about decision making implies a distributional judgement. CBA is quite explicit in "weighting" votes by ability to pay, just as the market-place does. Alternative rules can be accommodated, e.g. by seeing what would happen if everyone had the same income, or some other specified distribution. Basically, it is a matter of selecting the value judgements underlying the valuation procedure. Distributional adjustments are not unusual in CBA, although they are typically not undertaken.

Just as we can vary the result by adopting a particular distributional judgement, so we can adopt entirely different rules for CBA. We might prefer a rule which espouses fairness between generations. If so, CBA results as typically presented will not be a guide to rationality, for the adoption of discount rates tends to militate against future generations. Simply put, decision-aid rules adopt particular sets of value judgements. It is open to anyone to vary the judgements and rework the analysis. One reason CBA remains a powerful rational tool of analysis, however, is that its critics have generally failed to offer any practicable alternative. This does not mean their concerns are illegitimate, simply that they are difficult to translate into practice.

CBA, then, is founded in economic rationality. This is important, hence CBA becomes important. It informs us, and its approach to ordering our thinking is valuable in a world where a great many decisions are made without considering the pros and cons at all.

Valuation Techniques

The reason for devoting time and resources to valuation problems is that they tend to occur in non-market situations. Peace and quiet and clean air are not bought and sold in the open market, not obviously so anyway. This means we need techniques for uncovering values in non-market situations. The techniques of valuation have advanced considerably in the last decade. The most widespread technique now in use is *contingent valuation* (CV). This gets round the non-market problem by creating an artificial market. Crudely put, CV amounts to asking people what they would be willing to pay for the conservation of an environmental asset, an improvement in air quality, and so on. Hypothetical questions can be expected to elicit hypothetical answers and various tests are made to gauge the extent of hypothetical bias. These include testing the answers against other valuation techniques, and experimenting with controlled samples in which some people's answers are elicited using real money. CV techniques have been very successful in uncovering total economic values, although there is a general view that it is not possible meaningfully to separate out the component parts of TEV.

Another widely used technique is *hedonic pricing*. Hedonic pricing can take place using the property market or the labour market. In the property-market case, what is being sought is the influence of environmental quality changes on the prices of houses. Suitably carried out, this approach can provide measures of willingness to pay for environmental quality. Labour-market studies are used to tease out the extent to which risky jobs attract wage premiums. The aim is to see how people value changes in the risk of injury or even death, producing the much misunderstood "values of life". Economists are not in fact interested in the value of life, whatever that may mean. They are interested in the valuation of changes in the risk of death or injury, which is not at all the same thing.

For recreational benefits it is frequently possible to adopt the *travel-cost method*, which simulates a market for the site by looking at what people pay in travel costs to get to it.

Finally, there is a massive area of research which looks to actual markets for values. Soil erosion, for example, can be valued by looking at the impact on the value of crop output; the carbon-fixing values of trees can be assessed by looking at the damage done by global warming from CO_2 emissions, or the cost of reducing those emissions by other means; air-pollution damage can be partially measured by looking at the impact of air pollution on human health and then assessing hospitalization costs, and so on.

The essential message is that valuation is *possible*. Because valuation takes place in the real world of people, it cannot ever expect to have the accuracy of traditional sciences, although much experimental work now takes place in laboratories with individuals as respondents in much the same way as psychological tests take place. Overall, however, the demand to make valuation procedures scientifically accurate rests on a fundamental misunderstanding about the nature of social science. It can never be like the physical sciences precisely because it deals with human behaviour.

Using Benefit Estimation

However interesting the techniques of valuation are, and however controversial, they are not the focus of this volume. Instead, we ask a different set of questions. We are interested in the *uses* currently made of benefit estimation and the extent to which it might be used in the future. The projection of use depends on assessing its acceptability and the obstacles to its wider use. To assess this we report the results of case studies from six countries: Germany, Italy, the Netherlands, Norway, the UK, and the USA. The results make interesting reading, for they suggest that benefit estimation is still used only on a limited scale in many countries but extensively in several, notably the USA and Germany. The obstacles to use range widely.

Three main categories of obstacles seem to prevail although to a different extent in each country:

(1) ethical and philosophical;

(2) political;
(3) methodological and technical.

Ethical and philosophical obstacles proceed from a conventional criticism of the welfare foundations of CBA. In particular, "monetary reductionism", illustrated by the willingness-to-pay criterion, is strongly rejected in "deep ecology" circles or by so-called "institutionalists" who claim that natural resources (air, water, fauna, flora, etc.), human life and health are not economic assets and thus cannot be measured in monetary terms. As a one-dimensional concept, based exclusively on individuals' preferences, the principle of maximizing expected utility is judged inadequate and too reductionist a basis on which to make decisions involving environmental assets, irreversibilities and future generations. Such radical opposition does not seem to prevail in decision-making circles, although some distrust is sometimes manifested against monetarizing human health and natural resources. It may be, however, that public opinion would manifest some reluctance to accept a decision based on purely economic criteria in the absence of appropriate explanation by the decision-making authority. Another criticism of the cost-benefit criterion is that it fails to take into consideration distributive implications, i.e. equity concerns, as noted above.

There are also *political obstacles* to the use of benefit estimates. Three types of obstacle can be identified. First, policy makers may face opposition due to the philosophical and ethical concerns mentioned above. Second, the very objective and virtue of benefit estimates is to make explicit policy objectives and decision criteria, e.g. what are the actual benefits of a given course of action? what are the best alternatives? what is the cost-benefit ratio? is the government making an efficient use of environmental resources and public money? Introducing a public debate on such issues is not really attractive to technocrats and decision makers and may significantly reduce their margin of action and decision autonomy. Therefore, there may be some reluctance to introduce benefit estimates in the political debate. Third, decision-making structures may be ill adapted to processes where cost benefit analysis comes into play.

Methodological and technical obstacles are significant although over-estimated. Economic valuation techniques are somewhat complex but also largely unknown to policy analysts, decision makers, environmental pressure groups or non-governmental organizations (NGOs). Such lack of awareness and competence is clearly seen as a major obstacle to a consistent use of benefit estimates. In fact, alleged complexity, cost or duration-of-benefit studies are not mentioned as a real issue in the following case studies. Notwithstanding the need to elaborate further the valuation techniques, both information and training constitute most useful courses of action to take in promoting the use of benefit estimation techniques. This action could take three forms.

First, the development of *practical guidelines* and manuals, i.e. generic guidelines on background principles and general methodologies for CBA and risk assessment, as well as specific guidelines applicable to individual sectors or categories of issues providing a detailed, stage by stage approach to evaluation.

Second, the creation of *databases* as a support to the evaluation techniques, e.g. data on dose-response relationships (exposure to pollution and related effects), information on other physical data, and compendia of existing empirical estimates of damage and benefits.

Third, the elaboration of *training mechanisms*. The development of guidelines is in itself an educational device. But it is also of the greatest importance to educate both those who will have to interpret benefit appraisals (decision makers and their teams) and those whose responsibility it will be to carry out benefit studies. It seems at present that only a limited number of specialized economists have the capacity to undertake benefit valuation studies; this is particularly true in European countries. In addition, practitioners should be trained to adapt their methodologies to the specific environmental issues at stake, to the needs of their clients and, last but not least, to present their results in a comprehensible form. The educational situation in the field of benefit evaluation techniques seems, by and large, rather inadequate and a substantial effort must be made to develop training mechanisms and structures, both at university level and within government agencies.

We have briefly discussed what seems to represent the main current issues in the use of benefit estimates in environmental decision making. Details are contained in the case studies which follow. If one believes that cost-benefit analysis is a useful, though not unique tool for making informed and rational decisions, it is important to go beyond theory and draw lessons from existing experience.

2 The Federal Republic of Germany

Werner Schulz and Erika Schulz

Introduction

In the Federal Republic of Germany, research dealing with the economic assessment (monetarization) of the benefits derived from an improvement and of the costs resulting from a deterioration of the environment has received an unexpectedly strong impetus in recent years. Very few of the experienced cost-benefit analysts had reckoned with this trend. It was the intention of the Federal Minister for the Environment, Nature Conservation and Nuclear Safety, with a commitment of funds of over DM 3 million, to have the economic value of the environment monetarized as far as was possible, by 1990 at the latest. The symposium "Costs of environmental pollution" marked the beginning of the entire research programme and defined its direction. In the foreword to the proceedings of the symposium, which were published by the Federal Environmental Agency in 1986, Walter Wallmann – then Federal Minister for the Environment – stated:

> In the past, much too often only the costs directly incurred by environmental protection measures were discussed. The question as to the benefits to be derived from environmental protection, however, is just as important. We already know today that early and consistent protection of the environment is of great benefit to our economy in the areas of health, vegetation, buildings, works of art and materials. Failure to protect the environment, on the other hand, is a costly mortgage on our future. . . . The research programme will. . .mould our future environmental policy and will help objectify environmental policy discussions.
>
> Umweltbundesamt (1986)

Against this background, the question inevitably arises as to how relevant the cost-benefit considerations actually are or may become in the decision making on environmental policy in the Federal Republic of Germany. This chapter attempts to answer this question within its four main sections. Besides giving an outline of the general importance of cost-benefit analyses (CBA) in science and practice and on their concrete use as a tool for decision making on environmentally relevant measures, the authors illustrate different fields of application on the basis of selected case studies and subsequently discuss various obstacles which often impede the selective use of cost-benefit considerations. On that basis, a number of recommendations for action are made in the final part of the chapter which are designed to help eliminate present deficiencies in applying cost-benefit analyses.

The Importance of Cost-benefit Analysis as a Tool for Decision Making on Environmental Policy: an Overview

Cost-benefit analysis: theory and practice

Cost-benefit analysis is probably the most widely known procedure for the analysis of economic efficiency in the public sector. Its historical development is characterized by two fundamental influences. On the one hand, CBA is an application of welfare theory. The benefit concept in its classical form was prepared by Dupuit (1844), founded by Marshall (1907), and completely rejected by the advocates of Paretian welfare economics. It was rehabilitated by Hicks (1941), and debased by Little (1965) as a "theoretical toy". On the other hand, CBA is the very prototype of an applied science. In the USA, it initially came into its own as early as the 1930s. The main objective at that time was to assess water-management projects according to a criterion for macroeconomic efficiency. Finally, in the 1950s, the first guidelines for its standardization were issued in the USA, in the Green Book, Circular A 47.

In the Federal Republic of Germany, the issue in the early 1960s was to catch up on the lead that the Anglo-Americans had already gained in science and application. Recktenwald deserves particular credit in this connection. In 1966, he presented his first contribution, entitled "Undividable goods – their efficiency and distribution – cost-benefit analyses", at the World Congress for Financial Science held in York. In a path-finding collection entitled "Cost-benefit analyses and programme budgeting" (1970), he published the ideas of various theoreticians, predominantly from the USA. This initiative made it possible for a wide range of readers from German-speaking countries to gain access to discussions of problems such as choosing the "right" discount rate, taking risks and uncertainties into account, and how to identify and make allowance for distributive effects. Later, experts such as Stohler (1967), Stolber (1968), Georgi (1970), Fest (1971), Kirsch and Rürup (1971), Eekhoff (1972), Schussmann (1973), Hesse (1975), Andel (1977), Arnold (1980), Hesse (1980), Hofmann (1981), Witte and Voigt (1985), Pommerehne (1987) and Hanusch (1988) prepared concise scientific papers on cost-benefit analysis.

The budget reform which went into effect on 1 January 1970 was a milestone in the sector of applied CBA. Article 7, para. 2 of the Federal Budgetary Regulations (Bundeshaushaltsordnung) and Article 6, para. 2 of the Act on Budgetary Principles (Haushalts-grundsätzegesetz) – both Articles were passed in 1969 – stipulate that economic efficency studies be performed for all public projects of major financial relevance. The first CBA performed on this basis examined the macro-economic advantageousness of the Rhine-Main-Danube Canal (ECE, 1970). This was followed by various CBAs, particularly in the traffic sector, for example on the construction of an underground tramway in Hanover (Hesse and Arnold, 1970) and in the sector of water management, such as on the construction of a canal connecting the Saarland with the inland waterways system (Intertraffic, 1971).

Particularly at the Federal and Länder (Federal States) level, efforts were made to harmonize the procedural requirements and we give several examples of these:

● Within the framework of preliminary administrative regulations (Vorl. VV-BHO) of 21 May 1973 implementing the Federal Budgetary Regulations, the Federal Ministry of Finance issued "Explanatory notes for the performance of cost-benefit analyses" ("Erläuterungen zur Durchführung von Nutzen-Kosten-Untersu-chungen")
● In the early 1970s, the Road and Transportation Research Association developed an assessment scheme for traffic infra-structure investments. The 1986 edition of the "Guidelines for

road construction, section: cost-benefit analyses" ("Richtlinie für die Anlage von Straßen (RAS), Teil: Wirtschaftlich-keitsunt-ersuchungen (RAS-W)") superseded the "Guidelines for comparative economic calculations for road construction" ("Richtlinien für wirtschaftliche Vergleichsrechnungen im Straßenwe-sen (RWS)"), including the "1972 supplement".

• In 1977, a "Guide to cost-benefit analyses" ("Leitfaden für Nutzen-Kosten-Untersuchungen") containing information concerning the implementation of Article 8 of the Federal Budgetary Regulations, and in 1983, a "Guide to cost determination and cost-benefit analysis" ("Leitfaden für Kostenermittlung und Wirts-chaftlichkeitsprüfung") was published by the Civil Service Office of the Hamburg Senate.

• Since the early 1970s, a working group of the Federal Ministry of Transport and the Federal Highway Research Institute has developed macro-economic decision-making aids for the traffic sector. In connection with the Federal Traffic Infrastructure Plans (Bundesverkehrswegepläne (BVWP)) of 1980 and 1985, the Federal Ministry of Transport has had guidelines for the use of macro-economic assessment procedures developed.

• With a view to the problems encountered in the implementation of the provisions on CBAs contained in the Budgetary Regulations, the highest water authorities of the Länder which collaborated in the Federal States' Working Party on Water decided, in 1974, to establish a working group on "Cost-benefit analyses in water management". In fulfilment of this mandate, three fundamental sets of guidelines were prepared: "Guidelines for the performance of cost-benefit analyses in water management" ("Leitlinien zur Durchführung von Kosten-Nutzen-Analysen in der Wasserwirtschaft") (1979); "Basic elements of cost-benefit analyses" ("Grundzüge der Nutzen-Kosten-Untersuchungen") (1981); and "Guidelines for the performance of comparative cost calculations" ("Leitlinien zur Durchführung von Kostenvergleichsrechnungen") (1986).

More than a hundred CBAs used for decision-making purposes have been published to date in the Federal Republic. A publication listing selected literature on the subject of "Cost-benefit analyses for the traffic sector" ("Nutzen-Kosten-Analyse im Verkehrsbereich"), published by IRB-Verlag, 1985, contains more than 120 publications for the period 1976–85 alone, most of which are focused on specific problems. Such cost-benefit considerations deal with subjects like local transportation techniques (bus, dial-a-bus, track-bound cabin systems, elevated trackbound systems), measures for traffic safety (passenger safety, rumble strips), urban development planning (residential streets), the construction of major airports and highways, and the closure of railroad lines.

A large number of CBAs have likewise been carried out in the sector of water management (Table 2.1). The questions dealt with here include, in particular, flood control; the creation of water organization bodies; the activation of water organization bodies for recreational uses; drinking and industrial water supply; irrigation; hydro-electricity; facilitating transport; and the production of wood through land reclamation measures.

Monetary benefit and costs estimates as bases for environmental policy decisions

Legislative mandate
In accordance with the economy-of-effort principle, Article 7, para. 1 of the Federal Budgetary Regulations provides that the most favourable ratio be sought between the purpose pursued and the means used for its attainment, when measures are planned at the Federal level. In particular, such an investigation considers the costs, including social costs, and the benefit involved (the impact on the Federal budget is considered separately here). The assessment procedures provided for in Article 7, para. 2 of the Federal Budgetary Regulations include CBAs that are more than just micro-economic techniques for decision making on investments, in that they also consider the social benefits and costs in monetary form. The assessment is based on actual, adjusted or assumed market prices. In the annotations to the sample procedure comprising 11 stages, the legislator gives various examples which explicitly make reference to environmental aspects. This means that environmental effects which play a role in a great many constructional and/or legislative measures must, in principle, be taken into account within the framework of CBAs.

The once touted notion that cost-benefit considerations can be incorporated into the budgetary process without any problems, and made into an effective instrument for use by the Minister of Finance to ward off any unreasonable demands of the various ministries, has proved erroneous in practice. Furthermore, the

Table 2.1:   **Cost-benefit analyses for water-management projects in the Federal Republic of Germany (1969–83)**

Year	Water Organization body	Author/Publisher
1969	Fanle Heide	Wilhelm
1979	Rhine-Main-Danube Canal	ECE
1971	Altmühl by-channel	Klaus
1971	Chamb/Furth i.w.	Bayerische Landessiendlung GmbH
1971	Püttlach	Klaus
1971	Saarland Canal	Intergraffic GmbH et al.
1971	Wondreb	Bayerische Landessiedlung GmbH
1972	Sieg	Battelle Institute
1973	Rhine-Main-Danube Canal	Klaus, Fehm and Lerch
1973	Vils	Highest building authority of Bavaria
1974	Aller-Leine-Oker	Billib
1974	Elbe-Lübeck Canal	Seidenfus
1974	Waldnaab Gumpen	Schmidtke
1974	Kehlheim Harbour	Intertraffic GmbH
1974	Kiel Canal connecting the North and Baltic seas	Planco Consulting GmbH
1975	Mangfall	Billib
1975	Mosel Canal	Faber and Schmid
1975	Ochtum dam	WWA Braake
1975	Upper Isar region	Highest building authority of Bavaria
1976	Dollart harbour	Planco Consulting GmbH
1977	Upper Schwarzach Valley	Bayerisches Landesamt fur Wasserwirtschaft
1977	Neckar	Dornier System GmbH et al.
1978	Abickhafe/Dose	Wordemann
1978	Western part of Middle Franconia	Rincke and Klaus
1979	Wiehl dam	Rincke Rudolph
1981	Main/Danube Canal	Planco Consulting GmbH

1982	Main-Danube Canal	Ifo-Insitut
1982	Lake Tegel	Ewers and Schulz
1983	Leine	Klaus, März, Pflügner
		and Schöttner

Source: Pflügner (1988, p. 19). For additional sources and detailed descriptions, see Klaus and Vauth (1977); Günther et al.(1981); Klaus et al. (1981); Ewers and Schulz (1982); Klaus et al. (1983).

obligation to carry out CBAs is confined to projects which are "of considerable financial importance". The legislation thus grants ample scope for interpretation as to the cases in which CBAs have to be performed. Although the budget law requires them to be undertaken, third parties are not entitled to demand that this obligation be acted upon. When an airport is built, for instance, local residents may not object on the grounds that the authorities failed to carry out a CBA which would have revealed a more suitable site. On the whole, it should be noted that Article 7 of the Federal Budgetary Regulations does provide the possibility of performing CBAs that are of relevance to environmental policy. The extent to which they are actually used, however, is narrowly limited.

The sector which comes closest to fulfilling the legislative mandate is transport. The stipulations of the Federal Traffic Infrastructure Plans, which the Federal Government has passed at five-year intervals since the early 1970s, are based on comprehensive projections as well as on project assessments made according to macro-economic, traffic, regional policy and ecological criteria. The macro-economic assessment is based on a CBA which takes account of factors such as changes in operating costs, travel time, occurrence of accidents, and environmental quality. The monetary assessment of environmental effects which is mainly carried out on the basis of a cost-of-damage-abatement approach (for details and criticism see Schulz, 1989) covers noise and exhaust-gas pollution, the separating effects of thoroughfares on pedestrians, and the deterioration of living conditions and communications (Table 2.2).

The "Guidelines for road construction: cost-benefit analyses" ("Richtlinien für die Anlage von Strassen: wirtschaftlichkeitsunter-suchungen (RAS-W)") which were presented in 1986, constitute a standardized procedure for the monetarization of road construction

Table 2.2: **Consideration of environmental effects within the framework of the macro-economic assessment of traffic infrastructure investments. (Monetary assessment methods for the Federal Traffic Infrastructure Plan of 1985)**

Environmental effects	*Quantification*	*Monetarization*
Noise pollution	Results from the extent to which target noise levels are exceeded in each case (measured as dB (a)), the number of affected residents and the degree to which they are impaired	Is based on the market prices for noise-absorbing windows
Pollution by exhaust-gas emissions	Results from the traffic density at which the maximum permissible exhaust-gas emission (parameter: carbon monoxide) is exceeded, depending on the location of the housing unit	Is based on the market prices for exhaust-gas reduction devices for motor vehicles
Separating effects of thoroughfares	Results from the time that pedestrians have to spend waiting or taking circuitous routes to cross the street, depending on the type of road and the traffic density per hour	Is based on a uniform cost-of-time rate of approx. DM 5 per person and hour
Impairment of living conditions and communications	Results from the traffic density on a specific stretch of road and the number of affected persons	Is based on willingness to pay, derived from differences in rent

Source: Authors' compilation according to Hogrebe et al. (1986)

projects. The RAS-W allow a decision to be made under rational economic aspects by systematically recording the effects of the project, including noise and harmful substances pollution (Frerich, Emde and Vosdellen, 1988). In a general circular ("Circular on road construction", no. 13/1986, of 9 April 1986) to the highest road construction authorities of the Länder, the Federal Minister of Transport announced this new "Guideline", recommending its use particularly for the assessment of measures whose effectiveness is confined to fairly small areas (such as inner-city areas). In this respect, the RAS-W offer some refinements in relation to the assessment procedure of the Federal Traffic Infrastructure Plan of 1985. The Federal Minister of Transport furthermore indicates in the circular that the use of electronic data processing is required in order to apply these Guidelines in a practicable manner: "I would welcome your applying the RAS-W within your area of competence. I request that you inform me in due course of the experiences you have gained in using these Guidelines. In my view, the application of the Guidelines is only feasible with the aid of computer processing systems. I will therefore make a user manual and programs available within reasonable time, should a need for this be indicated." Heusch and Boesefeld, consulting engineers for traffic engineering and data processing, developed such a program for use on personal computers (Heusch and Boesefeld, 1987); hence, an efficient program covering the entire scope of RAS-W is now available.

Political and scientific importance
Up to the late 1970s, knowledge of the monetary benefit of environmental protection had still been comparatively slight in the Federal Republic of Germany. Thus, in its environmental report of 1978, the Council of Environmental Advisors pointed out in connection with a fundamental synopsis of problems associated with the determination of the costs and benefits of environmental protection that, in distinct contrast to the costs of environmental protection measures, the "benefits of environmental protection to our economy. . .have hitherto not been sufficiently substantiated empirically" (Bundestag Printed Matter, no. 8/1938, text no. 1726). Against this background, the Federal Environmental Agency first commissioned ten "Pilot studies for the assessment of the benefit to be derived from measures designed to improve the environment" in order to determine the economic value of

Table 2.3: **Pilot studies on the assessment of the benefit to be derived from measures to improve the environment**

Year	Title of the pilot study	Author
1980	Economic costs caused by air pollutants	Heinz
1980	Quantification and economic assessment of the damage caused by air pollution	Abstein and Birr
1982	Minimization of environmental pollution caused by the pulp and paper industry, taking account of the micro- and macro-economic costs and revenues resulting therefrom	Schußler and Seyfried
1982	The monetary benefits of measures designed to improve water quality – illustrated by the example of Lake Tegel in Berlin	Ewers and Schulz
1982	Approaches to the monetary assessment of the benefit of alternative noise-reducing measures, including the benefit to be derived from their secondary effects, in inner-city areas	Koppen, Krasser and Glück
1982	Determination of economic and environmentally relevant effects of the construction of Federal trunk roads on structurally weak areas	Walter
1983	The benefit to be derived from replacing individual heating systems by district heating – illustrated by an example carried out in a polluted area	Winje and Jahn
1984	Macro-economic cost-benefit analyses on the application of alternatives for active and passive noise-abatement measures in the traffic sector throughout the Federal Republic	Willeke, Hansmeyer, Kentner, Schild and Vorholz
1985	Better air, what is it worth to us? An analysis of society's requirements based	Schulz

on individual willingness to pay

1986	On the monetary assessment of environmental damage. Methodological study taking forest damage as an example	Ewers, Brabänder, Brechtel, Both, Hayessen, Jahn, Möhring, Moog, Nohl and Richter

Source: Federal Environmental Agency

ecological measures in specific problem areas which are quite different in nature from each other (Table 2.3). These studies made it possible to demonstrate that the economic assessment of environmental impacts (of a positive as well as a negative kind) is in fact feasible. Environmental measures, as well as other infrastructural activities initiated by the public sector, are monetarily justifiable even when the underlying assumptions are not extreme.

Various parliamentary inquiries, scientific conferences and essays illustrate the political and scientific importance that economic assessments are credited with in the Federal Republic of Germany. For example:

• In 1985 and 1986, the Federal Government received major inquiries from the opposition parties represented in the German Bundestag (Lower House of Parliament), namely, from the Social Democratic Party (SPD) on the subject of "Economic losses caused by air pollution" (Bundestag Printed Matter, nos. 10/3432 and 10/6075) and from the Green Party on the subject of "Ecological and social consequential costs of the industrial society" (Bundestag Printed Matter, no. 10/5849–53). The latter, consisting of more than 40 pages, is probably the most comprehensive inquiry submitted to the Federal Government by the Greens in the tenth legislative period. Recently, the Greens submitted a Minor Inquiry to the Federal Government on the subject of "Research contracts and research results on ecological and social costs resulting from industrial activities" (Bundestag Printed Matter, no. 11/2389). In its reply (Bundestag Printed Matter, no. 11/2627), the Federal

Government listed more than 70 relevant research projects, concluded or ongoing, which were commissioned by various Federal Ministries. Funds amounting to DM 14 million have been spent on these projects to date.

• As early as 1981, a conference was held in Loccum to discuss the economic importance of environmental protection (Jarre, 1983). The participants dealt intensively with the advantages and disadvantages of monetary and non-monetary assessment procedures. To further improve knowledge in this sector and to create awareness of gaps in research, a symposium on the subject of "Costs of environmental pollution" took place at the Federal Ministry of the Interior in Bonn on 12 and 13 September 1985. This conference, at which scientists from home and abroad reported on the state of uncertainty as to the monetary costs of air and water pollution, noise and soil contamination and the psycho-social costs of environmental pollution, was at the same time the prelude to a three-year focus of research from which decisive progress towards comprehensive knowledge is to be expected (see the section on The German Federal Comprehensive Research Programme, p. 22 below). One year later, the Greens organized a scientific symposium on the same subject. In the foreword to the proceedings (Beckenbach and Schreyer, 1988), Joschka Fischer (then Environmental Minister of the Land of Hesse) stated: "It [the analysis of social costs] shows the obvious irrationality of our way of production and life. Beyond the pathos of mere indignation, this analysis expresses the inefficiency of current economic practice in its own language, namely, the language of money. Thus, the analysis of consequential costs might become a guiding concept for a green alternative in economic policy beyond the job-oriented policy of the Social Democrats and the supply-oriented policy of the Christian-Democratic/Liberal coalition. The concept itself, however, still requires thorough elaboration. Furthermore, awareness of this problem must increase among researchers, economic-statistics experts, administrators, and, last but not least, politicians."

• Since the early 1980s German environmental economists have increasingly dealt with questions associated with the economic assessment of changes in the environment. Schulz and Wicke (1987) prepared a study giving an overview of the state of research conducted in the Federal Republic of Germany which dealt with the estimation of the benefit of environmental policy measures on the basis of damage prevented. More recent work – not included in Schulz and Wicke's study – was conducted by Leipert (1987), Hautau et al. (1987) and Pflügner (1988).

In summary, it can be stated that CBAs are undeniably of relevance to environmental policy in the Federal Republic of Germany. Particularly in the traffic sector, environmental effects have been systematically taken into account in monetary terms – albeit only rudimentarily – in the decision-making process. In the following section, selected examples which have influenced environmental policy discussions in different ways, that is, have initiated political action, will be described in more detail.

Concrete Areas of Application with Environmental Policy Relevance

Recent environmental economics literature nearly always points out that CBA can be employed as a useful aid in environmental policy decision making. Most frequently mentioned are five basic arguments which lend support to the method of monetizing environmental protection benefits with respect to environmental damage (Schulz and Wicke, 1986, pp 61ff).

(1) *The clarity argument* Monetary cost estimates demonstrate unequivocally to the public eye the socio-political importance of environmental damage.

(2) *The objectification argument* Rational environmental policy requires a careful weighing of the advantages against the disadvantages of environmental protection. Those who advocate less environmental protection do so by heaping staggeringly high costs on to one side of the scale. On the other side, however, the champions of more environmental protection often have only verbal arguments at their disposal; these scarcely provide a good counterbalance to offset the burgeoning costs cited by opponents of increased environmental protection.

(3) *The dosage argument* Available funds for environmental protection should be applied (dosed) in such a way as to ensure that the greatest amount of surpluses (benefits minus costs) will be achieved. However, these surpluses can be calculated

only when the amount of the environmental damage costs avoided is known.

(4) *The internalizability argument* Insofar as an economically optimal internalization of external effects via environmental charges is desirable, then extensive information is required on the reported net amount in monetary terms of environmental damage caused.

(5) *Correcting the gross national product (GNP)* It is increasingly argued that the GNP, traditionally the measure of societal affluence and economic growth, should be supplemented with additional data. In keeping with this aim, an expanded system of national accounting is envisaged which would include environmental as well as human health damage. This kind of national accounting is only reliable however if, for instance, environmental damages can be measured in monetary terms.

The German Federal comprehensive research programme, "Costs of environmental pollution: benefits of environmental protection" addresses each of these five basic arguments with varying degrees of intensity. The aims of this comprehensive research programme are: (a) to make the real dimensions of environmental damage patently clear; (b) to put the all too often one-sided environmental debate on a more factual basis; (c) to direct scarce resources to those areas of the environment where they are most urgently needed; (d) to show polluters the true costs (to themselves) of their actions; (e) to further develop statistical measures of welfare.

In addition to a series of selected case examples, the following section will examine the "Costs of environmental pollution: benefits of environmental protection" programme in greater detail.

The German Federal Comprehensive Research Programme "Costs of environmental pollution: benefits of environmental protection"

In 1985, the German Federal Ministry of Environment initiated a comprehensive research programme through which a complete, scientifically reliable determination of environmental damage in the Federal Republic of Germany was to be achieved, covering as many areas and aspects as possible. In its most recent expert opinion on environmental matters (SRU, 1987, Tz. 227), the German Council of Environmental Experts stated: "The Council welcomes the Federal Government's intention to support research for the purpose of registering and estimating the economic value of the environment, with an appropriation of over DM 3 million."

To this end, the German Federal Office of Environment developed a closed research model based on modules. Using these modules as building blocks in various basic combinations, it was then possible to examine the monetary costs of environmental damage from a given perspective. For instance, environmental costs may be investigated from a media-specific standpoint (e.g. air, water, soil, noise); from an aggregate-specific standpoint (e.g. private households, industrial concerns, the state); from an area-of-commerce-specific standpoint (e.g. agriculture and forestry, the fishing industry, the tourist industry, the building trade, the water supply industry); or from a damage-specific standpoint (e.g. human health and material damage, damage to flora and fauna, or other non-material damages). The approach pursued here can be seen as a landmark for the Federal Republic.

A special characteristic of this research programme is that analysis of damage includes not only material, but also non-material impacts which are particularly important in the area of environmental research. This dimension, hitherto considered to contain primarily only intangibles, includes for instance the psycho-social costs of pollution and, in particular, those individual losses resulting from an impairment of the so-called non-user benefits (option value, legacy value and existence value).

The option value is the worth the citizen ascribes to the possibility of having a specific kind of environment available for his or her use in the future, even if in the present it is not known whether he or she would actually make use of this option. If the option becomes less certain as a result of pollution, then the option value necessarily falls. Consider for instance the many employed people who, for want of available time, are not able today to partake in the leisure and recreational benefits of some unique, irreplaceable nature protection area. For a specific price, these potential users would be willing to ensure their possible future use of such an area, independently of whether or not they would actually ever visit it.

In contrast to the option value, the legacy value is not directly related to the affected individual's own claim to a specific level of environmental quality; rather, it relates to the claim of future generations. The legacy value is the worth ascribed by those affected to the possibility that future generations will be able to enjoy the luxury of a relatively unspoiled environment. This means that *vis-à-vis* future generations, the responsible and environmentally aware citizen rates longterm environmental damage higher than does the citizen who ignores their needs.

Finally, the existence value is a value which derives solely from knowledge about the continued existence of environmental goods. It is often expressed in statements such as "Protect the environment for its own sake!" This value is taking on increasing importance for many environmentally aware citizens.

In accordance with the present problem structure, the most suitable methods are being or will be applied in ten research projects staffed by some 70 natural scientists, social scientists and economists, from which as many as 50 possible valuations may be obtained (see Research Projects A-J, Appendix, p. 50). The Council on Environmental Quality (CEQ) proposed four alternative indices which, within the framework of the German Federal research programme, are of central importance for empirical cost estimation. These are damage costs, avoidance costs, transaction costs and abatement costs. The first category refers to those damage costs which cannot be limited through specific measures to avert harmful effects. The other three categories refer to those damage avoidance costs which must be accepted in order to prevent even higher resultant costs occurring.

All valuations are based on a market analogue valuation calculus. Thus the following basic alternative statements of the problem are possible, from which information about the monetary costs of polluting the environment or, conversely, the benefits from protecting the environment can be gleaned. One can determine either what amount of money the affected individuals would be willing to pay to improve the environment or to prevent further decline in environmental quality (the willingness-to-pay analysis); or one can determine what amount of money should be paid to those affected in order that they be prepared to relinquish their claim to improved environmental quality, or that would make them willing to accept a deteriorating environment (analysis of the demand for compensation). Within the framework of the German Federal comprehensive research programme, both approaches will be investigated on the basis of several national representative surveys.

Five Case Studies

Case study: The Tegeler See

Among the best known German-language CBAs in the area of environment is a study by Ewers and Schulz (1982), commissioned by the German Federal Office of Environment. At that time, former Berlin Senator for Environment Hassemer was hoping that the results of this investigation would provide him with supportive argumentation to back his application for funding for environmental protection. This study systematized previously developed monetary valuations used to calculate the benefits from water-quality improvement measures, and assessed these measurements of benefit in terms of their validity and practicability. In addition, the study developed two new methods of monetary valuation for leisure and recreational benefits and, using the example of the clean-up of the Tegeler See (one of a chain of lakes running north–south in the westernmost part of West Berlin), demonstrated the usefulness and efficiency of monetary valuation methods in general.

The water-quality improvement measures included among other things a phosphate removal system, a deep-water aeration unit, and the diversion of polluted waste water from the lake area into the Teltow Canal. Experts familiar with the relationships in the water economy of the Tegeler See have predicted – with a high degree of certainty – that after a maximum transitional period of 15 years, without water protection measures, in the worst case and under normal weather conditions the lake would be without oxygen at least 60 days per year. This would result in the formation of foul gases, longer-lingering foul smells, and fish production declining to virtually nil. (With certainty, therefore, under extreme weather conditions this lake would approach an oxygen-free state.) On the other hand, if water-quality improvement and protection measures are instituted, the majority of experts say that the water quality of the Tegeler See would be at least sufficient to satisfactory for every type of water use.

Altogether the expenditures for the clean-up including operating costs were estimated to amount to DM 400–600 million, with the operating units assumed to have a life of 40 years. These calculations assumed multiple use of the Tegeler See. Not only does it serve as a drinking-water reservoir for Berlin, it is also one of the favourite nearby recreation spots. On the basis of expected cost savings to be derived from drinking-water production, the increased leisure and recreational value of the lake area expressed in higher turnovers enjoyed by local restaurants and boat-hire businesses, the proceeds from commercial fishing and, finally, the assessed value of local residential property upon which rents are based, Ewers and Schulz calculated accrued benefits substantially greater than the amount of initial investment. Even a cautious estimate yielded a yearly net benefit of DM 29 million. Of this, DM 21 million could be attributed to the increased leisure and recreational value of the lake and surrounding area, while over DM 4 million is the direct result of cost savings from drinking-water production. However, surplus benefits in such high amounts can be anticipated only after a transitional period of 15 years.

This study, reporting a ratio of benefits to costs varying between about 1.7 to over 2.9, shows that on the level of individual projects, monetary valuation methods incorporate, for practical purposes, nearly all the benefits of water-quality improvement measures, with sufficient validity. Not included in the monetary calculus were the goals of biotope and species preservation, the dangers of exceeding global environmental thresholds and the problems associated with longterm effects of harmful substances emitted into the atmosphere, in water, or deposited in soil. According to Ewers and Schulz, in order to take these goals and problems adequately into account when deciding on individual water-quality improvement projects, a centrally regulated set of binding minimal and maximal requirements is necessary.

Case study: Cleaner air, what is it worth to us?

Up to the mid-1980s, willingness-to-pay surveys belonged to an area of research that had been sorely neglected and was for the most part under-developed. In order to narrow this gap, Schulz (1985a) commissioned by the German Federal Office of Environment, carried out an investigation on the subject of "Cleaner air, what is it worth to us?" This research work, reported nationwide in all the German media and translated into English for the Organization for Economic Co-operation and Development (OECD, 1987), was an attempt to demonstrate the efficiency of willingness-to-pay surveys even for such complex problems as air pollution.

To this end, Schulz polled 4,500 Berliners, using a written questionnaire to determine what they would be willing to pay for each of four kinds of air quality: Berlin air (where air quality may warrant a smog alarm); big city air (where air quality does not warrant a smog alarm); small town air; and vacation spot or holiday resort air. These are not scientifically defined categories of air quality; rather, they represent a distributional classification which is tied to the respondents' understanding and level of knowledge. For smoggy air, a willingness to pay of zero was assumed.

In order to be able to control the influence of the amount given over the respondents' actual willingness to pay (respondents were asked only to check off a value they thought appropriate for each of the four categories of air quality), two scale tests were carried out in which the indicated amounts in the main survey were halved and doubled respectively. Whereas doubling the scale yielded a 40 per cent greater willingness to pay, halving the scale left willingness to pay unchanged. Therefore the willingness-to-pay values used in the main survey did not result in any over-estimation of the respondents' actual willingness to pay.

In evaluating Berlin air, citizens were also asked how much in DM per month the prevention of even worse smog-filled air was worth to them. In addition, the target group was asked, on the basis of Berlin air quality, to rate three degrees of improvement:

(1) to the standard of big city air quality;
(2) to the standard of small town air quality;
(3) to the standard of vacation spot or holiday resort air quality.

Thus, with the aid of the survey results, it is not only possible to determine the general value of improved Berlin air quality, but also the value of Berlin air quality improved, for example, to the standard of big city or small town air quality.

These surveys also showed that the respondents' level of information or knowledge about the extent and consequences of air pollution was relatively low. Only one in three respondents were able to answer correctly both questions relating to specific harmful substances. In contrast to the averagely informed citizen, the better informed citizen demonstrated an approximately 70 per cent greater willingness to pay for improved air quality. Since, on the one hand, the level of information is critically important for willingness to pay and, on the other hand, the information deficit of the population is substantial, willingness to pay was therefore corrected upwards to take into account an improved level of knowledge of the population (Table 2.4).

The Berlin survey results were extrapolated onto the whole Federal Republic, using the average predominant West German air quality and average West German age. The investigation showed that willingness to pay for improved air was not only dependent upon the predominating air quality, but also to a very high degree upon the respondents. That is, with increasing age, the willingness to pay declined rapidly. On average, the willingness of an 18-year old to pay for vacation spot/holiday resort air quality was three times as high as that of a 75-year old.

The results from the Schulz investigation suggest that present German Federal clean air policy is not sufficient to meet public demand. The willingness to pay for an improvement from the status quo to the level of small town air quality is actually much higher than the minimal cost of such an improvement. Nevertheless, the argument that "as a rule there is a gap between hypothetical willingness to pay and a respondent's actual willingness to pay" is frequently invoked to dispute this claim. If the survey respondents

Table 2.4: **The monetary value of improved air quality from the viewpoint of the affected population (in billion DM per year)**

	Estimate of the benefit for nationwide air quality improved to the standard of small town air quality	*Estimate of the benefit for nationwide air quality improved to the standard of vacation spot/resort air quality*
Willingness to pay upwards for information deficit	DM 28 billion per annum	DM 48 billion per annum
Willingness to pay not corrected for information deficit	DM 14 billion per annum	DM 30 billion per annum

Source: Schulz, 1985b, p. 265ff

were subsequently asked to actually make a monetary contribution towards measures for cleaning up the air, some individuals would undoubtedly not be willing to give anything and, as a rule, most would probably actually contribute far less than they had indicated.

Nevertheless this argument, which in fact implies no more than that "free-rider" behaviour exists, does not provide sufficient proof that the willingness-to-pay amounts indicated in the study do not really reflect the true values held by the respondents. In other words, the survey instrument was not used in the study to determine the lucrativeness of fund-raising drives for environmental protection; rather, it was designed to determine the respondents' true preferences. To this end, the respondents were placed in a private buyer's market situation whereby it was up to each individual to determine the extent to which the air would be kept clean on the basis of monthly payments. Thus there was no longer any incentive for the respondents to exaggerate their true values as a strategic ploy. Another strong indication that respondents did not exaggerate is to be found in the fact that of the ten possible amounts a respondent could select, the lower values were largely chosen. This observation is inconsistent with the logic of the "free-rider" hypothesis because every individual whose intention it was to exaggerate (assuming that he or she is behaving rationally) would, in accordance with that goal, be much more inclined to fix attention on the higher values rather than on the lower ones.

Case study: The social costs of automobile traffic

Recently, a number of scientists have attempted for the first time to give rough overall estimates of the social costs of automobile traffic, an endeavour which has met with wide public response (Schulz, 1988a). These cost estimates suggest that automobile traffic in the Federal Republic is responsible for damages each year that go into at least the tens of billions. This figure signifies a substantial misallocation of economic resources and presents the politicians with a direct challenge to confront this issue.

Wicke, Scientific Director at the German Federal Office of Environment and Chairman of the Committee of Experts on "Urban Development and Environmental Protection" believes that the external social costs of automobile traffic total at least DM 50 billion each year. He sums it up thus: "Whether. . .this much higher

Table 2.5:   **Estimated yearly private and social costs of automobile traffic and local public transportation in Berlin (in million DM for 1985)**

Types of costs	Private cars	Local public Transpor- tation
Streets and bridges (maintenance, rebuilding, new construction, operation administration)	340	14
Parking garages (maintenance and operation)	80	–
Private car maintenance costs (excluding automobile tax)	1810	–
Private car operating costs (excluding mineral oil tax)	520	–
Traffic accident follow-up costs (excluding automobile insurance)	280	4
Costs for air pollution	280	11
Costs for traffic noise	550	25
Utilization of land for streets, paths, squares	410	18
Utilization of land for rail traffic	–	40
Utilization of land for parking places on private lots	80	–
Operating costs of the Berlin Transportation Company (BVG)	–	1486
Increased operating costs of the BVG from traffic obstructions	120	–120
Total (in mill. DM)	4470	1478
Costs per person kilometre	0.64 DM	0.38 DM

Source: Apel, 1988, p. 31

figure would be surpassed by the social surplus generated from automobile traffic and thus, upon comparison of social benefits to social costs, yield a positive balance sheet is a matter that I seriously doubt!" (Wicke, 1987, p. 7).

Apel, a member of the German Institute for Urban Studies estimated the private and social costs associated with automobile traffic (private cars) in Berlin and contrasted these with the respective costs of local public transportation (fiscal year 1985) (Table 2.5). According to these estimates, private automobile traffic in Berlin at a cost of more than DM 6 billion per annum is not only extremely expensive, it is also in a figurative sense "subsidized" by the State and the general public, who bear the external costs at the exceedingly high rate of DM 2.4 billion per annum – a rate higher than that allocated to local public transportation. If social costs are based upon transportation efficiency, then private automobile transportation will result in higher costs per person-kilometre than local public transportation.

On the basis of further calculations, Apel draws the following conclusion: "If the social costs of providing local public transportation have to be borne in full by the public transportation companies, which is in keeping with the principles of the market economy, and if this same principle were applied to private automobile transportation, for example, through a mark-up in the mineral oil tax, then the present tax rate would have to be increased nearly fivefold. The price of petrol would climb to more than DM 3 per litre. It is obvious that such 'adjusted' market conditions would bring about another form of transportation use. Among other things it would also raise substantially the level of cost coverage for local public transportation through better use of the available modes of transportation" (Apel, 1988, p. 34).

On the basis of their suggestions for ecological tax reform, Teufel et al. (1988) from the Institute for Environment and Prognosis in Heidelberg created a balance sheet of expenses for motor vehicle traffic. They contrast the monetizable costs of motor vehicle traffic of around DM 109 to 117 billion (fiscal year 1986) with revenues received by the state from motor vehicle traffic amounting to about DM 31 billion. According to their calculations, the yearly deficit would be equivalent to an increase in the mineral oil tax of at least DM 1.90 per litre. Based on estimated price elasticities, Teufel et al. calculate additional yearly tax revenues from the petrol tax of DM 49 billion and from the diesel tax of around

DM 21 billion. Therefore, as a result of the tax increase, they hypothesize a simultaneous yearly decline in petrol consumption of almost 8 billion litres and a decline in diesel consumption of nearly 4 billion litres (Teufel et al., 1988, p. 33).

Within the framework of road transportation of freight and related social cost accounting, Teufel (1989, p. 54) assumes costs for trucking in 1987 amounting to between DM 34.5 and 62.5 billion, as compared to revenues received by the state from trucking in that year amounting to between DM 6.7 and 7.4 billion. This results in a social deficit from trucking of DM 27.1 to 55.8 billion per year. In other words, according to Teufel every German citizen subsidizes trucking by some DM 500 to 1000 per annum.

Case Study: follow-up costs of economic processes

In 1987, Leipert, who participated in the Green faction's inquiry into the "Ecological and social follow-up costs of the industrial society in the Federal Republic of Germany" ("Ökologische und soziale Folgekosten der Industriegesellschaft in der Bundesrepublik Deutschland"), reported the empirical results of a research project "Environmental damage, defensive expenditure and net welfare measurement" ("Umweltschäden, defensive Ausgaben und Nettowohlfahrtmessung"). The starting point of his work, which sparked off a nationwide debate in political and scientific circles, was the recognition that the traditional way of calculating the national product distorted the economic performance measurement by a factor of two, resulting in cumulative distortion of the national product itself. According to Leipert (1987, p. 1) traditional national product calculation "not only 'supresses' the true costs of production and consumption (costs for harmful use of the environment), but also registers the follow-up costs of economic processes resulting from the negative environmental impacts of production as positive returns of trade and industry. Follow-up costs from the growth process feed the rate of growth of the gross national product." The author determined that the share of defensive or compensatory expenditures in the GNP increased from 5 per cent to at least 10 per cent between 1970 and 1985 (Table 2.6). Leipert anticipates that defensive expenditures will also climb more rapidly than the GNP in the future. Over the next 10 to 15 years a rapid rate of growth is pre-programmed, especially for pollution-related follow-up costs.

Table 2.6: **Estimated defensive expenditures in the Federal Republic of Germany (1970–85)**

Area of Defensive Expenditure	Amounts in billion DM based on 1980 prices				
	1970	1975	1980	1983	1985
Environment (total)					
* Investments and running costs					
(a) in the producing sector	3.00	7.05	7.81	9.36	
(b) in the state sector		9.60	12.75	10.29	
(c) total		16.65	20.56	19.65	20.00
* Follow-up costs of environmental damage			9.38	10.67	12.54
Traffic[1]	30.80	34.50	44.90	47.70	52.30
Housing[2]	5.45	7.50	10.14	11.10	11.57
Internal security[3]	3.91	8.58	14.92	17.69	19.80
Health[4]	19.50	31.80	37.30	38.70	40.70
Jobs[5]	0.90	0.60	0.70	0.70	0.70
Total	63.60	99.40	137.90	144.90	157.90
GNP (based on market prices)	1134.00	1258.00	1485.20	1497.80	1580.80

Source: Leipert, 1987, p. 144
Notes: 1 Follow-up costs from traffic accidents, defensive expenditures for roadways
2 additional compensatory charges on private households from expenditures for developed land, defensive rent outlays
3 defensive state expenditures for fighting crime, damage outlays of the insurer for break-ins and theft, plant security
4 defensive health expenditures
5 physical damage costs from occupational accidents (in a narrow sense)

There is no question that Leipert's calculations have political relevance. They can uncover ecological, technical, social and regional maldevelopments in an economy. The on-going discussion of this issue, already drawn out over a number of years, has led to the German Federal Office of Statistics attempting to supplement the national accounting system with an "Environment satellite system" ("Umwelt-Satellitensystem") (see especially, Stamer, 1988). Part of this set of figures will be concerned with observed past defensive expenditures resulting from environmental pollution.

Case Study: The ecological damage balance sheet

Wicke (1986) attempted for the first time to develop a systematic estimate of all environmental damage in the Federal Republic of Germany. His investigation dealt with a kind of interim balance sheet based on the present state of technology in the monetizing of environmental damage. On the basis of air pollution, water pollution, soil contamination and noise, Wicke determined that the levels of environmental pollution at that time accounted for damages amounting to some DM 103.5 billion per annum (Table 2.7).

Wicke's estimates have been used frequently in other investigations with a different problem formulation. This was done very recently in a study of the social costs of alternative energy sources (Hohmeyer, 1989). Nevertheless, a general assessment of these calculations is that they are still relatively rough (see SRU, 1987, Tz. 234). It cannot be claimed that the values of the data Wicke has established correspond exactly to some natural scientific measurement or valuation. This applies particularly to the assumption that through an improvement or worsening of environmental conditions, the output prices remain unimpaired (partial analysis approach). Even if we treat the costs of air and water pollution, soil contamination and noise as just a single entity, we are still confronted with the problem of the total approach. On this comparative-static analysis, basically two worlds are compared: one in which there is pollution and one in which there is not. But the relative prices of all other goods do not remain untouched.

Up to now, for all practical purposes no one has succeeded in incorporating all the possible social interdependencies resulting from some public measure into one all-encompassing model and then empirically evaluating that model. The damage costs Wicke

Table 2.7: **The environmental damage balance-sheet for the Federal Republic of Germany**

Damage category	Damage costs (in billion DM per year)
Air pollution	about DM 48 billion
Human health damage	greater than 2.3 – 5.8
Material damage	greater than 2.3
Damage to fauna	greater than 0.1
Damage to flora	greater than 1.0
Forest damage	greater than 5.5 – 8.8
Water pollution	much greater than DM 17.6 billion
Loss of earnings from fishing	greater than 0.25
Cost of drinking-water supply	much greater than 9.0
Decline in leisure and recreational value	greater than 7.0
Loss of aesthetic appeal/value	greater than 1.0
Other "calculable" damages (e.g. injury to water birds, oil spills from tankers)	greater than 0.35
Soil contamination	much greater than DM 5.2 billion
Chernobyl and "Chernobyl avoidance costs"	greater than 2.4
Waste disposal	greater than 1.7
Biotope and species preservation costs	greater than 1.0
Other types of soil contamination ("pro memoria" figures)	much greater than 0.1
Noise	greater than 32.7 billion
Decline in productivity	greater than 3.0
Noise compensation	greater than 0.4
Decline in value of residences	greater than 29.3
Total "calculable" damages	much greater than DM 103.5 billion

Source: A. Wicke (1986, p. 123)

has determined can only reflect a bottom line of all actual environmental damages because, of all the possible values one could assign, he has opted for the lower ones, that is, he has used the most conservative estimates. Furthermore, a whole set of intangible cost dimensions were not evaluated and hence could not be included in the damage balance sheet. The damages calculated amount to over 6 per cent of the 1985 GNP. Thus, the often cited OECD estimate from the 1970s – from which it was determined that environmental damage in the industrialized countries amounted to around 3 to 5 per cent of the GNPs – does not, at least for the Federal Republic, even reflect the lowest possible level of environmental damage.

The importance of this ecological damage balance sheet for the environmental debate and environmental policy was commented on by the author himself (Wicke, 1988, p. 1): "There is no doubt that the 'ecological billions'. . .have had an impact and indeed a strong one not only 'in the minds of the people' and on the environmental debate, but also to varying degrees on concrete environmental policy. . . . Moreover, the importance of environmental damage calculations as well as suggestions for market-oriented improvements to environmental policy are indeed not to be under-estimated in the coming years."

Obstacles to the Use of Cost-benefit Analysis

Our overview of the extent to which CBAs are used in the environmental sector and the more in-depth description of selected case studies have shown that, in the Federal Republic of Germany, CBAs can undeniably be rated as 'decision-making aids for environment-related measures' in individual cases. However, it is also true that their systematic application has been confined to a few sectors, such as traffic, and that even in these sectors they have only been used fragmentarily. This deficiency is, in particular, attributable to the following causes, which will be discussed in more detail in the subsequent sections:

● Environment-related cost-benefit estimates can be very time consuming and are often associated with high costs.
● A multitude of methodological difficulties can considerably limit the degree of accuracy of CBAs and thus their relevance as a tool for decision making on environmental policy.
● CBAs may lead to policy makers having to reveal their own "genuine" concept of values, although – especially with respect to the battle for votes – they are reluctant to do so.
● CBAs do not necessarily provide policy makers with the decision-making aids they are looking for.
● Thinking in terms of macro-economic costs is still very rare in administrative practice.
● CBAs occasionally founder due to a lack of capability or willingness to collaborate in an interdisciplinary manner.
● Some find a monetarization of environmental aspects unacceptable on moral grounds.

Time, costs and methodological causes

Cost-benefit analyses are very time consuming. They usually take at least one to two years to prepare, and quite often even up to five years to complete. It is self-evident that such long time lapses are of little value in the planning process. The amount of time and perseverance needed to conduct CBAs in the environmental sector is often under-estimated. Frequently, data are generated at great expense but partly lack the necessary relevance to the problems at hand. Planning-information systems often are an end in themselves and are not consulted during the actual planning and decision-making process. Many times, studies are too broad in scope, and the time allowed for the entire study is often only just enough to take stock of the situation at hand.

Environment related CBAs are expensive since they require, in principle, an interdisciplinary team of scientists. In the most simple case, an economist would deal with questions pertaining to the economic evaluation and a natural scientist would look into the environmental effects of the project. Allowing an average period of two years to perform the analysis, its costs would thus be at least DM 300,000. As already mentioned earlier, the Federal Government alone has spent at least DM 14 million to date for research on the determination of social costs. Added to that amount, there is the expenditure that the Federal Government has incurred in connection with the required budgetary and scientific supervision of the projects. Besides costs and time, there are the mainly methodological problems which most often impede the systematic application of CBAs in the environmental sector. It will not be possible here to address all methodological problems that may arise when environmental changes are monetarized (such as choosing a suitable discount rate, the determination of shadow prices, the assessment of risks and making allowance for uncertainties). Therefore, only the central problems of three important monetarization methods will be dealt with:

(1) the cost-of-damage approach;
(2) the cost-of-damage-abatement approach;
(3) the willingness-to-pay survey.

Methodological problems arising from the cost-of-damage approach

The derivation of damage functions is of crucial importance when empirical studies for the monetary evaluation of environmental aspects are conducted. One of the main problems of the cost-of-damage approach lies in the fact that a causal relationship between different environmental situations and the occurrence of damage is extremely difficult to prove. The problems inherent in this approach can be illustrated using the example of forest damage. In order to ascertain the economic value of measures designed to improve air quality, one would first have to quantify the complex chain of effects, starting with the reduction in emissions, via the distribution of pollutants, all the way to their effects on trees and the possible resulting changes in forest functions (as a recreational area, as a protected area, as a wood producer, etc.). Given the current state of knowledge of the relationship between these effects, such an analysis is extremely difficult to perform.

Compared with this problem, the economic assessment, that is, the transformation of physical damage functions into monetary ones, is a less demanding task. Where market prices are available (e.g. the price per solid cubic metre of different types of timber) and damage can be quantified (e.g. the loss of solid cubic metres for the types of timber concerned), the costs of damage can be ascertained by multiplying volume with prices. In many cases, however, the usual assessment on the basis of market prices is impossible to perform for environmental goods. A market for environmental services does not arise, because they possess the characteristics of collective goods and cannot be subjected to the exclusion principle of the market mechanism. In other words, since the beneficiaries of measures to improve the environment cannot be made to pay for an improved environment, no private entrepreneur will be prepared to produce the commodity of "a better environment". In such cases, economic analysts are forced to avail themselves of market-price surrogates.

Methodological problems arising from the cost-of-damage-abatement approach

With a view to the measuring of problems associated with the cost-of-damage approach, alternative measures are used to evaluate environmental aspects. These include the abatement costs and the transaction costs. All expenditures incurred to reduce existing pollution levels fall under these cost categories. In distinct contrast to the cost-of-damage approach, the cost-of-damage-abatement approach does not identify the benefits of an improvement in terms of costs saved, but as the expenditure which is accepted for protection of the environment. In other words, if people are willing to pay the necessary project costs for a reduction of pollution, then the environmental improvement achieved thereby is assumed to be worth at least that much to them. Thus, when the costs of damage abatement as an indicator of social benefit are determined, the question always arises as to what extent these costs are actually accepted by individuals. As long as the extent of such costs is determined by the authorities, social values can only be arrived at with this method more or less arbitrarily.

A precise determination of the macro-economic costs of environmental protection is met with considerable difficulties in practice. The opportunity costs which, strictly speaking, should be used as an indicator of economic losses – that is, the loss of benefits which a given ecological measure has caused due to its tying up of resources – can only be ascertained empirically with great difficulty. For one thing, the affected individuals or society are often unsure themselves of what the second-best alternative course of action is. For another thing, there are considerable problems in identifying the benefits lost.

This discrepancy between theory and practical application has led to a departure from the opportunity-costs principle, with basically the nominal costs of environmental protection (investment and operating costs) now being considered in CBAs. Given the large number of investments for expansion, conversion and rationalization projects which are of relevance to the environment, it is in many cases difficult to sift out those to be considered as environmental protection measures. Thus, because of possible differences in defining environmental protection investments, results of different empirical studies are not automatically intercomparable. Moreover, the operating costs (fixed expenses) resulting from environmental protection investments have not yet been systematically determined. The same applies to the environment related expenditure of private households.

Methodological problems arising from willingness-to-pay surveys

In principle, four problems arise in this approach – as in the assessment of environmental damage *per se*: the measuring, information, generation, and distribution problems.

The measuring problem concerns the question as to whether those participating in a survey are able and willing to explicitly articulate their values – as they would at an auction. For, in contrast to the indirect methods used to ascertain the individual's evaluation of environmental goods, a survey means that those questioned must be able to precisely specify their values. Four questions arise in this context:

(1) Can those questioned adequately conceive of the benefits to be derived from an improvement of the environment (such as enhanced well-being) and are they, moreover, capable of translating this conception into a monetary figure (the abstraction problem)?

(2) Will those questioned exaggerate their values for strategic reasons, thinking that an intact environment will be provided at no cost to them as long as the sum total of people's willingness to pay exceeds the actual costs of the project (the free-rider problem)?

(3) Are there – with a view to calculating the sampling error – enough people participating in an environmental survey (the motivation problem)?

(4) Is participation confined to fringe groups who are interested in environmental problems or does it extend – with a view to being able to generalize the results – to all sections of the population (the representativity problem)?

A possible argument against the validity of the results of surveys on the value of public goods, which is particularly often voiced in connection with environmental goods, is that those questioned are not sufficiently informed of the issues at hand (the information problem). It is certainly true that information on, for example, the adverse effects of environmental pollution on the affected people's own health decisively influences their appreciation of the commodity of a better environment. A further possible shortcoming of the willingness-to-pay survey as a social evaluation method is sometimes seen in the fact that it can only be used to record the preferences of the present generation, even though the current burdens on our environment also affect future generations (the generation problem). Taking into account that the willingness-to-pay concept is geared to spending power, its efficiency must inevitably be seen in relative terms. If identical willingnesses to pay of people with different incomes are weighted in accordance with the principle of "Mark equals Mark", this implies that the current distribution of incomes is fairly equitable (the distribution problem). If one does not share this view, one would have to give more weight to poorer people's willingness to pay than to richer people's.

Political and administrative barriers, ethical reservations

The literature published has hitherto mainly dealt with theoretical and methodological problems inherent in the performance of CBAs. However, the causes of the insufficient use of empirical CBAs are considered to include, in particular, political, administrative and other obstacles. Four examples are discussed below.

(1) Cost-benefit analyses may get politicans into an "unpleasant" decision-making situation. Such a situation arises, for example, when analysts have ascertained that the costs of a highly profitable environmental protection project would have to be mainly borne by the low-income section of the population, while it is mostly the higher-income section of the population that would benefit from it. If the decision maker sanctions the project, he or she inevitably shows a lack of commitment to a just distribution policy. It is not difficult to see why politicians are reluctant to define clearly and make known their distribution-policy objectives and programmes to the public, especially when the votes of the lower-income population are at stake.

(2) A politician's rationality primarily considers the political rather than the economic consequences of a project ("political cost-benefit analysis"). Working toward the realization of his or her ideas – such as the aims of the political party and of the people he or she represents – a politician is concerned with improving the political rationality of decisions. Decision-making aids strictly geared to economic values do not necessarily provide him or her with the information which is looked for. In other

words, decision makers are not only interested in ascertaining a project's effects in terms of efficiency and distribution, but also, for example, its longterm effects on the economic system and the distribution of power within the state and on federalism.

(3) In administrative practice in the Federal Republic of Germany, thinking in terms of micro-economic costs is still predominant. For one thing, there is a lack of qualified individuals who are able to systematically apply CBAs in evaluating and selecting public investment projects. Furthermore, to the author's knowledge, it is not possible for non-operational cost components to be taken adequately into account when fees are fixed under public law in the Federal Republic. Thus, for example, the fees to be paid for the landfilling of waste are still being exclusively calculated on the basis of the costs that the municipality has incurred directly as a result of the operation of the waste-management facility. The social costs of the landfilling practice are disregarded when fees are fixed.

(4) Environmental protection is a task which can only be tackled satisfactorily with the joint expert knowledge of different branches of science. Numerous disciplines are represented in the nationwide research programme "Costs of environmental pollution/benefits of environmental protection", which was dealt with above. Besides economics, they include medicine, psychology, sociology, statistics, hydrology, che.nistry, physics, limnology and landscape planning. But not always are these branches able and willing to collaborate to the extent required.

In conclusion, a further obstacle to the use of CBAs in the environmental sector should be mentioned – the ethical reservations against a monetarization of environmental assets. Time and again, cost-benefit analysts are confronted with the question as to why phenomena such as the dying of forests and the pollution of the North and Baltic Seas, which are so obviously undesirable, should require any economic-costs calculations. Non-economists, in particular, sometimes emphatically insist that nature and health are "unestimable" assets. As they see it, an intact environment is "a value in itself" and should not be tainted by an association with money.

Summary and recommendations

Summary

Cost-benefit analysis is probably the most widely known procedure for the analysis of economic efficiency in the public sector. In the Federal Republic of Germany, the issue in the early 1960s was to catch up on the lead that the Anglo-Americans had already gained in this field in science and application. The budget reform which went into effect on 1 January 1970 was a milestone in the sector of applied CBAs. Article 7, para. 2 of the Federal Budgetary Regulations (Bundeshaushaltsordnung) and Article 6, para. 2 of the Act on Budgetary Principles (Haushalts-grundsätzegesetz) – both articles were passed in 1969 – stipulate that economic efficiency studies be performed for all public projects of major financial relevance. Many more than a hundred CBAs used for decision-making purposes – particularly in the traffic and water-management sectors – have been published to date.

The once touted notion that cost-benefit considerations can be incorporated into the budgetary process without any problems and made into an effective instrument for use by the Minister of Finance to ward off any unreasonable demands of the various ministries, has proved erroneous in practice. Furthermore, the obligation to carry out CBAs is confined to projects which are "of considerable financial importance". Legislation thus grants ample scope for interpretation as to the cases in which CBAs have to be performed. On the whole, however, it should be noted that Article 7 of the Federal Budgetary Regulations does provide the possibility of performing CBAs that are of relevance to environmental policy. The extent to which they are actually used, however, is narrowly limited.

The sector which comes closest to fulfilling the legislative mandate is transport. The stipulations of the Federal Traffic Infrastructure Plans, which the Federal Government has passed at five-year intervals since the early 1970s, are based on comprehensive projections as well as on project assessments made according to macro-economic, traffic, regional policy and ecological criteria. The macro-economic assessment is based on a CBA which takes account of factors such as changes in operating costs, travel time, occurrence of accidents and environmental quality. The monetary assessment of environmental effects which is mainly carried out on the basis of a cost-of-damage-abatement approach covers noise and exhaust-gas pollution, separating effects, and the deterioration of living conditions and communications.

Up to the late 1970s, knowledge of the monetary benefit of environmental protection was still comparatively slight in the Federal Republic. Against this background, the Federal Environmental Agency first commissioned ten "Pilot studies for the assessment of the benefit to be derived from measures designed to improve the environment" in order to determine the economic value of ecological measures in specific problem areas which are quite different in nature from each other. These studies made it possible to demonstrate that the economic assessment of environmental impacts (of a positive as well as a negative kind) is in fact feasible and that environmental measures as well as other infrastructural activities initiated by the public sector are financially justifiable.

To further improve knowledge in this sector and to create awareness of gaps in research, a symposium on the subject of "Costs of environmental pollution" took place at the Federal Ministry of the Interior in Bonn on 12 and 13 September 1985. This conference, at which scientists from home and abroad reported on the state of present knowledge as to the monetary costs of air and water pollution, noise and soil contamination and the psycho-social costs of environmental pollution, was at the same time the prelude to a three-year focus of research. It was the intention of the Federal Minister for the Environment, Nature Conservation and Nuclear Safety, with a commitment of funds of over DM 3 million, to have the economic value of the environment monetarized as far as possible.

To this end, the Federal Environmental Agency developed a closed research model based on modules. Using these modules as building blocks in various basic combinations makes it possible to examine the monetary costs of environmental damage from a given perspective (from a media-specific, aggregate-specific, area-of-commerce-specific, or from a damage-specific standpoint). The approach thus pursued can be seen as a landmark for the Federal Republic. Some 70 natural scientists, sociologists and economists worked on the ten research projects, for which the best suited method for each was selected from approximately 50 evaluation approaches.

Recent literature on environmental economics nearly always points out that CBA can be employed as a useful aid in environmental policy decision making. Its particular value is mainly seen in the fact that it may help:

(1) to make the real dimension of environmental pollution patently clear (the clarity argument);
(2) to put the all too often too one-sided environmental debate on a rational basis (the objectification argument);
(3) to direct scarce financial resources to those areas of the environment where they are most urgently needed (the dosage argument);
(4) to make polluters aware of the costs arising from their own actions (the internalizability argument); and
(5) to further develop statistical measures of welfare (the correcting the-GNP argument).

Our more in-depth analysis of six selected case studies has shown that, in the Federal Republic, environment related CBAs make a considerable contribution to clarity and objectification. As far as the clearly more ambitious aims of proper dosing and internalizability are concerned however, environment related CBAs are neither now nor will be in the foreseeable future close to attaining these aims.

In the short to medium term, such analyses might contribute to the further development of statistical measures of welfare, provided that they are confined to recording the pollution related abatement costs which have already been incurred (defence expenditures).

The fact that environmentally relevant CBAs have hitherto only been systematically applied to quite a limited extent is, in particular, attributable to the time and money they require, to methodological problems, political and administrative barriers and, finally, to ethical reservations. The performance of CBAs is in many cases very time consuming and costly. Furthermore, many methodological problems have not yet been solved satisfactorily; especially, the knowledge of ecological cause–effect relationships is still quite sparse. The economic evaluation of environmental aspects likewise poses difficulties, particularly if market prices are unavailable and market-price surrogates have to be used.

Cost-benefit analyses may lead to policy-makers having to reveal their own "genuine" concept of values, although – especially with respect to the battle for votes – they are reluctant to do so. Moreover, CBAs alone do not necessarily provide politicians with the decision-making aids they are looking for. Further obstacles to the use of CBAs are encountered in the administrative sector. For one thing, there is a lack of sufficiently qualified personnel in administration who are familiar with thinking in terms of macroeconomic costs. For another, fees set under public law, such as for the landfilling of waste, are based on strictly operational cost components. Finally, people are easily led to the conclusion on ethical grounds that the protection of the environment is of unlimited, supreme importance and thus not accessible to any monetary evaluation. This can be countered as follows. If an infinitely high value were to be ascribed to nature, then correspondingly high sums of money would have to be provided for air-quality control, water protection and noise abatement. In addition, production processes which inevitably emit environmental pollutants would not be allowed to operate. From this perspective, if nature were to be given this value of infinitely high priority, then the supply of goods to society would become impossible. On the other hand, if an assessment of the environmental aspect were waived altogether, this would mean no less than our implicitly ascribing nil value to it. Both extremes are unacceptable. Therefore, here too, cost-benefit analysts can only be advised not to waste effort in espousing these arguments to the opponents of monetarization.

Recommendations

In the following section, various recommendations for action to help diminish existing deficiencies in applying CBAs will be outlined. The key to a broader use of environmentally relevant CBAs could be standardized guidance material – for example, the "Technical instructions on cost-benefit analyses in environmental protection (TI-CBA-EP)". To employ such guidelines in a practicable manner, it is necessary to use electronic data processing and to ensure that those involved in planning practice – particularly in the sector of public administration – receive the appropriate professional training.

Technical instructions on cost-benefit analyses in environmental protection
There is considerable theoretical, methodological and practical knowledge available today of the economic evaluation of projects, so the possibility exists of standardizing the various techniques for routine use. For each type of measure with relevance to

the environment, a number of standardized guidance materials should be developed which would provide cost-benefit analysts with an effective as well as cost- and time-saving set of tools. The guidelines should cover as many planning factors and conditions as possible. The recommended procedures should only be geared to data which can be obtained at reasonable cost and effort. For each of these data, a basic (best estimate) method and an approximation (second-best estimate) method should be developed. This principle has already been implemented in the "Guidelines for road construction, section: cost-benefit analyses (RAS-W)", which were mentioned above (p. 15). For example, to assess traffic noise using the basic method, a map of noise pollution for light night-time traffic (in the form of an isogram) and figures on the number of residents affected are required. If this information is not available, the approximation method can be used to calculate the costs brought on by noise pollution on the basis of town-model modules. In the event that the data required for this is likewise unavailable, further approximation options are proposed.

The "Guidelines for the performance of cost-benefit analyses" mentioned earlier (p. 15) already contain some fundamental techniques (such as for the calculation of future costs and benefits) whose methodology is well developed and generally recognized. What is still lacking, however, is a comprehensive system of methods which addresses the problem of risk and uncertainty. The simple rule-of-thumb practice of, for example, adjusting uncertain benefits downwards by a randomly fixed percentage or of systematically under-estimating the service life of the projects to be assessed, cannot be considered adequate. Therefore, it is recommended to conduct first a number of evaluations with respect to risk and uncertainty (using, for example, the scenario and delphi techniques) in order to subsequently derive standardized guidelines from the data and experience thus gained.

As far as the monetary evaluation methods are concerned, efforts towards their systematization have progressed to quite an advanced stage. As early as the beginning of the 1980s, Ewers and Schulz (1982) developed a multi-tiered system for the classification of methods which might serve as a basis for a generally applicable procedural guidelines (Table 2.8). The authors' first classification criterion refers to the question of whether the method used to perform a monetary evaluation of a specific effect or of the overall effect of a measure is based on the individual willingness to pay

Table 2.8: **Systematology of methods for monetary evaluation of environmental values**

Authoritarian method: public obligation to a payment				expenses method alternative expenses method time-serving expenses method
Non-authoritarian methods: methods to evaluate the profit for consumption or for producers	estimate the profit for consumption with the willingness-to-pay-method	direct methods: questioning persons concerned	pure questioning	simple questioning simple structured questioning complex structured questioning
			priority-evaluator-method	priority-evaluator-technique
		indirect methods: individual expenditure method	without consideration of the revenue for consumers	entry price method cross-expenditure-method aggregate-expenditure-method user time method land value method
			with consideration of the revenue for consumers	travel cost approach demand curve estimation
	estimate the profit for producers with the value-added-method			net product method producers revenue method cost saving method

Source: Based on Ewers and Schulz (1982)

of the persons affected, or, whether it considers the collective judgement of the persons involved in the decision making on this measure. Only the group of methods mentioned first assumes consumer sovereignty. Ewers and Schulz have therefore described them as non-authoritarian. On the other hand, the cost methods belonging to the second group do not estimate the willingness to pay of the persons affected, but rather the commitment made by public authorities for political reasons to pay for an environment improvement project, irrespective of user preferences. They have therefore described this group of methods as authoritarian.

Ewers and Schulz (1982, pp. 42–95) give an overview, in the form of uniformly structured tables, of the monetary evaluation methods they have classified. In this overview, methods are first differentiated with respect to the underlying indicators of benefit, followed by a description of the basic idea of each method. Subsequently, the methods are checked for their validity by comparing the benefit actually measured by the respective method with the benefit to be measured theoretically. This is followed by a review of the methods' practicability (especially with a view to the problems encountered in determining the necessary data). A summary of important points of criticism of the method, specific information on certain fields of application and literature references are given at the end of the discussion of each evaluation method.

Accompanying measures
The manageability of the guidelines developed can be considerably improved by the use of data processing. The work of the user is confined here to the proper selection and compilation of input data. The work involved in performing the complex calculations, hitherto a time-consuming task, can be shortened and previous sources of error eliminated. The analysis and interpretation of the results can be utilized in further planning without much loss of time. The Federal Minister of Transport commissioned the consultants Heusch and Boesefeldt (Aachen) to develop a personal-computer program for the performance of cost-benefit calculations in accordance with the "Guidelines for road construction, section: cost-benefit analyses (RAS-W)". In a modified form, this program could also be used for the environmental sector, which would substantially facilitate the complicated and data-intensive calculations to be performed for environmentally

relevant CBAs. The program is used with the aid of masks and menus and consists of different modules (such as project loading, securing, working, computing, output and erasing). The advantages of the system are: well-designed menus, user-friendly masks for data input, fast processing of the data, functional administration of different alternatives of a project, automatic pre-storage of known data, duplication of data by means of function keys, fast and precise computing, well-presented printouts of the results and printouts of the input data.

The broad-scale performance of environment related CBAs requires well-trained personnel. There is no doubt that this is where the main bottleneck is to be found, and not – as is often assumed – in methodological shortcomings. As this field of knowledge only receives marginal attention in administrative training, or is not dealt with at all, selective further training is advisable. The courses conducted in the Federal Republic of Germany at the Academies of Administration (Verwaltungs-akademien) have proved to be particularly suitable for such further training. In this context, reference is made to the courses held at the Verwaltungsakademie in Berlin in the subject of "Cost-benefit Analyses" (14 double periods in one semester). By building on such training, the knowledge necessary for the performance of CBAs can be gradually increased.

Appendix: Research Projects A-J

Research Programme "Costs of environmental pollution: benefits of environmental protection" of the Federal Government: Problem formulation, aims and study approaches

The ten research projects of the research programme are outlined below. The presentation of the projects is uniformly structured (giving title, performing institution, sponsor, problem formulation and aims, study approach and results). Further information can be obtained from the Data Base for Environmental Research (Umweltforschungsdatenbank – UFORDAT) of the Federal Environmental Agency. The agency is also responsible for the scientific supervision and co-ordination of the entire research programme. In addition, the Federal Ministry for the Environment has established a group of economic experts to accompany the programme. This group consists of representatives of the Federal Ministry for the

Environment, the Federal Environmental Agency and the Federal Statistical Office as well as these four independent economic experts: Professor Dr Paul Klemmer (Chairman, President of the Rheinisch-West-fälisches Institut, Essen); Professor Dr Alfred Endres (Technical University, Berlin); Professor Dr Jan Jarre (Fachhochschule Münster); Professor Dr Klaus Zimmermann (University of the Federal Armed Forces, Hamburg).

A: Cost of air pollution in the sector of public health

Title Economic assessment of health damage caused by air pollutants
Performed by Institute for Environmental Protection of Dortmund University
Sponsored by Federal Environmental Agency
Problem formulation and aim of the project There are still considerable gaps in knowledge of the cause–effect relationships between environmental pollutants (such as sulphur dioxide in air) and diseases (such as diseases of the respiratory tract). Given these uncertainties, the central aim of the study was to develop an approach for the determination of health damage and the associated health costs (costs for out- and in-patient treatment, sickness benefits, continued payment of wages), taking influencing parameters (such as smoking) into consideration, and to roughly estimate the damage on that basis.
Approach On the basis of health insurance data on some 70,000 employees obliged to pay social security contributions, the probability of falling ill and the duration of the illness was estimated exemplarily for the eastern part of the Ruhr District (the polluted area) and for the bordering areas of Münsterland and Sauerland (the control area). Different types of diseases (of the respiratory tract as well as heart and circulatory diseases) and different groups of the population (by age, sex, profession, education, income) were differentiated. Multiple regression analysis was the statistical method used to evaluate the extensive data.
Results Distinct differences were determined with respect to the frequency and duration of certain diseases. Thus, diseases of the heart and the circulatory system occurred more frequently and were of a longer duration in the polluted areas than in the control areas. Against this background and including the rates for out- and in-patient treatment (including prescribed medication, sickness

benefits, continued payment of wages), the additional health costs incurred in the polluted areas in 1984 were calculated at DM 7.7 million, or DM 270 for each health-insured employee.
Source Data Base for Environmental Research (UFORDAT) and Institute for Environmental Protection, Dortmund University

B: Damage to material caused by environmental pollution

Title Economic losses resulting from pollution-induced damage to material in the Federal Republic of Germany
Performed by Federal Institute for Material Testing (BAM), Berlin
Sponsored by Federal Environmental Agency
Problem formulation and aim of the project Since the early 1950s, considerable damage to buildings and monuments has occurred in the Federal Republic of Germany, and the trend is sharply increasing. This damage is attributed to the impact of aggressive pollutants, particularly air pollutants, on the environment. Utility metals, for instance, can be particularly affected by air pollution. At the sulphur dioxide levels occurring in industrialized areas, the wearing away of zinc – which is frequently observed, for example, in the case of steel structures – is five times as high on an annual average as in rural areas with low pollution levels. This study serves to demonstrate the orders of magnitude of the monetary losses that may be incurred nationwide as a result of pollution-related damage to material.
Approach The necessary data are evaluated on the basis of a secondary statistical analysis. In particular, the study is designed to estimate physico-chemical corrosion functions and the number of affected buildings and building components at different sites and for different types of exposure situations. The damage-prone objects under consideration are: buildings, infrastructure facilities, industrial plants, and monuments. Finally, the additional costs for material maintenance and the additional expenditure for material restoration and repair work (including costs), where attributable to environmental impacts, are estimated.
Results The study is expected to be concluded by the end of 1989.
Source Data Base for Environmental Research (UFORDAT) and Federal Institute for Material Testing (BAM), Berlin

C: Economic value of nature conservation

Title The economic importance of the decline in species and

biotopes in the Federal Republic of Germany
Performed by Kassel Polytechnic (Faculty of Economic Sciences)
Sponsored by Federal Environmental Agency
Problem formulation and aim of the project Natural biotopes that are rich in species are an indispensable basis of the ecosystem and are thus the safeguard of human life. They stabilize the ecosystem, serve as a gene resource and are of practical value to humans in that they maintain the food supply and furnish the basic materials for the manufacture of drugs. In addition, they help clarify ecological processes and serve as models for technical procedures. The central aim of the empirical study is to illustrate, for the first time, the economic value of the protection of species and biotopes for the Federal Republic of Germany. The envisaged scope of the study includes, *inter alia*, a theoretical discussion of the ecological aspects of nature conservation as well as a systematic compilation of available information on the usefulness of species.
Approach The study pursues the controlled costs-for-damage-avoidance approach. First, the required measures are summarized and the economic costs of an effective nature conservation policy (and thus the loss of benefits in other areas) are estimated for the Federal Republic (determination of the costs for damage avoidance). The second stage investigates the extent to which the estimated costs are accepted among the population (determination of latent willingness to pay). In this context, people are to be confronted with scenarios of different levels of nature conservation and with the expected effects of a higher or lesser willingness to pay. Furthermore, the motives underlying the willingness to pay (in particular, categorization into experiental value, option value, legacy value and existence value) are to be ascertained.
Results The study is expected to be concluded by mid-1990.
Source Data Base for Environmental Research (UFORDAT) and Kassel Polytechnic

D: Economic losses caused by noise

Title Costs of noise in the Federal Republic of Germany
Performed by Institut für Verkehrswissenschaften at Cologne University
Sponsored by Federal Environmental Agency
Problem formulation and aim of the project Noise levels as low as approximately 30 decibels may be annoying and disturbing;

noise levels between 40 and 60 decibels may interfere with communication; excess of 60 decibels may cause stress reactions; and excess
of 85 decibels may damage the inner ear. Epidemiological studies
have found a higher incidence of high blood pressure in people living
in noise-polluted areas than in control groups from comparatively
quiet areas. The aim of the study is to determine the economic
impact of noise in the Federal Republic of Germany.

Approach The main element of the study is a nationwide willingness-to-pay survey. Using this approach, the overall loss of benefits
which noise causes among the affected population is to be expressed
in monetary units. Further objectives of the survey are: (a) to
obtain an indication as to the magnitude of the losses to the
economy which may be incurred as a result of a noise-related
decline in labour productivity; (b) to determine the total annual
expenditure on noise-induced pensions in the form of compensation
paid to workers who have become hard of hearing due to noise at
the workplace; (c) a literature study on investigations into noise-
related depreciations of real estate and residential buildings; (d)
to determine the expenditure for noise-reduction measures which
the public sector, industry and the affected citizens have to shoulder
annually for protection against noise pollution.

Results The study is expected to be concluded by the beginning of
1990.

Source Data Base for Environmental Research (UFORDAT) and
Institut für Verkehrswissenschaften at Cologne University

*E: Losses caused by environmental pollution in the sector of
leisure and recreation*

Title Economic costs of an impairment of leisure and recreational
values as a result of environmental pollution in the Federal
Republic of Germany

Performed by Prognos AG, Basle

Sponsored by Federal Environmental Agency

Problem formulation and aim of the project The demand for leisure
and recreational activities depends on a multitude of conditions and
factors, such as living conditions and work situation, the leisure
needs of the individual, and the quality of the recreational facilities
and options offered. Environmental pollution, particularly of a
visual, acoustic or odorous kind, may limit the experience value
of a leisure and recreational activity (such as walking, hiking,

swimming, sailing and rowing) to a considerable extent. The aims of the investigation are first to monetarize the loss of benefits suffered by those seeking outdoor leisure and recreation in the vicinity of or at a distance to home, and second to ascertain the revenue losses incurred by the tourist industry.

Approach The project deals with the following issues: (a) the influence of environmental pollution on the leisure and recreational behaviour of the population; (b) identification and evaluation of available leisure activities and options which constitute a burden on the environment; (c) estimation of the annual decline in demand (thoughout the Federal Republic); and (d) monetarization of the damage in the sectors of consumption and production. Difficult problems, such as the question of substitution (pollution-induced shift from environmental-quality-dependent to environmental-quality-independent leisure activities), are dealt with interactively in the form of intensive verbal interviews with 1,450 persons throughout the Federal Republic.

Results The study is expected to be concluded at the beginning of 1990.

Source Data Base for Environmental Research (UFORDAT) and Prognos AG, Basle

F: Loss of income in the fishing industry caused by environmental pollution

Title of the project Loss of income incurred by the fishing industry in the Federal Republic of Germany as a result of environmental pollution

Performed by Futuras, Hamburg

Sponsored by Federal Environmental Agency

Problem formulation and aim of the project Marine pollution contributes to a decline in fish stocks, especially in river mouth areas but also in the oceans. In recent years there have been many reports on incidences of diseases in fish (also in mussels, oysters and other crustaceans) occurring in highly polluted marine waters. This project serves to demonstrate the monetary magnitude of the losses of income incurred by the fishing industry nationwide as a result of environmental pollution (primary effect). In addition, the resulting changes in associated branches of industry (suppliers and processors) are to be quantified (secondary effect).

Approach The following sectors of the fishing industry are differentiated: German deep-sea fishing outside and within the North and Baltic Sea areas; German coastal fishing in the North and Baltic Seas; German mussel fishing, fishing in rivers and lakes, and fish farming in ponds. Up to five categories of different losses of income are considered in the investigation: reduction in stocks, quality losses, material damage, control costs and avoidance costs. To check the impact of water pollution on the fishing industry, three additional anthropogenic determinants are investigated: excessive fishing, fishing technique, and fishing policy.

Results The study is expected to be concluded by the end of 1989.

Source Data Base for Environmental Research (UFORDAT) and Futuras, Hamburg

G: Water-supply costs caused by water pollution

Title of the project The impact of water pollution on the costs for the drinking-water and industrial-water supply in the Federal Republic of Germany

Performed by Technical University, Berlin (Fachgebiet Energie- und Rohstoffwirtschaft)

Sponsored by Federal Environmental Agency

Problem formulation and aim of the project As late as the beginning of the 1950s, the water supply in the Federal Republic of Germany provided by public or private water supply companies hardly involved any costs. Since then, the average costs for water conditioning have increased thirty-fold. This development is mainly attributable to the increasing pollutant load in surface and groundwater. This study serves to show the monetary magnitude of the additional costs for the water supply system (avoidance costs that arise when switching to long-distance water supply) and for water conditioning (abatement costs incurred by conversion of the process) which water pollution causes nationwide.

Approach The study is performed in two stages. Within the framework of a micro-analytical approach, a number of typical water supply companies (ensuring a high degree of representativity) are investigated with respect to the costs incurred as a result of water pollution. Within the framework of a macro-analytical approach, the water pollution-related determinants of the increases in water supply prices and costs which have occurred since 1950 are ascertained by means of regression analysis.

Results The study is expected to be concluded in mid-1989.

Source Data Base for Environmental Research (UFORDAT) and Technical University, Berlin

H: Economic losses caused by soil contamination

Title of the project Economic losses caused by soil contamination in the Federal Republic of Germany
Performed by Institut für Stadtforschung und Strukturpolitik, Berlin
Sponsored by Federal Environmental Agency
Problem formulation and aim of the project In the Federal Republic of Germany, several million tonnes of sulphur dioxide and nitric oxides, some thousands of tonnes of lead and several hundred tonnes of cadmium end are deposited each year in soil, either through direct inputs or via air and water. Besides the widespread contamination by not readily biodegradable chemicals and heavy metals, there is mechanical stress, soil erosion caused by wind and water, the depositing of waste, and land consumption, all adding to the burden placed on soils. This study serves to illustrate the economic consequences resulting from such burdens.
Approach As a first step, the causal chains of different areas of damage (such as groundwater, species and biotopes, food and human health) are to be described on the basis of an analysis of available literature. Second, the physical values are transformed into monetary values. The assessment approach used is essentially based on the determination of the costs that have to be accepted as a result of soil contamination, categorized into avoidance costs, costs for planning and supervision (transaction costs) as well as the costs for prevention or elimination (abatement costs), all of which can be quantified and monetarized.
Results The study is expected to be concluded at the beginning of 1990.
Source Data Base for Environmental Research (UFORDAT) and Institut für Stadtforschung und Strukturpolitik, Berlin

I: Psycho-social costs of environmental pollution

Title of the project Psycho-social costs of environmental pollution
Performed by Gesellschaft für angewandte Sozialwissenschaft und Statistik (IST GmbH), Heidelberg
Sponsored by Federal Environmental Agency

Problem formulation and aim of the project In the course of the past decades, various studies on the economic evaluation of the physiological effects of environmental pollution, such as damage to health, have been conducted. Nuisances and irritations which do not manifest themselves in the form of an acute illness have hithero not been taken into consideration in such studies. The environmental nuisances and irritations referred to include those, for example, that can be directly perceived as noise or as an unpleasant sight or odour. Such pollution is physiologically harmless to a large extent, but – in a given area – there are normally many more people whose well-being is impaired than people whose health actually is endangered. Therefore, a welfare-oriented economic CBA must be designed so that such immaterial effects are likewise taken into account in monetary terms. The aim of the research project is to estimate the psycho-social costs of environmental pollution in monetary terms as far as is possible.
Approach In order to be able to relate environmental pollution to psycho-social well-being, different levels of impact are differentiated as follows: the perception level (which describes symptoms such as headache or insomnia); the effect level (which addresses things such as a loss in the diversity of aesthetic experiences, annoyance about and fear of environmental hazards); and the action level (which refers, for example, to a change of residence and to the taking of medicine). In addition, a larger number of people are questioned by way of a computer interview as to their personal assessment of these effects. For this purpose, te.minals are used which are programmed in such a way that environmental effects which are of psycho-social relevance successively appear on the screen in the form of pages of a questionnaire, which then have to be assessed by the participants in terms of DM amounts.
Results The study is expected to be concluded in mid-1989.
Source Data Base for Environmental Research (UFORDAT) and Gesellschaft für angewandte Sozialwissenschaft und Statistik (IST GmbH), Heidelberg

J: Demand for environmental quality

Title of the project The demand for environmental quality in the Federal Republic of Germany
Performed by Institut für Stadtforschung und Strukturpolitik, Berlin

Sponsored by Federal Environmental Agency

Problem formulation and aim of the project In principle, different questions can be asked in order to obtain information on the welfare benefits or losses resulting from improvements or deteriorations of environmental quality. One either ascertains what amount the affected citizen would be willing to pay for an improvement of environmental quality or for preventing it from deteriorating (willingness-to-pay analysis), or one ascertains what amount would have to be paid to the affected citizens in order for them to be prepared to do without an improved environmental quality or to tolerate a deterioration of environmental quality (willingness-to-sell analysis). This study serves to determine the extent to which citizens are willing to pay for different environmental qualities in different sectors of the environment.

Approach The first stage of the study is based on an experimental survey conducted within the framework of market simulations. This approach is especially suitable for determining the over-estimation effect which can be expected when the persons questioned are asked in isolation about their willingness to pay for specific goods that they want. The second phase of the project involves a standardized representative survey questionning 3,300 citizens. Another central aim of the study is to determine the influence of environmental pollution on real estate prices.

Results The study is expected to be concluded at the beginning of 1990.

Source Data Base for Environmental Research (UFORDAT) and Institut für Stadtforschung und Strukturpolitik, Berlin

References

Andel, N. (1977) "Nutzen-Kosten-Analysen", in *Handbuch der Finanzwissenschaft* (eds, Andel, Haller and Neumark), Band I., 3 Aufl., 475–518. (Tübingen).

Apel, D. (1988) *Zweiter Bericht für die AG "Fläche" der Enquete-Kommission Bodenverschmutzung, Bodennutzung und Bodenschutz – Verkehrsflächen.* (Deutsches Institut für Urbanistik: Berlin).

Arnold, V. (1980) "Nutzen-Kosten-Analyse II: Anwendung", in *Handwörterbuch der Wirtschaftswissenschaft, Band 5* (eds, Albers et al.), 382–99. (Stuttgart, Tübingen und Göttingen).

Beckenbach, F. and Schreyer, M. (1988) *Gesellschaftliche Folgekosten. Was kostet unser Wirschaftssystem?* (Frankfurt and New York).

Dupuit, J. (1844) "On the measurement of the utility of public works", *International Economic Papers*, 2 (1952), 83–110.

ECE (1970) *Die wirtschaftliche Bedeutung der Rhein-Main-Donau-Verbindung, Studie der Berichtergruppe der Wirtschaftskommission für Europa (ECE) in Genf.* (München).

Eekhoff, J. (1972) *Nutzen-Kosten-Analyse der Stadtsanierung. Methoden, Theorien.* (Bern).

Ewers, H.J. and Schulz, W. (1982) "Die monetären Nutzen gewässergüteverbessernder Massnahmen – dargestellt am Beispiel des Tegeler Sees in Berlin", Berichte 3/82 des Umweltbundesamtes. (Berlin).

Fest, H.E. (1971) *Zur gesamtwirtshaftlichen Konistenz des Entscheidungskriteriums für die Auswahl öffentlicher Investitionen. Ein Beitrag zur theoretischen Grundlegung der gesamtwirtschaftlichen Nutzen-Kosten-Analyse.* (Berlin).

Frerich, J., Emder, W. and Vosdellen, L. (1988) "Das Verfahren der RAS-W zur wirtschaftlichen Bewertung von Strassenbauprojekten", in *Strassen und Vekehr 2000* (Band 3: Verkehrsokonomie), Internationale Strassen- und Verkehrskonferenz. (Berlin).

Georgi, H. (1970) *Cost-benefit-analysis als Lenkungsinstrument öffentlicher Investitionen im Verkehr.* (Göttingen).

Grundzüge der Nutzen-Kosten-Untersuchungen (1981): *Ausgearbeitet von der LAWA-Arbeitsgruppe Nutzen-Kosten-Untersuchungen in der Wasserwirtschaft.* (Bremen).

Günther, W., Schmidtke, R.F., Klaus, J. and Lindstadt, H.J. (1981) "Monetäre Bewertung wasserwirtschaftlicher Massnahmen – Systematik der volkswirtschaftlichen Nutzenermittlung", *Schriftenreihe des Bayerischen Landesamtes für Wasserwirtschaft*, H. 2/81. (München).

Hanusch, H. (1987) *Nutzen-Kosten-Analyse.* (München).

Hautau, H., Lorenzen, U., Sander, D. and Bertram, M. (1987) *Monetäre Bewertungsansätze von Umweltbelastungen.* (Göttingen).

Hesse, G. (1975) "Nutzen-Kosten-Analyse und souveränes Individuum", in *Jahrbücher für Nationalökonomie und Statistik*, vol. 189, 498–521.

Hesse, H. (1980) "Nutzen-Kosten-Analyse I: Theorie", in *Handwörterbuch der Wirtschaftswissenschaft*, Band 5 (eds, Albers et al.), 361–82 (Stuttgart, Tübingen und Göttingen).

Hesse, H. and Arnold, V. (1970) "Nutzen-Kosten-Analyse für städtische Verkehrsprojekte – dargestellt am Beispiel der Unterpflasterstrassenbahn in Hannover", *Kyklos*, 23, 520–57.

Heusch, H. and Boesefeldt, J. (1987) "Programmsystem zur Durchfuhrung wirtschaftlicher Vergleichsrechnungen nach den RAS-W", in *Auftrag des Bundesministers für Verkehr.* (Aachen).

Hicks, J.R. (1941) "The rehabilitation of consumers' surplus", *Review of Economic Studies*, 8, 108–16.

Hofmann, J. (1981) *Erweiterte Nutzen-Kosten-Analyse. Zur Bewertung und Auswahl öffentlicher Projekte.* (Göttingen).

Hogrebe, P., Platz, H. and Rieken, P. (1986) "Gesamtwirtschaftliche Bewertung von Verkehrswegeinvestitionen. Bewertungsverfahren für den Bundesverkehrswegeplan 1985". Gutachten im *Auftrag des Bundesministers für Verkehr.* (Bonn–Bad Godesberg).

Hohmeyer, O. (1989) *Soziale Kosten des Energieverbrauchs. Externe Effekte des Elektrizitätsverbrauchs in der Bundesrepublik Deutschland.* (Berlin, Heidelberg, New York, London, Paris and Tokyo).

Intertraffic (1971) "Wasserstrassenanschluss für das Saarland. Nutzen-Kosten-Analyse", *Auftrag des Bundesministers für Verkehr.* (Bonn).

IRB-Verlag (1985): *Kosten-Nutzen-Analyse im Verkehrsewsen* (ed. Fritsch, H.). (Stuttgart).

Jarre, J. (1983) (ed.) *Die wirtschaftliche Bedeutung des Umweltschutzes. Zur ökonomischen Bewertung von Umweltschäden und Umweltverbesserungen.* Loccumer Protokolle 31/81, Rehburg-Loccum.

Kirsch, G. and Rürup, B. (1971) "Die Notwendigkeit einer empirischen Theorie der Diskontierung in der Kosten-Nutzen-Analyse öffentlicher Projekte", in *Zeitschrift für die gesamte Staatswissenschaft*, 127, 432–58.

Klaus, J., März, F., Pflügner, W. and Schöttner, G. (1983) *Ökonomische Bewertung der Gewässergüte in Fliessgewässern. Methodische und empirisch quantitative Ergebnisse für das Flussgebiet der Leine.* UBA-Text 31/83. (Berlin).

Klaus, J., Lindstadt, H.J. and Pflügner, W. (1981) "Methodische und empirische Ansätze zur Bewertung wasserwirtschaftlicher Infrastruktur", *Schriftenreihe des Bundesministers für Ernährung, Lanwirtschaft und Forsten*, Reihe A, Heft 258. (Münster-Hiltrup).

Klaus, J. and Vauth, W. (1977) *Wirtschaftlichkeitsüberlegungen in Flussgebietsmodellen. Studie für das Umweltbundesamt.* (Nürnberg).

Leipert, Ch. (1987) *Folgekosten des Wirtschaftsprozesses und volkswirthcaftliche Gesamtrechnung. Zur Identifikation von steigenden kompensatorischen Ausgaben in der Sozialprodutrechnung.* IIUG rep 87–22, Wissenschaftszentrum. (Berlin).

Leitfaden für Kostenermittlung und Wirtschaftlichkeitsprüfung (1983) (eds, Gührs, E. and Hünerberg, G.): Herausgegeben von der Freien und Hansestadt. (Hamburg).

Leitfaden für Nutzen-Kosten-Untersuchungen (1977) (eds, Gührs, E., Linder, K., Pagels, J. and Reissmann, W.). Herausgegeben von der Freien und Hansestadt. (Hamburg).

Leitlinien zur Durchführung von Kosten-Nutzen-Analysen in der Wasserwirtschaft (1979) Ausgearbeitet von der LAWA-Arbeitsgruppe Nutzen-Kosten-Untersuchungen in der Wasserwirtschaft. (Stuttgart).

Leitlinien zur Durchführung von Kostenvergleichsrechnungen (1986) Ausgearbeitet vom LAWA-Arbeitskreis Nutzen-Kosten-Untersuchungen in der Wasserwirtschaft. (Stuttgart).

Little, J.M.D. (1965) *A Critique of Welfare Economics*, 2. (Oxford).

Marshall, A. (1907) *Principles of Economics*, 5. (London).

OECD (1979) "OECD Environment Committee at Ministerial Level". Press Release, Press/A(79)23. (Paris).

OECD (1987) "Better Air, how do we evaluate it? A social demand analysis based on willingness to pay". Translation of a report written by Werner Schulz in 1985 for the Federal Environment Agency. Working Paper. (Paris).

Pflügner, W. (1988) *Nutzen-Analysen im Umweltschutz. Der ökonomische Wert von Wasser und Luft*. (Göttingen).

Pommerehne, W.W. (1987) *Ansätze zur Erfassung der Präferenzen für öffentliche Güter: Ein Beitrag zur Verbesserung der kollektiven Willensbildung*. (Tübingen).

RAS-W (1986): *Richtlinien für die Anlage von Strassen RAS*. Teil: Wirtschaftlichkeitsuntersuchungen RAS-W. Forschungsgesellschaft für Strassen- und Verkehrswesen, Arbeitsgruppe Verkehrsplanung. (Köln).

Recktenwald, H.C. (1970) *Nutzen-Kosten-Analyse und Programmbudget*. (Tübingen).

Schulz, W. (1985a) "Bessere Luft, was ist sie uns wert? Eine gesellschaftliche Bedarfsanalyse auf der Basis individueller Zahlungsbereitschaften". Texte 25/85 des Umweltbundesamtes. (Berlin).

Schulz, W. (1985b) *Der monetäre Wert besserer Luft*. (Frankfurt, Berne and New York).

Schulz, W. (1988a) "Die sozialen Kosten des Autoverkehrs", in *Polizei, Verkehr und Technik*, 33. Jg., Heft 12, December, 370–4.

Schulz, W. (1988b) "The Economic Costs of Air Pollution", in *A Selection of Recent Publications* (vol. 2), Federal Environmental Agency, 26–42. (Berlin).

Schulz, W. (1989) "Ansätze und Grenzen der Monetarisierung von Umweltschäden", in *Zeitschrift für Umwelpolitik*, 12 Jg., H. 1, 54–78.

Schulz, W. and Wicke, L. (1986) "Die Kosten der Umweltverschmutzung – Beispiel: Waldesterben", in *Umwelt und Energie*, 7 Jg., Heft Nr. 4 v. 14.8., 52–85.

Schulz, W. and Wicke, L. (1987) "Der ökonomische Wert der Umwelt", in *Zeitschrift für Umweltpolitik*, 10 Jg., H. 2, 109–55.

Schussmann, K. (1973) *Die Paretianische Nutzen-Kosten-Analyse*. (Kallmünz).

SRU (1978): *Umweltgutachten 1978 des Sachverständigenrat für Umweltfragen*. (Stuttgart and Mainz).

SRU (1987): *Umweltgutachten 1987 des Sachverständigenrat für Umweltfragen*. (Bonn).

Stamer, C. (1988): "Umwelt-Satellitensystem zu den Volkswirtschaftlichen Gesamtrechnungen", in *Allgemeines Statistisches Archiv*, Jg. 72, 58– 71.

Stohler, J. (1967) "Zur Methode und Technik der Cost-Benefit-Analyse", in *Kyklos*, 20, 218–45.

Stolber, W.B. (1968): *Nutzen-Kosten-Analysen in der Staatswirtschaft. Wasserwirtschaftliche Projekte.* (Göttingen).

Teufel, D. (1989) *Gesellschaftliche Kosten des Strassen-Güterverkehrs. Kosten-Deckungsgrad im Jahr 1987 und Vorschläge zur Realisierung des Verursacherprinzips.* UPI Bericht Nr. 14. (Umwelt- und Prognose-Institut: Heidelberg).

Teufel, D., Bauer, P., Becker, G., Gauch, E., Lenz, H., Wagner, T. and Vilja, S. (1988) *Ökosteuern als markwirtschaftliches Instrument im Umweltschutz. Vorschläge für eine Steuerreform.* UPI Bericht Nr. 9. (Umwelt- und Prognose-Institut: Heidelberg).

Umweltbundesamt (1986) "Kosten der Umweltverschmutzung". Symposium 12 and 13 September in Bundesministerium des Innern. Berichte 7/86 des Umweltbundesamtes. (Berlin).

Vorläufige VV-BHO (1973) Vorläufige Verwaltungsvorschriften zur Bundeshaushaltsordnung, 21 May 1973. Ministerialblatt des Bundesministers der Finanzen und des Bundesministers für Wirtschaft Nr. 13, 11 July 1973, 194–302.

Wicke, L. (1986) *Die ökologischen Milliarden. Das kostet die zerstörte Umwelt – so können wir sie retten.* (Kösel-Verlag: Munchen).

Wicke, L. (1987) "Soziale Nutzen und soziale Kosten des Automobils – Eine positive Bilanz?" Referat auf der Internationalen Automobilausstellung, 18 September 1987 in Frankfurt-am-Main.

Wicke, L. (1988) *Die ökologischen Milliarden. Das kostet die zerstörte Umwelt – so können wir sie retten.* (Goldmann-Verlag: München).

Witte, H and Voight, F. (1985) *Die Bewertung von Infrastruktureinrichtungen. Dargestellt am Beispiel von Verkehrsinvestitionen.* 2 Aufl. (Berlin).

3 Italy

Giorgio Panella

Introduction

Environmental policies often require the allocation of large amounts of private and public resources which must be withdrawn from other purposes. The private sector complains about the difficulties, at both micro- and macro-economic level, caused by such policies. At the same time, public authorities find it increasingly difficult to apportion budgetary resources for environmental improvements at a time of growing fiscal restraints and economic difficulties. It seems therefore necessary to weigh thoroughly the total impact that a particular environmental project would have on both sectors.

In order to determine whether the welfare of the society would rise or fall as a result of a contemplated project, it is necessary to identify and measure the social benefits and costs of the project under consideration. Accordingly, cost-benefit analysis (CBA) emerges as a valuable tool in environmental decision making.

Applying CBA to environmental concerns is not without problems, especially in the area of benefits evaluation. This is why CBA adopts related decision tools, such as effectiveness analysis or environmental impact statements, in the evaluation of the benefits expected of various environmental projects. Decisions are normally made by considering only the costs directly imputable to the activities or the quantitative physical impacts (damages) to the environment. There are no generally acceptable rules for translating all foreseeable effects to a common monetary measure as, typically, there is no agreement about the possible consequences of alternative choices.

Benefits estimates serve as helpful indicators to compare the environmental consequences of alternative projects. They are often used to organize data and summarize information on environmental effects and thus afford a measure of rationality to environmental decisions. Attempts to estimate monetary benefits as correctly as possible not only propel rationality but may generate additional information which may benefit the entire decision-making process.

Appropriate techniques abound, but they can seldom be applied in a mechanical manner. Despite a fairly extensive list of readings, on both theoretical and practical levels, standardized approaches are clearly missing. Handbooks prepared by the staffs of concerned international organizations have recently offered valuable insights into how to use damage estimates as an environmental policy tool and how to perform a CBA (see Pearce and Markandya, 1989; OECD, 1989; OECD, 1976; OECD, 1974; Little and Mirrless, 1968; Dasgupta et al, 1972). Nevertheless, benefit estimates in environmental decision making seldom play an important role. It is only from the beginning of the 1980s that we have observed in Italy some interest in CBA as an environmental decision-making tool in general, and the evaluation of the environmental benefits in particular. In fact, most of the theoretical and empirical literature at national level deals with the traditional aspects of CBA: see Allione (ed.), 1977; Buratti, 1978; Sobbrio, 1978; Cassone et al., 1981; Tenembaum, 1982; Gronchi, 1984; Pennisi (ed.), 1985; Tenembaum, 1987; Formez, 1987; Nuti, 1987.

The purpose of this chapter is to trace the origins of this new interest, explore the technical and political obstacles which still seem to limit the general diffusion of the applicable evaluation procedures, and suggest what could be done in order to improve the decision-making process. More specifically, in line with the guidelines set forth by the Organization for Economic Co-operation and Development (OECD) study (Miltz, 1988), the objectives of this report are the following:

• to analyse the obstacles to a wider use of the environmental benefit estimates for decision making;
• to investigate the ways and means of producing benefits estimates in a form usable and meaningful to decision makers;
• to assess various decision-making tools and methodologies which can be used as a complement or a substitute when little or no benefits estimates are available.

The structure of the chapter is as follows. The first section introduces the problem of public expenditures in Italy, the need for rationalization, and the role of CBA in the decision-making process in relation to specific environmental projects. The sphere of applicability of CBA and other decision-making tools has broadened considerably both at national and regional level since 1980, especially in relation to the evaluation of public expenditures.

The second section reviews briefly the conceptual basis of CBA as it has been applied in Italy to environmental projects. Attention is given to the experience of the "Investment and Employment Scheme" ("Fondo Investimenti e Occupazione" – FIO) and the activities of the Public Investment Evaluation Group set up by the Ministry of Budget and Economic Planning. Particular emphasis will be placed on the description of the benefit estimate procedures developed by this group. Additionally, the conceptual difficulties and information requirements necessary in order to implement CBA will be stressed.

The third section considers some case studies which it is hoped will illustrate the methodology used to evaluate the benefits and the discrepancy, when present, between theory and practice. These successful examples will, in turn, serve as sources for developing useful guidelines to improve the decision-making process.

Finally, in the fourth section, the obstacles to the more widespread use of benefits estimation will be reviewed by considering some technical limitations as well as some rather theoretical objections raised against the use of CBA. The attitudes of decision makers towards the benefits estimation approach will be presented and ways to better incorporate benefit estimations in the decision-making framework will be suggested.

Public Expenditure and Cost-Benefit Analysis in the Environmental Sector: an Overview

Public expenditure: the need for efficiency

According to official statistics, capital expenditures of the public administration in Italy are important in relation to the gross national product (GNP) and to those incurred by the other OECD countries. The magnitude of capital expenditures is mostly due to the inefficiency of these expenditures themselves and is often artificially inflated by the very expenditure process, the revision of the prices (Galimberti, 1988).

Budgetary constraints and the public budget deficit call for improvement of the efficiency of these expenditures and to value the social profitability of the public projects.

This is a need which also concerns environmental projects. Environmental expenditure in Italy, as shown in Table 3.1, has almost reached the same dimension as in other OECD countries. Expenditures have been used in order to increase aggregate demand in adverse economic situations; however, scant attention has been given to their quality and profitability. The debate on public expenditures in Italy has concentrated too much on the aggregate variables, to the detriment of the efficiency of expenditure (Gerelli, 1987). It is important to observe that the data reported in Table 3.1 present the expenditures *planned* by the government and not those which have been realized. The spending capacity of the public sector is in fact very limited: only 54 per cent of the total expenditures will normally be realized (Gerelli et al., 1989).

Institutional efforts have recently been made in order to solve this problem. One of the measures worth mentioning is the use of new investment procedures – a systematic consideration of costs and benefits of the projects to be realized. These measures are supposed to improve the efficiency and effectiveness of environmental expenditures.

These measures have also facilitated the integration of environmental policy with the other political economic objectives. Such an outcome has been explicitly called for by public authorities. The reduction of the current expenditures, because of the budgetary deficit, is expected to be associated with the increase of the

Table 3.1:   **Environmental expenditures in Italy (billion lira)**

	1981	*1982*	*1984*	*1986*	*1987*	*1988*
Central authority	1377	1418	1145	1316	1461	3022
FIO	–	420	563	1793	1793	1600
Regions	1414	1462	1500	1786	1514	1500
Total	2791	3300	3208	4895	4768	6122
Local community	n.a.	n.a.	1686	2786	n.a.	n.a.
Grand total	–	–	–	4894	7681	–

Source: Gerelli et al. (1989)

fiscal pressure and of the capital expenditures. An increase of investments, however, is likely to be smaller than the reduction of current expenditures; but the higher capital expenditures multiplier will probably offset the negative effect of the reduction of the current expenditures (Galimberti, 1988, p. 6).

This strategy requires an improvement of the spending capacity of the government, which is quite low. The introduction of a new decision-making process and, more specifically, the use of CBA will probably help the government to attain these objectives.

Planning by projects and cost-benefit analysis

In the 1980s the public authority embraced a new planning approach based on a decentralized system: planning by projects (See Pennisi, 1985, pp. 593–603; Lamanda, 1986, pp. 237–250; Lamanda, 1987, pp. 235–246; Florio, 1986, pp. 553–558.) With this new approach, investment projects are proposed directly by relevant operators. The consistency of the particular projects with macro-economic objectives is then evaluated by *ad hoc* agencies using decision analysis tools.

This is not a wholly new approach: the Agency for the Development of the South of Italy (Cassa per il Mezzogiorno) was already using this method; however, the level of the financing involved was limited.

The traditional planning model, based on the allocation of funds for specific purposes managed by the concerned administrations, was not completely abandoned, but interest in it was clearly diminished. This new approach is the public authorities' answer to the failure of the traditional concept of planning used in other OECD countries as well (Gerelli and Pola, 1979). The advantage of this approach is that decisions are market oriented. In other words, investment decisions are left to the market with public authorities assessing, through decision analysis tools, the validity of the proposed projects and their consistency with the economic objectives. More specifically the features of the approach are as follows (Lamanda, 1986, pp. 242–3):

• it is required that each project be evaluated from the point of view of efficiency;
• efficient resource allocation requires that projects compete with each other. This requires a screening of all projects and the

application of transparent criteria of choice;
• the procedure is relevant also from a macro-economic point of view because projects are also valued according to their capability of meeting macro-economic objectives;
• it is a decentralized procedure in that projects are proposed by a multiplicity of subjects.

Because of these features a great deal of benefit has been gained. Through the projects proposed at local level, demand for new investment has emerged. The majority of the projects have concerned environmental development (hydro-geological engineering and anti-pollution activities) and public instruction (university infrastructures) (Lamanda, 1986, p. 244). Another beneficial aspect has been the use of decision analysis in the decision-making process.

It is within this frame of reference that the FIO scheme was set up in 1982. The objectives of the fund were twofold:

• in the short run, to sustain public investments and the rate of employment;
• in the long run, to improve the quality of the capital expenditures and maintain their consistency with economic planning (Pennisi in Muraro, 1987, p. 173).

In a mixed economy system, where the market mechanism prevails and economic planning has mainly the role of "defining" the objectives, CBA can help make the directives of the economic planning more concrete. It may specify the directions in which the public sector has to move in order to guarantee an efficient allocation of the existing resources (Petretto in Formez, 1987).

The use of decision analysis techniques at national and regional level

The appraisal of public investments has been adopted in the public administration since 1960 in relation to investment programmes of the Agency for the Development of the South of Italy. Guidelines were elaborated by the agency. Evaluation of the public investments carried out by the Agency concerned the following sectors:

• hydraulic engineering;

- infrastructures;
- promotion of industrial activities;
- roads construction and land protection;
- irrigation projects.

The methodology used did not take into consideration estimates of environmental benefits: the computation of the rate of profitability (internal rate of return and net present value) was based on market prices. The objective of the analysis was to evaluate the incremental production, the increase of the per capita income and employment, and the public revenue originated by the tariffs of the services produced through the projects.

After that experience, the Investment and Employment Fund (FIO) was set up by Law n.181 of 26 April 1982. In order for an investment to be financed by the fund it should be in conformity with the law to promote employment. Both central and regional bodies are entitled to this fund. FIO funds can be used for environmental protection and have indeed been used to such an extent that this instrument has become the most important source in Italian environmental policy.

As a result, funds going to environmental protection are high. In the 1982–5 period, 34 per cent of FIO funds, (3000 billion out of 8850 billion lira) was spent on environmental protection. In the 1986–8 period, environmental projects planned to be financed totalled 3686 billion lira, most of which (1450 billion lira) was for water treatment. For 1989, expenditures for 2000 billion lira were authorized, with a possibility of qualifying for the funds of the European Investment Bank for 1500 billion lira. A substantial quota of these funds was reserved for environmental projects: 900 billion lira for waste water treatment, 350 billion for solid waste treatment, and 150 billion for less polluting agricultural activities.

Only those environmental projects costing between 10 and 100 billion lira can be financed. Projects have to be carried out within four years from the delivery of the plans.

The demand of funds concerns only projects which are "immediately feasible", that is, projects with technical and legal qualifications which permit the delivery of the plans within 120 days of the issuing of the concession in the Official Gazette.

The investments are the subject of a prior CBA in accordance with the 1982 Law n.181, which also set up the Public Investment Assessment Group under the Economic Planning Secretariat. This

Group appraises the technical and economic merits of public investment proposals and, particularly, their costs and benefits. This application of CBA is an innovation worth mentioning since it constitutes the first case of its use by the authorities to any great extent.

The Group is expected to appraise not only FIO but also other funds, such as the Environmental Plan of the Environmental Department, the Anti-pollution Plan for the River Lambro, projects for the development of the South of Italy (Law n.64, 1986) and virtually all public investments.

The objectives and the operational guidelines of the Group were stipulated in 1986 with Law n.878. The same law set up the final organization of the Inspectors Group (care of the Budget Department) and the Technical Commission of Public Expenditure, (care of the Treasury Department). The former was in control of the realization of the projects financed through the FIO and the latter in charge of the study of the economic rentability of the current public expenditure.

Some other funds that have been created in the same period use decision analysis tools for the allocation of their funds. In addition to the Department for the South of Italy, the National Scheme for the Environment and the Bank for Deposits and Loans (Ministero del Tesoro, 1986; Di Maio, 1988) should be mentioned. However, the procedures set up by these later schemes do not have the same importance as those of the FIO.

Methodological problems raised by the intervention of the FIO as regards the evaluation of anti-pollution projects and cultural goods have led to the institution of independent evaluation groups, set up in the competent departments (that is, the Department of the Environment and the Department of Cultural Goods). These evaluation groups were initially set up with the limited function of advising the Public Investment Assessment Group of the Budget and Economic Planning Department. But, afterwards, they assumed a larger capacity and this gave rise to the possibility of autonomously managing the decisions on public expenditures. For this reason, the opportunity of managing specific funds from the FIO has increased considerably. This happened, for instance, in relation to the so-called "cultural deposits" plan set up through the 1986 financial law. The Assessment Group of the Cultural Goods Department has to collaborate in evaluating costs and benefits with the Assessment Group of the Labour Department, which is entitled to check the impact on employment of the projects.

According to one point of view, the proliferation of the assessment groups' overseeing of different departments of the public administration has been determined by politicians' fears of losing control of public expenditure.

Increases in the number of the assessment groups without there being co-ordination of the evaluation methodologies will produce further obstacles to the necessary rationalization of public expenditure. Because of this, Article 14 of the 1986 financial law established that the environmental projects proposed at regional level be jointly evaluated by the Assessment Group of the Environmental Department and by the Technico-Scientific Commission for the Assessment of Environmental Projects of the Environment Department.

The same procedures used by the Assessment Group of the Budget Department have been adopted in other public administrations: the Agricultural and Forestry Department, the Foreign Affairs Department, the Transport Department, and the Ministry of Education. The methodology used in these later cases is not satisfactory in that it introduces an insufficient amount of rationalization in the decision-making process.

Assessment procedures have also been introduced at regional level. Emilia Romagna set up a regional scheme for the financing of local infrastructures (Regione Emilia Romagna, 1985, Friest). Lombardy is applying CBA in financing public projects in relation to the Lombardy Investment Fund (Bollettino Ufficiale Lombardia, 1985). Finally, Latium is planning to use decision analysis techniques in respect of economic planning activities (Buffoni, 1983; Formez, 1983).

The need for co-ordination of the assessment procedures

All these examples show the interest of the public authorities in assessment procedures and in ameliorating the problems associated with their implementation. These procedures have the aim of producing collaboration between different levels of government. However, it is not enough to specify some rules that would govern such a collaboration. These rules and procedures have to be sound and capable of fostering collaboration. (It has already been mentioned that there is the feeling that the assessment groups have been instituted to keep under control the resources of their respective departments.)

Besides this problem, the interest in the FIO experience is related to the innovative aspect of the procedures which were adopted in order to realize public investments. Because different actors participate in the investment process, this could constitute an example of integrated procedures where the interdependencies between the different bodies may create serious complications.

A simplified version of this process is as follows:

- every year the FIO funds are determined by law;
- the Inter-ministerial Committee for Economic Planning (CIPE) sets up the conditions of access to the FIO funds;
- the Assessment Group of the Budget Department arranges and brings technical evaluating procedures up to date;
- central authorities and regions put forward financing proposals, accompanied by CBA;
- the Assessment Group of the Budget Department controls the technical admissibility of the proposals on the basis of the validity of the CBA;
- in a parallel fashion, as far as the environmental projects are concerned, the Technico-Scientific Commission for the Assessment of Environmental Projects of the Environment Department also assesses the validity of the CBA and, according to the results of the analysis, defines a priority list of projects to be financed. This list is sent to the Assessment Group of the Budget Department for further methodological analysis;
- within the Inter-ministerial Committee of Economic Planning, the Budget Ministry takes into consideration the technical investigation of their Assessment Group and puts forward the political proposal for financing the projects;
- this is followed by an assignment of funds to the central authorities or the regions and a control by the Inspectors Group of the Budget Department on the start of the work.

Other decision analysis techniques

There are other types of decision analysis which are used by the public authorities but they do not have the same importance. Environmental impact assessment (EIA) has recently been adopted by the government. This procedure requires that environmental impacts be assessed for any major project likely to have significant effects on the environment. A list of the projects and specific guidelines has been adopted by the public authorities.

It is not the purpose of this chapter to discuss the guidelines established by the Ministry of the Environment or to comment on specific regulations. However, it is emphasized that environmental impacts should be assessed in physical terms and that their appraisal should be subject to the same limits that are encountered in the benefit estimate procedure used in the CBA.

EIA surely constitutes a progress in the better understanding of the environmental impacts of the projects. However, these impacts are defined only in qualitative or physical quantitative terms. Dealing with homogeneous impacts, we can expect that when certain limit values are exceeded projects have to be rejected. But if the impacts are not homogeneous – such as when we have to compare the impact of a project on the physical and social environment – we need a common criterion.

Cost-benefit Analysis in Italy: Theory and Practice

Environmental projects and cost-benefit analysis: some theoretical aspects

We have already anticipated that the primary goal of CBA is to show a project's net effect on the value of output and other flows of "welfare". The basic criterion to be satisfied is that the value of goods and services produced be ultimately increased.

In order to achieve this result the following procedure should be followed:

- identification of the various effects of the proposed project or programme;
- quantification in physical terms of these effects;
- evaluation of costs and benefits in monetary terms;
- presentation of the relevant information in a reasonably straight-forward manner that clearly spells out the important assumptions underlying the analysis, and the implications of these assumptions for the study's conclusions.

These stages are the same for all types of project, but, when dealing with environmental projects, special problems emerge.

Environmental projects create a wide variety of benefits: their identification and evaluation requires knowledge both of physical and biological processes and of the economic responses to these effects. For example, determination of the effects of changes in pollutant concentrations on agricultural productivity requires knowledge of the effects of pollutants on the yields of various crops and on the responses of farmers in choosing which crop to plant. Changes in environmental quality will affect the amount of output obtained from given amounts of other inputs, and thus will shift the supply curves for the affected commodities. In order to ascertain these effects and to measure them accurately, monitoring activities are necessary. (For the general aspects of these problems see Barde and Gerelli, 1980; Nuti, 1987, chap.9; Pennisi in Muraro (ed.), 1984.)

The benefits and costs of public sector activities depend upon individuals' willingness to pay. When the commodities involved are exchanged in straightforwardly competitive markets, then market prices would measure the willingness to pay for the last unit consumed, and the area under the demand curve would represent the total willingness to pay. What is needed is to consider how the contemplated project would affect the availability of the commodity.

Dealing with environmental projects, a market may not always exist and therefore we cannot refer to the market indicators. Even if such indicators do exist, they may fail to reflect appropriate substitution ratios, for several reasons discussed in the literature:

• the existence of market distortions means that special interpretations will have to be placed on market-demand curves;
• there is often less than complete information on demand curves;
• the existence of non-market goods poses special problems in the conceptualization and measurement of demand curves.

These problems introduce the use of shadow prices and indirect methods of evaluation which recall the concept of willingness to pay (McKean, 1968). There has been considerable work done at both theoretical and practical level on problems related to shadow prices and on opportunities for applying analytical techniques in evaluating environmental benefits. There can be divergencies and/or contradictions between the actual individual behaviour and what is socially desirable. The willingness-to-pay approach used in order to evaluate the environmental benefits implies that individuals are able to judge the effects of an environmental improvement project upon their welfare. This might not be the case. As an example, the individuals may be incapable of judging the damage caused by toxic substances accumulation. Thus, to the Paretian approach of the willingness to pay, a paternalistic approach based on technical expertise may be preferred, but even technical experts may have an insufficient amount of knowledge regarding the relevant problems. Nevertheless, the paternalistic approach has one advantage: it may stimulate general evaluation. Because of the interdependency between the environmental resources at national level, the project by project approach can be limiting.

Although methods of evaluation have been developed and discussed for almost all categories of environmental benefits, the application of any such methodology is still difficult (Johansson, 1987; Dorfman, 1965). As will be seen in relation to the FIO experience, without better resolution of the methodological problems and without specific guidelines, a serious problem may occur. Proponents of an action tend to assign inordinately high values to those benefits which are important but hard to measure, while opponents tend to over-emphasize the benefits which are easiest to quantify and value them relatively low.

Another theoretical problem encountered in CBA is the determination of the net impact of the benefits and costs on social well-being. This requires a criterion for determining what does constitute an increase in social well-being and procedures for aggregating effects that occur at different points in time.

Environmental projects have effects that extend over a number of years. The actual distribution of benefits and costs over time will depend on several factors: the length of the installation period; the relative magnitudes of capital, operating and maintenance costs; the length of life of the equipment, and so on. Therefore, decision rules are required for choosing among policies that have different distributions of benefits and costs over time, and one of the inescapable features of decision-making processes in the environmental sector is the presence of significant uncertainties.

Once all benefits and costs are expressed in present values they can be readily and justifiably compared with one another. This implies a choice of discount rate, which poses no problem for the analyst because government agencies specify what discount rate is to be used in cost-benefit studies. This does not necessarily mean that there are no theoretical problems however, since there is considerable controversy among economists over what criteria to employ in selecting the proper discount rate.

Discount rates can either reflect society's preference for present benefits over future benefits or the rate of return forgone in the private sector. In the former case we talk of social-time preference rate, whereas in the latter of social-opportunity cost of capital (Pearce, 1986; Pearce and Nash, 1981).

The experience of the Investment and Employment Scheme (FIO)

Although some of the problems mentioned in the previous section have been solved from a theoretical point of view, a lot of questions still remain when passing from the theoretical analysis to the implementation phase.

When comparing different projects or ranking them according to their profitability we have to be sure that the methodology and the parameters used are identical. For this reason the Public Investment Assessment Group, on behalf of the Budget and Economic Planning Department, attached great importance to the issuing of a manual (Ministerio del Bilancio, 1983). The objective of the manual is to help the departments, expenditure agencies and regions to prepare plans and investment projects which meet efficiency criteria and are consistent with the priorities set up by the Medium-Term Economic Planning Group. In order to reach these objectives, the manual (a) defines the methodology to be used by the analyst and (b) points out which activities of the Assessment Group should be used to help the analysts in formulating plans and projects.

The manual does not pretend to elaborate new methodologies but only to synthesize the most common accepted approaches. As will be seen in the next section, emphasis will be put on the theoretical problems of CBA such as the shadow prices, the national parameters and the method to be used for evaluating the benefits. All these problems have been carefully taken into consideration when comparing the different solutions adopted by other manuals e.g. those of UNIDO and OECD.

The manual was prepared at the beginning of the 1980s when public operators were concerned with so-called "planning by projects"; for this reason attention is given to the relation between CBA and economic planning (Pennisi, 1985).

In addition to the manual, which is mostly theoretical, the government issued precise guidelines to be used by the analyst in performing a CBA, as required by FIO rules (Official Gazette Supplement n. 161, 1988). Unless care is taken in the preparation of the report, valuable information about the assumptions and evaluation methods underlying the study may be overlooked or misunderstood. For these reasons, formats were prepared by the Assessment Group which were to be used in developing a cost-benefit report so that all reports should ultimately convey essentially the same information. Special formats were prepared for the projects concerning waste and water treatment plants. Detailed instructions were also given for environmental projects such as aqueducts, irrigation, transport projects and waste-water treatment plants.

These formats, approved by the Inter-ministerial Committee for Economic Planning (CIPE), have undergone a long process of refinement. One recent improvement allows the analyst to use a specific computerized program for the representation of tables and an electronic computation of the indicators of the project.

The formats, once filled in, are sent to the Assessment Group and the details of the environmental projects to the Technico-Scientific Commission for the Assessment of Environmental Projects of the Environment Department. Projects are ranked according to the internal rate of return and the net present value. However, as will be seen in the following sections, projects, in order to be financed, should also be consistent with other criteria.

Methodological and procedural aspects
We have anticipated that the manual and the guidelines provide guidance on the methodology and procedural issues related to the CBA. The presentation which follows will therefore take both of these into consideration. We will first introduce the procedural aspects and subsequently some of the methodological aspects covered by the manual.

The use of the allocative criteria based on the comparison of economic costs and benefits requires that an empirical content be given to these elements. It is therefore essential to indicate that generally accepted criteria concerning the methodology have been used to identify and assess costs and benefits.

In the case of environmental projects, the acceptance of the allocative principle based on the comparison of costs and benefits requires a close correlation between technical and economic criteria.

For these specific reasons the guidelines require that, in order to produce a correct CBA, three aspects must be considered:

(1) technico-analytical aspects which are necessary for a correct identification of the environmental effects;
(2) engineering aspects for the identification of the best technical alternatives which will be useful for solving the environmental problems;
(3) economic aspects for the computation of profitability indicators of the project (internal rate of return and net present value).

The areas concerned are characterized by the use of generally accepted methologies. The weak point lies in the third area: the evaluation of the impacts of the projects.

Guidelines underline the importance of initially considering the nature of the problem and the general objectives stated by the economic and physical plans of the sectors concerned with the project. For instance, as far as water treatment plants are concerned, it is necessary to supply evidence about the relevance of the water resources concerned in the projects in relation to the objectives stated by the Water Reclamation Regional Plan. A description of the priorities stated by these plans is also relevant, as is how the proposed projects are related to these priorities.

One of the initial steps is the recognition of all resource inputs and final outputs of the projects, and the time at which they will occur. This market analysis should show the quantities which will be demanded at various prices and under various conditions. It should recognize, therefore, not only the current demand for goods and services, but also the expected growth in population, income and economic activity in the area of influence of the proposed project. All the underlying assumptions in the market estimate must be clearly defined.

The objective of the demand analysis is to determine the potential value of the anti-pollution measures applicable to the area indicated by the project. Because of this it is necessary to identify all the direct and indirect users of the environmental resources and the most relevant parameters in order to determine the pollution level that can be ascribed to the economic activities.

In the case of irrigation projects, the demand analysis should consider the amount of water to be provided by the project and the additional agricultural production which can result. The alternative uses of the water should be considered only if they will be affected by the project.

The analysis of the supply should take into consideration the existing environmental infrastructures *vis-à-vis* the project. In the case of water treatment plants, the situation *without* the project should give a picture of the main features of the sewerage system, existing water treatment plants, etc. A description should be given of the actions necessary to improve the operating conditions of the existing infrastructures without modifying the ratio between demand and supply capacity. The situation *with* the project is supposed to determine the value of the anti-pollution measures in relation to the total demand and to the existing supply.

Another relevant step considered by the guidelines concerns the technical aspects and the operating conditions of the project. Relevance is given to the managerial aspects of the project: operating conditions have to be carefully indicated for the entire life of the project. While problems of cost evaluation are less difficult than those of benefit evaluation, it is particularly important that costs of competing projects be rigorously and fairly compared.

A revision of prices can be made; this is based on the trend of the general level of prices and can be computed only from the second year of the project if the inflation rate is greater than 10 per cent in relation to the adjudication of the project. A revision of prices is also indicated for the operating costs for the initial five years of the project.

As far as economic life is concerned, this may be defined as the period over which useful benefits will be derived from the project. Different assumptions of life periods may be quite appropriate for different types of projects, depending on the physical facilities involved and the state of technology.

It is however assumed that the significant period of economic life should not exceed 25 years.

Finally, in order to perform the financial and economic analysis, costs and benefits should be evaluated. An analytical explanation should be given of the procedures used in the determination of the conversion factors necessary to translate financial costs into economic costs.

The correct identification and the sound measurement of project benefits are important and they should be set out in detail. Benefits may be classified in several ways. Classificatory schemes are provided by the guidelines; they are useful in that classification helps to identify effects. Knowledge of the various classificatory schemes can eliminate problems of double counting. To the greatest extent possible, the value of goods and services should be expressed in monetary terms, determined through the market system. Some goods and services, however, are not bought and sold in the market. In many cases, it is possible to attach a monetary value to them by methods largely discussed in the literature on shadow prices. As is shown in the next section, some of these methods are considered within the guidelines.

Shadow pricing

Shadow pricing aims to establish a set of prices reflecting the real scarcity of the domestic resources. In order to assess the corrective factors, we need to know on the basis of a social demand function the social value of the goods and services considered. For a first approximation, this value can be drawn from the indirect taxation. Successively, it can be calculated by subtracting from the unity the ratio between the social and the economic value of the goods. The correction is than added to the value of the goods. In summary:

market prices − imports = gross value added
gross value added − indirect taxes − transfer payments − direct taxes on salaries and wages = net value added
(market prices/net value added) − 1 = conversion factor

It was suggested that conversion factors which are used in the evaluation of shadow prices be calculated by the experts of the Assessment Group for the most important inputs and outputs of the project. This task remains to be performed.

In many situations, market prices do not exist. In these cases, explicit values must be imputed. Unfortunately, as is shown in the next section, subjective judgements often weigh heavily in this regard; this is the reason why the Assessment Group is trying to elaborate new guidelines.

Analyses
Additional instructions are given in relation to the sensitivity analysis, risk analysis, analysis of the alternatives, and the impact analysis.

• Sensitivity analysis: Whenever there is considerable uncertainty about the reliability of a predicted benefit or cost, the analyst should recalculate the net present values for some alternative values within some upper and lower bound estimates of the variable in question. An advantage of this approach is that it allows the analyst to identify those estimates that are crucial to the analysis.

Among the variables to take into consideration, the guidelines suggest the productive capacity of the project, the delay in the execution and the time optimization. The rate of capacity utilization is normally over-estimated for new technologies. The same miscalculation happens for the assessment of the length of the construction period. As far as the optimization time is concerned, the sensitivity analysis should be carried out whenever doubts exist about the rate of increase of the real demand for the output of the project (Ministero del Bilancio, 1983, p. 125).

• Risk analysis: in many cases it is necessary to take explicitly into account the fact that the exact outcome of an environmental decision cannot be predicted. The programme's effects are experienced over a period of time, so naturally there are uncertainties or risks associated with any attempt to predict the precise magnitude of those effects. The measurement of benefits and costs requires the analyst to predict such things as changes in consumption patterns, population movements and trends which cannot be known for certain. The role of the analyst in this regard is to provide the best estimates he or she can obtain, and, when necessary, acknowledge any uncertainties so that the decision maker is warned that the outcomes depend on less than perfect knowledge.

If the internal rate of return does not vary significantly when the main variables are modified, it may not be necessary to proceed with risk analysis. When the profitability indicators do vary considerably, the analyst should identify the variables to use in the analysis and give them a probability distribution derived from the available information and experience.

• Evaluation of the alternatives: this procedure examines alternative projects in order to supply evidence that the proposed solution is preferable to competitive technical solutions. The

reasons that the alternatives have been excluded have to be indicated by specifying the technical, managerial and economic aspects of the projects.
• Economic impact analysis: the analysis provides the basis for judging the importance of some of the assumptions underlying CBA. The guidelines consider the effects of the project on employment, on the revenue and on the balance of payments, both in the short and long term.

Identification and evaluation of the project benefits

The evaluation of the benefits is strictly connected to the possibility of being able to identify the effects of the project and determine the ways these effects would modify economic activities.

Two considerations should be put forward:

(1) Techniques used in defining the value of environmental projects emphasize the benefits either according to the use of the recovered or protected resources or to the cost of the resources when they are no longer usable. In other words, the value of the generated benefit can partly or totally coincide with the cost of the avoided damage.
(2) The value of the environmental resources tends to increase during the life of the projects whereas that of the economic goods tends to decrease in real value. The hypothesis of constant prices of the environmental resources has to be considered conservative (official Gazette Supplement n. 152).

The analysis of the effects of the project on the environment should produce information to define two specific functions:

• a function which relates the polluting activities to environmental quality;
• a damage function which takes into consideration the qualitative changes of the resources and the effects on the behaviour of the socio-economic subjects (the damages to be estimated are those perceived by those who currently suffer the damage).

This procedure, which tries to identify the benefits through the identification of the environmental effects of the projects associated with the potential users of the resources, has the advantage of avoiding the risk of double counting. One error usually made by the analyst consists of computing the benefits of the environmental services twice, once through the tariffs or other revenues associated with the use of the environment, and again through the benefits to the same subjects as users of the environmental resources recovered through the project.

Both direct and indirect effects should be considered. A critical problem in evaluating these effects is that markets generally do not exist. As a result, the assignment of monetary values to changes in environmental quality requires either the use of market data for related commodities or the use of non-market data, such as the results of surveys. Many authors present an excellent review and critique of the theoretical bases for a number of procedures that have been, or could be, used (Freeman, 1979).

Moreover, the handbook prepared by the Assessment Group and the guidelines issued by the CIPE describe a number of techniques of benefits assessment that are normally used. The aim is to provide a useful catalogue of methods to assist the practitioner in selecting the basic approach that seems most appropriate for his or her needs in carrying out specific benefit assessments.

A short description of some benefit assessments in two areas, water resources and tourism, is given below.

• Water resources: Direct economic benefits stemming from the use of water resources are strictly related to final consumption of water and the nature of the inputs.

In the first instance, the value can be attribted to the willingness to pay of the consumer and, in the second instance, to the productivity of the input. In both cases, however, the value depends on the scarcity and the opportunity cost of the supply. Accordingly, in evaluating the uses of water, these aspects have to be taken into consideration: the degree of scarcity, the features of the particular area, and the technological opportunities that are available. An alternative approach is to consider the most expensive tariff to be paid by the consumer with the maximum level of consumption.

In evaluating the situation without the project, the value of the water would depend not only on the present use but also on plans of alternative uses. The value is zero only if the water supply exceeds the present needs. In all other cases, the value should be computed considering the net forgone benefits of the alternative uses of water.

Indirect benefits of water must also be considered. Water can always be reused, even if considered as a final good; accordingly, the value should be appraised on the basis of costs and benefits stemming from subsequent uses.

As far as irrigation projects are concerned, environmental effects assume particular importance. Such effects can be positive in the case of underground water, but normally they are negative because of the lower quality of the surface water returned to the main system. The value of these effects should be discounted by the lack of benefits for the downstream users or by the additional costs that the users have to bear in order to protect their uses.

If the information necessary for an accurate evaluation is lacking, the effects should be presented in quantitative physical terms (quality of the surface waters, quantity of fertilizers or pesticides in the water, etc.) in order to allow the Assessment Group to make the proper corrections.

• Tourism: Environment is affected by tourism demand. However, the hypothesis based on a high reduction of the value added of the sector does not seem justifiable except in extreme situations.

Normally, the market mechanism tends to smooth out the impact on the number of tourists by increasing the investments on alternative supplies and modifying the prices. Just as an approximation, benefit evaluation procedures try to determine the trend of the tourist demand and the average cost of a day spent by the tourist, or, the cost increase borne by the tourist operators in order to supply alternative services able to sustain the level and the quality of the demand.

In order to harmonize the methods used for the evaluation of direct benefits, the following parameters apply:
• a shadow price of 10,000 lira for each user;
• 95,000 lira for each day spent by the tourist;
• each additional day spent by the tourist due to the project will be multiplied by a factor of 1.38.

In order to apply this factor, the analysis should demonstrate that the existing tourist capacity is able to satisfy the incremental demand originated by the project. For the communities with more than 300,000 inhabitants, the demand of tourism should also be assessed for the resident population. The incremental factor, however, should be applied to foreign visitors.

Finally, in the evaluation of the net benefits stemming from the incremental expenditures of tourism thus computed, it is necessary to subtract the value of the cost of production of the goods bought by tourists. The net benefit is not equal either to the total expenditure of tourists nor to the value added at input prices, because the value added includes the payment of inputs such as labour and capital which are cost elements. In order to evaluate the costs of these inputs, which have to be subtracted from the value added, shadow prices can be used.

Selected problems in benefit estimation: the role of the national parameters

The implementation of CBA in a situation where economic planning is missing requires the determination of suitable parameters by the political authority. These parameters furnish the value that society would attribute to consumption, investment (the rate of development), employment, foreign currency, and the distribution of the revenue.

These parameters can be identified through a process of revealed preferences. In some cases they are elaborated by the public authority on the basis of *ad hoc* studies on the opportunity cost of the capital, the marginal productivity of work, the implicit exchange rate, and fiscal pressure, etc, which help define the values that society attributes to consumption, investment, employment, foreign currency and the distribution of the revenue (Pennisi, 1985, p. 64). Parameters defined in this manner comply with the criterion of transparency of the decisions. However, they should be re-examined periodically in the face of ever changing economic conditions.

These parameters differ from shadow prices in that they reflect the social value that citizens attribute to principal economic variables. They constitute the medium-term objectives of the political economy of a country (Pennisi, 1985, p. 65).

Once approved, these parameters must be applied uniformly in order to have choices based on the same criteria. In the manual developed by the Assessment Group, specific instructions are given in order to elaborate the shadow prices of the exchange rate, the employment and the discount rate. In actuality, precise indications are given only for the social discount rate.

The *social discount rate* is the national parameter which assures the intertemporal distribution between consumption and investment. The evaluation of the social rate of discount in a market economy creates many problems concerning the difficulty of building a social welfare system that accurately represents the objectives of the public economy. Distortions that exist in the economy result in a discrepancy between the market interest rate and the marginal productivity of the capital (internal rate of return) and between the marginal productivity of the capital and the intertemporal rate of preferences of the society.

There are a number of methods which can be used to evaluate the social discount rate which reflect various meanings accorded to it by different theorists. According to some theories, one must use more than one social discount rate depending on the type of project or the incomes of those who have to bear the costs or reap the benefits. In Italy, only one rate of discount has been adopted. From an empirical point of view, the use of one social discount rate simplifies the comparison of competing projects even though this may result in some errors, especially when there is a large difference between average and marginal return.

Econometric evaluations of the marginal productivity of the capital for the periods 1951–70 and 1970–82 have been performed. These evaluations have been subsequently compared with empirical estimates both for the whole industry sectors and for some specific industry sectors. These estimates were then controlled for the effect of technical progress on the GNP in the period 1951–82. The conclusion drawn from this analysis is that in Italy the social rate of discount is larger than the rate of productivity of the system: it is between 10 and 12 per cent. The rate determined by the Assessment Group was 10 per cent between 1984 and 1986 and 8 per cent from 1986 onwards.

Four Case Studies

The following sections present some case studies which concentrate on the analysis of the benefits estimates and demonstrate the problems encountered in their estimation. The emphasis is upon the direct effects of the projects considered. Accordingly, technical description and cost analysis are not taken into consideration.

Case study: A solid-waste treatment plant in a Southern Italian Region

Until now, solid waste in this area has been subject to

non-controlled disposal. This practice has created a number of environmental problems. The project considers the construction of a compost plant, three treatment plants and an inertization plant for industrial sludge.

The project considers only the direct benefits. Tariffs were deemed not to reflect the real social value of the service provided by the waste treatment plant since they cover only the average cost of the treatment. Therefore, a price was calculated which expressed the opportunity cost that society is willing to pay in order to remove the pollution originated by solid waste. For this reason, tariffs have been considered as transfers and therefore have not been included in the economic analysis.

The opportunity cost represents, as a good approximation, the shadow price of the treatment activity to be applied to the output of the project. The procedure compares the operating and maintenance costs of the treatment associated with the two options considered:

- a centralized treatment plant and three small plants for the treatment of specific wastes;
- different controlled discharges over the entire territory affected by the project (situation without project).

Shadow prices of the two options have been computed with the method of average incremental cost:

$$AIC = \frac{\sum_i (Ii + OMi)/(1 + r)^i}{\sum_i (Vi + Vo)/(1 + r)^i}$$

where:

i	$= 0, 1, 2, \ldots 30$ – the life of the project;
Ii	= investment costs for the ith year;
OMi	= operating and maintenance costs;
Vi	= the quantity treated in the ith year;
Vo	= the quantity treated in the o year;
r	= the social discount rate (8 per cent).

The difference between the two AIC parameters represents the social value that society attributes to the centralized treatment compared to controlled discharges over the territory. Such a difference is the willingness to pay of society for better environmental protection.

Another direct benefit considered in the analysis is the value of the land used for the discharges which, when the discharges cease, is recovered and used as a recreational resource. The intangible benefits are not easy to measure. The ideal measure of the benefits to the user is the sum that he or she would be willing to pay soley to enjoy a recreational opportunity. The analysis must attempt to estimate the amount that could be collected from the users of recreational areas, provided that it were possible to price their services and amenities.

The method used consisted of evaluating the cost of the expropriation. This represented the capitalization of the "social revenue" associated with the use of the area by the public. This method is likely to produce an under-estimation rather than an exaggeration of the amount which users are willing to pay to retain the recreational area or amenity. The net present value was 1 billion lira and the internal rate of return 10.44 per cent, which was larger than the discount rate used in the analysis (8 per cent).

As stated previously, the procedures established by CIPE require the implementation of other forms of analysis. Risk analysis is not relevant in the case of a solid waste treatment plant, since the only parameters which can assume probabilistic behaviour are the rate of population growth and the daily quantity of solid waste per capita produced. The two parameters have the same sign because they have a negative impact on the tariffs and on the benefits considered. The only significant hypothesis is that the quantity of solid waste delivered to the plant is smaller because population numbers are diminishing. However, this is not in fact the case because the rate of indigenous population growth is stationary. Indeed, we can consider a small increase in the quantity of solid waste delivered to the plant because of tourism and the development of economic activities.

A sensitivity analysis has been carried out in order to check whether the modification of the benefits influence the performance of the project. The analysis has been limited to the identification and quantification of the benefits, because as far as technology is concerned this is standardized, and the revision of the prices has already been taken into consideration by the project according to the CIPE guidelines.

Different alternative hypotheses have been considered for calculating the benefits:

• the sum of the benefits has been diminished by 10 per cent in order to analyse the sensitivity of the managerial conditions;
• investments costs of the situation with the project and the operating costs of the situation without costs have been reduced by 10 per cent;
• finally, two scenarios have been considered, one negative which foresees an increase of 10 per cent of all costs and benefits and one positive with a reduction of 10 per cent.

Table 3.2 summarises the results of the sensitivity analysis.

Case study: European Centre for Environmental Training Activities

In this case, we are not dealing directly with pollution problems. The objective of the project is to establish a centre for the training of the personnel in charge of managing environmental equipment.

Direct benefits were assessed using the tariffs that the users of the centre would have to pay; this demonstrates the willingness of the public administration and of the industry to pay for well-trained personnel. This service would result in cost saving for the management of the infrastructures, in terms of reduced consultancy fees, higher productivity, etc. This cannot be considered double counting because the indirect benefits concern capital expenditures of the public administration in the environmental sector, whereas

Table 3.2: **Sensitivity analysis of the social benefits of solid-waste treatment plant**

	Var.%	*NPV (billion)*	*IRR (%)*
Investment costs	+10	−1	6.2
	−10	3	16.0
Operational costs	+10	−7	not sig.
	−10	9	23.0
Benefits	+10	11	26.8
	−10	−9	not sig.
Positive scenario		21	45.1
Negative scenario		−18	not sig.

the expenditures taken into consideration by the project concern public and private current expenditures.

As for indirect benefits, the only benefit considered is the cost saving for the central and local authorities as a result of the environmental programmes. In addition, one may consider the effects of the project on public health, the development of the rate of employment, the development of new professions, less damage to the environment and increase in tourism. Yet, these effects have not been considered because they did not seem to be relevant. For, even though the relevant literature offers valuable methodology for the assessment of these secondary effects, their appraisal will create considerable probabilistic error or, again, a high margin of subjectivity in the evaluation.

The hypothesis adopted in assessing the indirect benefits is that through the training activity there would be an improvement in knowledge of the environmental problems and an increase in the efficiency of the environmental operators and, consequently, a saving in the public current expenditure.

In an attempt to quantify this effect, the trend of environmental public expenditure for the period concerned in the investment was considered to be equal to the average expenditures registered in the period previous to the investment. This yields a 1 per cent saving in expenditure. In other words, the benefit stemming from the project is the amount of public expenditure saved and which can be attributed to the satisfaction of the supply generated by the proposed investment:

$$Bct = \frac{Oct.Sat}{Dt}$$

where:

Bct   = benefits with the project at year t;
Dt   = training activity demand at year t;
Oct   = training activity supply with the project at year t;
Sat   = public expenditure foreseen at year t.

The same method is applied for the appraisal of the indirect benefit without the project. The benefit is determined by the public expenditure saved to be ascribed to the satisfaction of the demand generated in the situation without the project. That is:

$$Bst = \frac{Ost.}{Dt} \quad Sat$$

where:

Bst   = benefits without project at year t;

Ost   = supply of training activities at year t.

Net benefits are determined by the difference between the situation with and without the project:

[Bnt = Bct – Bst = (Ost/Dt – Oct/DDt) Sat]

As shown in Table 3.3, benefits rapidly increase in the first ten years because of the development of the centre and then, after the sixth year, benefits progressively decrease because of the physical constraints of the centre, which would not be keeping up with the increase in the supply in relation to the trend of the demand.

Table 3.3:   **Direct benefits of the European Centre for Training Activities (million lira)**

Years	With	Without	Net benefit
1	75150	75150	0
2	74777	73760	1017
3	74417	72420	1998
4	75052	71128	3924
5	74700	69881	4819
6	73729	68677	5052
7	72480	67514	4967
8	71273	66390	4884
9	70106	65302	4804
10	68976	64250	4726
–	–	–	–
23	57028	53120	3920
24	56278	52422	3856
25	55548	51741	3806

Case study: Water supply system in the Venice region

This project consists of increasing the potable water supply for some small communities in the Venice region. The project involves a network of water collectors and a canalization system.

Only direct benefits have been assessed and they are represented by the value of the water supplied. Tariffs are not considered to represent the benefit for society because they do not reflect market prices. In fact they are largely below the user value (price) that society is willing to pay.

The shadow price, which is 912 lira, has been assessed using average prices in various European countries (Table 3.4).

In order to avoid double counting, tariff revenues have not been considered. The evaluation carried out in the analysis is quite conservative because the benefit has been considered to be constant for the entire life of the project.

Another benefit is the improved quality and quantity of the underground waters. The increase of water supply would reduce the pressure to use well water. The benefits have been calculated considering the saving in the expenditure actually incurred for hydro-geological protection. This is based on a percentage of expenditures carried out in the previous years.

There are, of course, other indirect benefits such as the increase

Table 3.4: **Water prices in Europe (exchange rate at 3.9.88)**

City	Lira cm
Bilbao	256
Copenaghen	428
Munich	768
Lille	850
Vienna	1030
Lyon	1033
Marseille	1099
Paris	1287
Brussels	1457
Average	912

in quality of life for the residential population. Tourism would also benefit from the improved water supply. These effects could all be evaluated; nevertheless, they have been omitted because of their susceptibility to a high degree of subjectivity during assessment.

Case study: Coastal water reclamation in a southern region of Italy

On the Italian southern coast, pollution problems are mostly due to tourism activities which are concentrated into a few months of the year. This creates serious pollution in the summer period and poses many problems for the operators of waste-water treatment plants whose capacities are based on the peak load of pollution to be treated.

The objective of the project concerns the completion and the renovation of the sewerage system and the construction of a waste-water treatment plant according to the Water Regional Reclamation Plan. The project considers not only the benefits stemming from the building of new infrastructures but also those that are related to the optimization of the operating conditions of the existing plants.

The demand for anti-pollution measures is determined by the load on the system created by the residential population and tourism in addition to the local economic activities. The supply without the project satisfies only 33 per cent of the total demand for anti-pollution activities of the relevant area. The existing infrastructures have to work at full capacity with high operating costs. The sewerage system covers only part of the region. The supply with the project has been determined by considering two alternative types of waste-water treatment plants.

Most of the benefits of pollution abatement projects appear to fall into the category of intangibles, in the sense that a price is not usually charged for the services provided.

Direct benefits are mainly related to the tariffs of the service provided, whereas indirect benefits are connected to the possibilities of using environmental services, plus the increase in tourism activities.

The hypothesis adopted in order to assess the impact on tourism is that tourism flow will not decrease with the realization of the project. The increase in tourism activities has therefore been omitted. The situation without the project considers the possibility that without an intervention from the public authorities there will be a reduction in the number of tourists.

Indirect benefits associated with tourism consist of avoiding the decrease in the number of tourists of about 8 per cent (1 per cent yearly for the economic life of the project). The value has been assessed using the coefficient issued by the CIPE guidelines, that entail:

• an average expenditure for each tourist in the amount of 95,000 lira;
• a quota of 49,500 lira to pay for inputs of this expenditure. (This has been calculated using a value-added coefficient of 0.5216 drawn from the input/output tables of the Italian economy.)

Some indirect benefits have been identified as the improved quality of the services provided to the tourists and better quality of life in general. But these benefits have not been quantified; the analysis has provided only a description of them.

In spite of the fact that the assessment of the indirect benefits has been limited only to the most relevant ones, the net present value – based on the difference of the benefits that would occur in the situation with and without the project – came out as positive (34 billion, 1988 lira) and the internal rate of return was calculated to be 15.62 per cent. Also, the sensitivity analysis confirms the social profitability of the project. Considering a reduction or an increase of the direct benefits (tariffs) of 10 per cent, the internal rate of return is still 8 per cent larger (social discount rate), assuming values around 14–17 per cent.

Difficulties and Problems Arising in the Application of the Estimation Procedures

Lessons arising from the FIO experience

The work performed by the Assessment Group has facilitated the implementation, transparency and consistency of the economic and technical criteria used in the analysis. The number of projects presented to the Group has increased considerably – from 227 in 1982 to 708 in 1988.

The ratio of projects approved over the total projects presented has also improved. This is partly due to the procedures adopted by the Group (Ministero del Bilancio, 1988, p. 21):

1982	38.3 per cent
1983	28.7 per cent
1984	31.6 per cent
1985	51.6 per cent
1986	53.1 per cent

Because of the applicable procedures, analysts have made a considerable effort in the technical and economic definitions of the projects.

In analysing the requests presented to the FIO, it is immediately noticeable that, from a theoretical point of view, environmental projects were best endowed. In most cases, the proponents have carefully assessed the direct and indirect effects of the proposed projects, as they knew that they were in competition with other sectors (such as agriculture) where CBA and the cost-efficiency techniques are easier to apply (Pennisi, 1984, pp. 177–8).

In spite of this, the analyses were not uniformly satisfactory. In some cases, they took into consideration both the direct and indirect effects, whereas in other cases they considered only the direct benefits. One reason for this inconsistency is that guidelines provided by the Assessment Group do not cover the entire spectrum of possible benefits.

One of the negative factors encountered in the FIO experience is related to the budgetary reserve which must be set up in order to promote specific sectors. According to one point of view, while this has directed the demand toward under-financed sectors, it has limited the effectiveness of the procedures.

These comments are confirmed by the indicators elaborated by the Assessment Group which measures the ratio between the net present value and the average financing of the sector (Ministero del Bilancio, 1988, p. 25). As seen below, the indicators of the environmental sectors for which financing has been assessed are low compared to the average of the projects financed (1.43):

cultural assets	1.63
anti-pollution activities	0.81
solid waste treatment	1.05
hydraulic engineering	0.84
irrigation	1.17

However, it should be remembered that the budget reserves set up by the central authority are useful instruments if they are in line with the objectives of the economic plan. Anyway, some sectors have high priority in the social preference function of the society (CER-CENSIS, 1987).

Economic efficiency is only one criterion used in the adoption of a project. The Assessment Group is giving a high degree of relevance to operating conditions and the size of the projects. The optimum scale of the project and the actual capability of the proponents for managing the project are deemed extremely relevant. The last point is borne out by the fact that most of the water treatment plants which have been built in southern Italy are not in operation, due to a lack of managerial expertise and higher operating conditions (Ministero dell'ambiente, 1987). It is for this specific reason that emphasis is placed on the technical analysis of the procedure, and on the computation of the incremental benefits and costs when the scale of the project or programme components is increased or decreased or, again, when alternative projects are considered.

Fundamental objections to the use of cost-benefit analysis

The growth in interest in the use of CBA and in the evaluation of environmental benefits has generated a number of criticisms. From the beginning, CBA has suffered serious criticism, directed mainly towards the distributional effects of costs and benefits, the choice of an appropriate rate of discount, the evaluation of a damage function, and the assessment of the intangible benefits.

Considerable concern was raised about the fact that CBA might become an instrument of interference by the public in the private sector. For the social parameters used in the appraisal of the projects rely on a system of prices that are completely different from those of a competitive market.

Difficulties relate also to the technical specifications of environmental impacts. We simply cannot discern, given the current state of scientific and technical knowledge, all the systematic environmental impacts of the proposed activities. The availability of adequate knowledge emerges as a critical issue in carrying out the analysis. Even when appropriate data are available, it becomes necessary to determine whether physical functional relationships can be based on them with a given degree of reliability.

Another set of difficulties concerns the evaluation of the effects of a policy and framing these into economic terms. Such estimates can seldom be made with accuracy because of the poor quality or non-existence of objective measurements. This may lead the analyst to serious bias in selecting critical values, which may not be apparent to a reviewer.

As has been emphasized, in order to establish a monetary measure of environmental damage we have to use the willingness-to-pay concept. The problem remains that it is not always easy to calculate people's willingness to pay. It may be extremely difficult, in practice, to evaluate specific dangers to health and amenities, and damage to cultural assets and properties, in the face of the fact that the impact in question is likely to occur in the future. In some cases, individuals are largely unaware of the environmental dangers caused by one or more pollutants to which they are subjected. In such cases, it is maintained that the concept of willingness to pay will not help determine the price of environmental protection for the society.

Technical difficulties

In order to overcome the problems connected with the assessment of the benefits, it is necessary to adopt sophisticated techniques which challenge the principle of standardization and the speed of execution required by the CIPE's assessment procedures. The existence of these problems has favoured the opinion that the schemes concerning the financing of projects for which budgetary reserves were set up should be managed without assessing the benefits. In other words, the emphasis should be put on the technical feasibility of the projects and their consistency with regional plans (Lamanda, 1987, p. 246).

We have seen in the previous paragraphs that several methods can be used for the measurement of environmental damage. The choice of methods depends upon the type of damage being estimated, the availability of information and the purpose of the study.

A general problem concerns the evaluation of the physical damages: it is impossible to survey each category and physical area under study for all types of damage. Hence, in many areas, one is forced to make a set of assumptions and these assumptions are not always realistic. In such cases where even physical effects are unknown, it is unrealistic to expect that monetary values closely reflect social values.

From a theoretical point of view, monetary estimates of environmental benefits can be useful even if they are not accurate. In practice, the behaviour adopted by most analysts has been to limit the monetary evaluation to the most important effects and give just a description of intangible effects. There is therefore a need for more knowledge about the quantitative effects of changes in environmental quality.

Another problem which is highly relevant is connected with the objectives that the projects are supposed to meet. The objectives indicate the aspects that have to be taken into consideration and the method by which to assess their value. The projects financed through the FIO funds have to meet multiple objectives dealing with environment, employment, economic development, etc. The list of objectives has grown considerably longer. This has led to an increase of the time needed for the technical investigation and the information available to the political decision maker. The increase in the number of objectives may introduce some element of arbitrariness in the technical investigation of the Assessment Group, while the excess of information may give rise to the risk of incoherent decisions at the political level (Muraro, 1988).

Political and institutional difficulties

The institution of the FIO and the Assessment Group has generated a reaction by some groups whose interests were contrary to the rationalization of the public expenditures. In this respect it has been emphasized that the work carried out by the Assessment Group could be improved if it operated as an external body independent of the Secretary General of Economic Planning who, normally, is under political pressure (Pennisi and Peterlini, 1987). It has been proposed to set up the board under the care of the Treasury Department, where assessment procedures such as CBA may favour the introduction of merit valuation instead of merely on-paper controls.

Another difficulty relates to the limited capability of the local administration of performing correct CBAs. The evaluation of a public investment project through a CBA which can be defined "honest", from the point of view of the definition of the costs and benefits of the project, is not always easily achievable without technical bodies with specific and qualified professional capabilities (Giarda, 1988).

Until now most of the technical procedures have been elaborated by external consultants. Economists are lacking in experience of public administration. Only recently have technical officers of the regions sought to improve their capabilities, thanks to the pressure exerted by the Assessment Group.

From the beginning of the institution of the FIO, requests for funds presented by the regional administration have been consistently larger than those of the central administration (68.8 per cent). This trend has even increased over recent years as southern regions have become familiar with the new procedures. Initially, in 1982, southern regions presented 31 per cent of the total regional demands, whereas in 1986–8 their proportion increased to 51.5 per cent.

However, considering only the requests that have been approved, those that have the necessary requisites in order to be financed are limited. The projects of the central administration have registered a larger rate of success than those of the projects proposed by regional authorities (Ministero del Bilancio, 1988, p. 23). These results suggest that the action of the Group in promoting and standardizing the methodology should intensify, especially at the local level.

Another aspect which emerged from the inquiry is related to the increase of the powers of the administrative bureaux *vis-à-vis* the politicians. Because of the procedures, the role of technicians has considerably increased. In spite of this, engineering aspects of the projects still remain more important than those of the economic aspects.

Finally, another aspect which limits the effectiveness of CBA and the assessment of the benefits is the poor quality of the planning activities at regional and central level. These activities represent the frame of reference for evaluating relevant procedures. We have seen that in order to evaluate the project's capability of satisfying needs at local level, relevance is put on the regional plans such as the Aqueduct Plan, the Regional Water Reclamation Plan and so on. Most of these plans are based on poor qualitative information.

Has the decision-making process really been improved?

Having considered the experience of the Employment and Investment Scheme and of the other funds, we are now in a position to
draw some conclusions.

From an empirical point of view, decision tools such as CBA
are being progressively used both at the national and regional
level. We have advanced the hypothesis that these evaluation
techniques were helpful in implementing what has been called
"planning by projects" and that they were useful in improving
the decision-making process and therefore the efficiency of the
public expenditures.

As far as planning by project is concerned, these tools surely
represent a significant step towards its realization. However, it
has become evident that most of the theoretical work necessary to
adapt the evaluating techniques to the objectives of the economic
planning has not been done.

Nevertheless, the quality of public decision making has certainly
improved. A lot of effort has been put into identifying and
evaluating both costs and benefits, even though a gap remains
between the development of the theory and what is really applied.

Most of the projects have correctly identified and quantified
tangible and intangible effects. In some instances, it has not been
possible to do more than list the intangibles because of the lack of
adequate knowledge of the local environmental conditions.

Most analysts have applied disproportionately more effort to the
evaluation of the direct effects than of intangible effects. This did
not affect the usefulness of the analysis to any great extent. However, there is a need to improve this aspect of the analysis. Because
the type of information varies from study to study, it is difficult
to provide specific guidelines as to what kind of information should
be used and in what detail it should be presented.

After all, the purpose of CBA is merely to provide useful
information to public decision makers rather than providing abso-
lutely accurate measurements of every possible effect. It is simply
uneconomical to continue refining the measurement of a project's
effects unless the benefits of the improved information are worth
the cost.

Problems still remain in relation to some other aspects of the
decision-making process. Shadow prices play a relevant role in
evaluating benefits. Guidelines developed by the Assessment

Group are useful but they are not enough. There is need for additional theoretical and empirical work. Precise instructions should be given in order to compute shadow prices for different sectors. They should reflect the willingness to pay of the consumers but should also take into account the objectives of economic planning. For example, manpower should be valued differently if the project is situated in the north or south of Italy.

Finally, other beneficial effects are related to the engineering and managerial aspects of the projects. It has already been mentioned that the decision maker gives a high degree of relevance to the technical aspects, i.e. to the operating conditions of the project. In this respect, the decision-making process can be further improved if guidelines are also developed for the evaluation of the cost functions.

Concluding Comments

Economic efficiency is the basic criterion used in CBA. In spite of the fact that it provides an important starting point in evaluating public projects, it is not the only relevant criterion used in the decision-making process. There are many other aspects that must be considered. These are income distributional effects, technical and political acceptability, etc. More precisely, the following elements have to be considered:

• the consistency of the project with regional plans which constitute the frame of reference for the proposed project. We have seen in previous sections that significant steps of the CBA are related to the demand and supply analysis and to the planning activity of the public authority;
• technical characteristics are also relevant. In this respect, evaluation of the alternative projects plays a significant role. They are extremely useful for describing the cost behaviour and how a project affects existing infrastructures;
• managerial consideration is another relevant element. In the past, we have assisted the financing of a number of projects, especially water treatment plants, which were inefficient both from the technical and the economic point of view. Operating conditions and managerial aspects should therefore have equal importance with the other elements.

In conclusion, the use of CBA shows that, although considerable progress has been achieved in coping with the difficulties and problems of environmental projects, much remains to be done.

It is necessary to improve and enlarge the specification of environmental impacts. It is equally necessary to refine, through actual case studies, the analytical tools for evaluation in order to deal effectively with uncertainties, longterm consequences or irreversible negative effects.

The decision-making process can therefore be further improved if some actions can be taken:

• a clear definition of the role of analysts with respect to the political power;
• the definition of standardized methods for the benefit estimates: they already exist but they should be further improved;
• the elaboration of shadow prices for the main inputs concerning the environmental projects.

References

Allione, M. (ed.) (1977) *Le Decisioni di Investimento Pubblico*, (Angeli: Milan).

Barde, J. Ph., and Gerelli, E. (1980) *Economia e Politica dell'ambiente*, (il Mulino: Bologna).

Bollettino Ufficiale della Regione Lombardia, n. 2, 12 January 1985; n. 22 29 May 1985; n. 39 25 September 1985.

Buffoni, F. (1983) "La valutazione economica dei progetti regionali di intervento", *Bollettino IRSPEL* n. 3–4.

Buratti, C. (1978) "La valutazione economico-sociale degli investimenti autostradali", *Economia pubblica*, 501–11.

Cassone, A., Grisoli, V. and Tasgian, A. (1981) *Una analisi costi-benefici nel campo della viabilità d'attraversamento di un'area urbana*. (Angeli: Milan).

CER-CENSIS, (1987) "Analisi di strumenti di intervento: il Fio", *PubblicoPrivato*, vol. II, Ediz. Sole-24 ore, (Milan).

Dasgupta, P., Sen, A. and Marglin, A. (1972) *Guidelines of Project Evaluation*. (UNIDO: Vienna).

Di Maio, A. (1988) "Una nota sulla procedura per la valutazione degl investimenti in opere pubbliche: l'esperienza della Cassa per il Mezzogiorno e della legge 64/1986", in *Rassegna Economica*, n. 3, 629–40.

Dorfman, R. (ed.) (1965) *Measuring Benefits of Government Investments*. (The Brookings Institution: Washington).

Florio, M. (1986) "La programmazione per progetti: problemi metodologici dell'esperienza italiana", *Economia Pubblica*, n. 12 dic., 553–8.

Formez, (1983) *La Programmazione di Bilancio: Stato di Attuazione a Livello Regionale*. (Naples).

Formez, (1987) *Lezioni di Analisi Costi-benefici*, Strumenti Formez n. 3. (Naples).

Freeman, A. (1979) *The Benefits of Environmental Improvement: Theory and Practice*, (Johns Hopkins Press: Baltimore).

Galimberti, F. (1988) Sintesi introduttiva a CER-CENSIS, *Stato ed Economia. Istituzioni, Efficienza, Sviluppo*, vol. II, Ediz. Sole 24 ore, 3–15. (Milan).

E. Gerelli, (1987) "Note sull'introduzione dell'analisi costi benefici in Italia", in Formez, *Lezioni di Analisi Costi-benefici*. (Naples).

Gerelli, E. and Pola, G. (1979) *La Programmazione Poliennale della Spesa Pubblica. Esperienze Europee a Confronto*. (il Mulino: Bologna).

Gerelli, E., Cellerino, R. and Ghessi G. (1989) *La Spesa Ambientale*. (Econpubblica: Milan).

Giarda, P. (1988) Introduction to Formez, *Applicazioni dell'analisi Costi-benefici. Agricoltura, Acquedotti, Ambiente e Viabilità*, Quaderni Regionali 48. (Naples).

Gronchi, S. (1984) *Tasso Interno di Rendimento e Valutazione dei Progetti: un'analisi Teorica*, (Collana dell'Istituto di Economia: Siena).

Johansson, P.O. (1987) *The Economic Theory and Measurement of Environmental Benefits*. (Cambridge University Press: London).

Lamanda, G. (1986) "La programmazione per progetti", in CER-CENSIS, *Il Governo dell'economia. Rapporto 1986*, Ediz. Sole- 24 ore, 237–50. (Milan).

Lamanda, G. (1987) "La programmazione per progetti a carattere decentrato e concorsuale, in CER-CENSIS, *Pubblico e Privato*, Ediz. Sole- 24 ore, 235–46. (Milan).

Little, I.M.D., and Mirrless, J.A. (1968) *Manual for Industrial Project Analysis in Developing Countries*, (OECD: Paris).

McKean, R.N. (1968) "The use of shadow prices", in Chase, S. (ed.) *Problems in Public Expenditure Analysis*. (The Brookings Institution: Washington).

Miltz, D. (1988) *The Use of Benefits Estimation in Environmental Policy*, Organization of Economic Co-operation and Development (OECD), Environment Directorate, Report ENV/ECO/ 88.8

Ministero dell'ambiente (1987) *Nota Preliminare alla Relazione sullo Stato dell'ambiente*, April, 27. (Rome).

Ministero del Bilancio e della programmazione economica (1983) *Manuale di Valutazione dei Progetti per la Pubblica Amministrazione Italiana*. (Rome).

Ministero del Bilancio e della programmazione economica (1988) *Rela-*

zione sull'attività del Nucleo di Valutazione degli Investimenti Pubblici. (Rome).

Ministero del Tesoro, Cassa e Depositi e Prestiti (1986) *Scheda di Valutazione.* (Rome).

Muraro, G. (1988) "Il problema degli obiettivi nella valutazione degli investimenti pubblici", *Economia Pubblica*, Jan.-Feb., n. 1–2, 3–10.

Nuti, F. (1987) *L'analisi Costi-benefici.* (il Mulino: Bologna).

Official Gazette (1988) Direttive per l'applicazione della normativa per il finanziamento di interventi pubblici di rilevante interesse economico immediatamente eseguibili ed atti applicativi, *Supplement to the Official Gazette, n. 161*, 11 July.

Official Gazette, Supplement to the Official Gazette, n. 152.

OECD, (1974) *Environmental Damage Costs.* (Paris).

OECD (1976) *Economic Measurement of Environmental Damage.* (Paris)

Pearce, D. (1986) *Cost-benefit Analysis.* (Macmillan: London).

Pearce D.W. and Markandya, A. (1989) *Environmental Policy Benefits: Monetary Valuation* (OECD: Paris).

Pearce, D. and Nash, C. (1981) *The Social Appraisal of Projects. A Text in Cost-benefit Analysis.* (Macmillan: London).

Pennisi, G. (1984) "I progetti per la tutela dell'ambiente nell'esperienza del Fondo Investimenti e Occupazione", in Muraro, G. (ed.) *Criteri di Efficienza per la Politica Ambientale*, (Angeli: Milan).

Pennisi, G. (1985) "La programmazione fattibile", in *Rivista di Politica Economica*, May 593–603.

Pennisi, G. (ed.), (1985) *Tecniche di Valutazione degli Investimenti Pubblici.* (Istituto Poligrafico dello Stato: Rome).

Pennisi, G. and Peterlini, M. (1987) *Spesa Pubblica e Bisogno di Inefficienza*, 157. (il Mulino: Bologna).

Petretto, A. (1987) "La valutazione dei costi e dei benefici dei progetti di investimento pubblico: premesse teoriche", in Formez, *Lezioni di Analisi Costi-benefici.* (Naples).

Regione Emilia Romagna, L.R. 24 maggio 1984 n. 25; L.R. 12 dic. 1985, n. 29.

Sobbrio, G. (1978) "Analisi costi-benefici e redistribuzione dei redditi", *Economia Pubblica*, n. 9, sett. 375–82.

Tenembaum, M. (1982) "Distribuzione del reddito e sviluppo economico nell'analisi costi-benefici", *Note economiche*, n. 3

Tenembaum, M. (1987) "Un nuovo manuale per la valutazione e la selezione degli investimenti nei trasporti", *Economia Pubblica*, n. 11, Nov. 521–30.

4 The Netherlands

Onno Kuik, Huib Jansen & Johannes Opschoor

Introduction and Background

The environmental impacts of human activities can be categorized into:

(1) changes in the quality of air, water,soil;
(2) impacts on the supply of natural resources;
(3) other alterations of structure, infrastructure and processes in ecosystems and landscapes.

Insofar as these impacts are negatively valued (in themselves, or in their consequences), they are said to lead to environmental damage or loss of environmental quality. Environmental policy aims at preventing and reducing such damage by improving environmental quality relative to the situation without such policy, and thereby leads to environmental benefits. Environmental benefits are, as a rule, prevented environmental damage.

Estimates of environmental damage and benefits can be used in the decision-making process at various levels:

(1) policy
(2) regulations
(3) projects

The functions of such estimates are:

(a) to stimulate awareness
(b) to justify decisions
(c) to make trade-offs between alternatives

Dutch estimates of environmental damage in monetary terms have primarily been used for functions (a) and (b), at level (1). Here the need for accuracy and reliability is not as urgent as in the other levels/functions. For function (a), the "softer" valuation methods (e.g. contingent valuation, hedonic approach) are more easily allowed, but for function (b) and, more so (c), accuracy and "hardness" are desirable features. At the present state of the art, accuracy and hardness are to a large degree mutually exclusive: the harder valuation methods are primarily based on market prices and financial data. Non-marketable goods, consumers' surplus and non-user values, estimated with softer valuation methods, are mostly not included in hard estimates. Therefore, hard estimates have a strong tendency to under-estimation. Due to this bias, hard estimates lack accuracy.

For function (c) at levels (2) and (3), not only hardness and accuracy are required, but also the form of a monetary damage function should be known, so as to allow comparison between alternatives. Moreover, regulations and projects influence, as a rule, a number of different environmental qualities. Consequently a number of hard and accurate estimates of damage functions are needed. Such requirements encumber the use of monetary estimates of environmental benefits at levels (2) and (3) and in function (c) (Jansen, 1988). Therefore, with the exception of the case of estimation of damage due to an accident in a nuclear plant (see p.131) no monetary estimates of environmental benefits have been made in the Netherlands for evaluation of regulations and projects or for making trade-offs. In the contexts mentioned, decision making is based on other assessment methods, which we briefly outline. To assess the consequences of *regulations* for industry, so-called "basic documents" are prepared. These documents spell out a number of economic consequences at the micro- and meso-level of, for example, stricter environmental standards. Economic aspects covered by the basic documents include impact on cost levels, price impacts, changes in competitiveness, etc. The economic value of environmental benefits of the regulation are not included, hence these documents are not within the scope of this paper. For specified types of large *projects*, environmental impact assessment is required; but as a rule, no monetary estimates of environmental benefits are made and environmental consequences are only described in qualitative and, where possible, in quantitative physical terms.

If environmental benefits are not expressed in monetary terms in order to make *trade-offs* through benefit criteria analysis (BCA), an alternative method to make trade-offs of projects or regulations can be found in multi-criteria analysis (MCA). MCA includes various techniques which are to different degrees based on ordinal rather than cardinal figures and on weighing factors for the various criteria. An early application of MCA was used to evaluate the proposed project to transform Lake Markerwaard into a polder (Vos, 1975). Although MCA was not often used in Dutch policy making, the method seems to have become more popular now. For a description, see the case of "Electricity production", p. 135.

In the remainder of this chapter we give a broad-brush analysis of Dutch benefit studies, looking at the relevance of the studies from a policy point of view. Later we analyse specific Dutch benefit studies. The selected studies form a broad spectrum with different levels of decision making (policy, regulation, project), different functions, different objects affected and different valuation methods used. The studies are summarized and we try to answer the following questions:

- What type of analysis is carried out and what are the main results?
- Are the results of the study usable and meaningful to decision makers?
- What is the cost and complexity of the study?
- What publicity is generated by the study?
- What is the influence of the study on decision-making processes?
- What other (side) effects are there of the study?

Finally we draw conclusions on the use of benefit assessment for decision making.

Practical Use of Benefit Assessments in the Netherlands

Use of benefit assessments in the 1970s

The history of damage and benefit estimates in the Netherlands dates back to the 1970s. Early Dutch economic damage studies did not lead to very optimistic conclusions regarding the possibilities of finding monetary equivalents of welfare changes (Hueting, 1974; Opschoor, 1974; James, Jansen and Opschoor, 1978). The studies mentioned gaps in knowledge, lack of data and biases in the perception of the consequences of environmental change, especially of the long-run implications. The ethical side of valuation based on individual utility was also questioned.

Benefit assessments in the 1980s and their use

Despite this early pessimism, research on benefit estimates gained momentum in the 1980s. Since then, the Dutch environmental department has tried to get a wider view on the potential benefits of assessment of environmental pollution in all major areas of environmental policy by issuing benefit studies to independent research institutes. Results of most studies (until 1985) have been summarized in the Environmental Programme of the Netherlands 1986–90. The programme evaluates various elements of pollution: Dfl. 5.7–13 billion for past or accumulated damage, and Dfl. 2.1–3.7 billion p.a. for current damage, i.e. damage at current levels of pollution (see Table 4.1). The programme also estimates that re-use of a number of waste substances is currently yielding benefits valued at Dfl. 1.1 billion p.a., potentially to become Dfl. 1.3 billion p.a. In addition to the benefit estimates in Table 4.1, the monetary benefits of recovery and protection of soil quality have been estimated at Dfl. 34–155 million in the short run, and Dfl. 102–424 million in 2020. A more recent attempt at valuing air-pollution damage to agricultural production has resulted in a lower figure than is presented in Table 4.1: Dfl. 135 million (in 1983) including consumers' surplus within the Netherlands. Inclusion of damages suffered abroad as a consequence of air pollution in the Netherlands would have added another Dfl. 290 million (in 1983), including consumers' surplus. The willingness to pay for the conservation of Dutch forest and heather was estimated at Dfl. 1.4 billion p.a. (Van der Linden and Oosterhuis, 1988).

From a policy point of view it is interesting to assess which degrees of "completeness" and "comprehensiveness" have been reached by the various damage and benefit estimates. "Degree of completeness" refers to the coverage by benefit studies in terms of categories of environmental changes/receptors affected. "Degree of comprehensiveness" refers to the coverage of these studies of the various elements of value that are potentially relevant from a welfare perspective (i.e. user value without surplus, user surplus, non-user values). Thus, completeness is increased when hitherto ignored pollutants or impacts are investigated;

Table 4.1:   **Damage (million Dfl.) from environmental pollution**

Category	Nature of damage	Explanation	Accumulated past damage	Current and future damage per year
Air				
● people	health	c	p.m.	700–1,300
● agriculture	extra lime in soil	c	p.m.	15–50
	damage to cultivated crops	b	p.m.	565–655
	incidental damage to crops	b	p.m.	0.3–3
● nature	management of heather regions	c	p.m.	3–30
management	other nature regions	b	200–500	p.m.
● forestry	yield-reduction wood	b	p.m.	20–50
	capital loss/recovery costs	b	3000–10,000	p.m.
● cultural goods	monuments	b, c	120–200	15–30
	stained glass windows	b	20	p.m.
	carillons	c	p.m.	0.25
	textiles	b	20	p.m.
	paper	b, c	620	10
● use goods	steel and sheet zinc	c	p.m.	40
	value reduction of residences	–	p.m.	p.m.
● materials	metals	c	p.m.	113
	automobile tyres	c	p.m.	50–100

Category	Nature of damage	Explanation	Accumulated past damage	Current and future damage per year
	concrete damage	b	p.m.	175–350
	cleaning façades	c	p.m.	12–25
	Subtotal Air ca.		3980–11360 + p.m.	1730–2781 + p.m.
Surface water				
● recreation	swimming, sport fishing	a	p.m.	110–350
● professional fishery	income loss	b	p.m.	2–4
● navigation	disposal dredge spoil	c	p.m.	10–40
	damage to underwater soil	–	p.m.	p.m.
● industry	demineralization, etc.	c	p.m.	11
● agriculture	discharge of fertilizer	b	p.m.	20–60
● greenhouse horticulture	increasing salt content	b	p.m.	25–50
● households	corrosion	b	p.m.	10–30

Category	Nature of damage	Explanation	Accumulated past damage	Current and future damage per year
	Subtotal Water ca.		p.m.	188–545 + p.m.
Drinking and industrial water	modification of surface water purification systems	c	p.m.	85
	modification of groundwater purification systems	c	p.m.	23–300
	damage distribution network	c	p.m.	1.5
	Subtotal Drinking water	ca.	p.m.	110–387
Noise	value reduction of residences	b, b	1674	80

Category	Nature of damage	Explanation	Accumulated past damage	Current and future damage per year
	Subtotal Noise ca.		1674	80
Other	well-being		p.m.	p.m.
	Total damage		5650–13030 + p.m.	2107–3793 + p.m.

Key:
a = based on willingness to pay;
b = material damage (unrecovered);
c = cost of compensation measures;
p.m. = ???

Almost all numbers from studies since 1982 are given in prices of the year of publication of the study. Given the large margin of inaccuracy, it was decided not to index to 1985 prices. Health damage from air pollution was estimated at one billion in 1974. This amount is included for 1985 with an uncertainty margin.

Source: Environmental Programme of the Netherlands, 1986–90

comprehensiveness is enhanced when surpluses, "existence" or "option" values are added to previous estimates of expenditure impacts of environmental change.

Analysing benefits/damages in terms of completeness and comprehensiveness requires that the following aspects are looked at:

• environmental changes or impacts (three main categories and several sub-categories will be distinguished);
• objects affected by environmental change (six types of objects and receptors will be distinguished);
• elements valued (three such elements will be distinguished).
In addition, the valuation methods applied will be referenced.

Environmental changes
Environmental changes (or changes in environmental quality) have been categorized as:

(1) changed levels of pollution;
(2) changed resource potentials;
(3) improved or decreased ecosystem/landscape integrity.

These main categories can be subdivided into various sub categories such as air pollution, mineral reserves, or even lower levels of aggregation, e.g. sulphur dioxide concentrations, nickel reserves.

Objects affected
Environmental change may affect various objects and receptors, which have been classified as:

(1) human health;
(2) living environment;
(3) reproducible output flows;
(4) reproducible stocks;
(5) non-reproducible stocks;
(6) ecosystems and landscapes.

By "living environment" is meant the immediate surroundings of residential areas and working places. "Landscapes" refers to rural situations and artificially maintained ecosystems. "Non reproducible stocks" refers to unique, once-produced objects of artistic or historic value (historic buildings, paintings, libraries, monuments, etc.), whereas in "reproducible stocks" other-produced objects are included, such as painted surfaces, concrete foundations, other buildings, etc. "Reproducible output flows" incorporate produced consumable goods and services from affected economic sectors (e.g. agricultural produce, timber, cars, etc.).

Elements valued
We follow Pearce and Markandya (1989) in defining Total Economic Value of a benefit as the sum of user benefits (willingness to pay by users, including consumers's surplus and option value) and non-user benefits (existence value, bequest value). Comprehensive valuations of benefits must include the following elements (even if one limits oneself to the value to the present generation as perceived by the individuals involved):

(1) volume of actual money transactions (e.g. market value of improved crop yields due to reduced nitrogen oxide pollution, changed maintenance costs on historical buildings, etc.);
(2) consumer surpluses in addition to transaction volume (e.g. surplus value on houses);
(3) user values of non-marketable goods;
(4) "non-user values":
    (a) existence value: value given to objects, species, systems, etc. merely for their existence, on ethical grounds;
    (b) option value: willingness to pay for the future availability for use of an amenity, good or service;
    (c) bequest value: willingness to pay for the availability to future generations of objects, species, systems, etc.

Valuation methods used
Methods used in Dutch damage and benefit estimates include:

(1) market values (observed or estimated changes in input or output flows times observed prices);
(2) implicit market values (observed or estimated output flows multiplied by values based on changes in behaviour in other markets);
(3) stated willingness to pay (contingent valuations of well-defined changes in environmental conditions, by "translating" these

Table 4.2: Potential benefits by object and type of pollution (Dfl million)

Pollution Type of object	Health	Living conditions	Flows of products	Reproduceable stocks	Non-reproduceable stocks	Ecosystems and landscapes
Air						
SO_2	xx[1]	xx	xx}	x}340–528	x}	xx}
NO	x	xx	xx}650–858	x}	}25–40	xx}3–30
O_3	x	x	xx}	x	x}	xx}
NH_3			x}	x	x	xx}
C_xH_y	x		x		x	
Particulates	x[1]	x	x			
Pb	xx		x			
CO	x		x			
F	x		x			
Carcinogens	xx					
Odour		xx[2]	x			
Undivided	700–1300[1]		12–105			
Water						
O_2		x	x			x
Euthrophic	x	x	x}25–302			xx
Inorganic substances	xx		xx}151–245	x		xxx
Organic substances	xxx12–42		xx			

Temperature			x		xx	
Other		x				
Undivided			x	122–384[3]		
Soil						
Odour/view	xxx		xx			
Acidification			x	15–50[4]	xx	
Eutrophication					xx	5–25[4]
Metals	xxx		xx	4–15	xxx	
Other inorganics			xx		xx	
Organo-halogens	xxx		xx		xx	
Other organics	xx		xx		xx	
Undivided			x	10–75		
Other pollution						
Road traffic noise	x	xx 80			xx	
Aircraft noise	x	xx			xx	
Industrial noise	x	x				

Pollution Type of object	Health	Living conditions	Flows of products	Reproduceable stocks	Non-repro stocks	Ecosystems and landscapes
Safety/hazards	xx	x				x
Radiation	xx	x				
Waste	x	x		x		xx

Key: x = damage expected; xxx = substantial damage expected (adapted from Baan 1983; Oosterhuis 1985)

Notes

[1] The exact figure as calculated by Jansen et al. (1974) is Dfl. 862 million; due to the often debatable assumptions used, they suggest using the 1 billion figure as an indication of the order of magnitude involved. The Dfl. 700–1300 million range mentioned by the Environment Report is a range arbitrarily picked, around Dfl 1000×10^6, for which the researchers are not responsible.

[2] Dissatisfaction with air pollution was, via empirical estimates of house price depreciation in the Rotterdam industrial area, estimated at an annual sum of Dfl $1,4 \times 10^5$ (Jansen et al., 1974). The best explanation available was an indicator of odour complaints and the estimate was made for 1970. Odour problems have become much less since then.

[3] Mostly recreation: Dfl. 110–350 million (Baan, 1983).

[4] Values coinciding partly with estimates for acidification related to air pollution.

Source: Environmental Programme 1986–90 and background documents; Oosterhuis, 1985

Table 4.3: **Elements of benefits expected and evaluated, per object**

Aspect or level / Object	Transaction values/cost differentials	Consumer surplus	Non-user values		
			existence	option	bequest
Health: mortality	xx 493[1]→	xx	xx		
illness	xx 370[1]	xx			
Living conditions	x (1400)[2] 90–155[3]	xx		x	
Reproduceable product flows	xx 723–973[5]	(x) 110–350[4]			
Reproduceable stocks	xx 470–985	xx		xx	
Non-reproduceable stocks	(x) 15–30	x	xx	xx	xx
Ecosystems/landscapes	(x) 23–80	xx	xx	xx	xx

Key:

x = benefits expected

xx = substantial benefits expected

→ = figure also contains estimates for element indicated

Figures: maximum damage estimates (See Table 4.1) in D*fl* million.

Notes:

1 Jansen et al., 1974, p. 35

2 Not officially quoted estimate of impacts of air pollution on house prices in 1970 (Jansen et al., 1974)

3 Totals for noise and soil pollution

4 Recreational value (fishing, swimming) related to air pollution: this estimate contains some elements of consumer surplus

5 Aggregate of appropriate items, as labelled "b" and "c" in Table 4.1; 68–78% is contributed by crop-damage estimates

hypothetically into some change of condition or of behaviour that can be assessed in money terms).

Analysis of Dutch benefit studies: a broad-brush approach
Of the three categories of environmental changes that potentially yield benefits, the Environmental Programme 1986–90 contains estimates related mainly to pollution. The benefits associated with re-use could be regarded as an example of increased availability of resources but also as an attempt to optimize waste management – which relates this activity to the category of (reduced) pollution as well.

Table 4.2 redistributes the damages/benefits as summarized in Table 4.1 over various sub-categories of (reduced) pollution of air, water, etc. and of affected classes of objects; the more recent estimates of soil benefits are added. In addition, Table 4.2 indicates (with x's) where damages/benefits are expected or already in evidence. Comparison of these indications with the listing of money values gives an impression of what could be labelled as the completeness of benefit estimates. Even within the pollution-related categories, coverage is far from complete.

A final aspect to be dealt with in this section is the extent to which the benefit or damage evaluations reviewed here incorporate all relevant elements of damage/benefits. Table 4.3 provides a first approximation of this. For each of the objects and elements distinguished, x and xx indicate very roughly the extent to which benefits are expected of improved environmental quality, as covered by the categories of Table 4.1. The money values in Table 4.3 are the results of a regrouping exercise based on an analysis of the various damage studies on which Table 4.1 is actually based. As in the discussion of Table 4.2, the (lack of) coincidence of x's and money values is a qualitative indication of the (lack of) "comprehensiveness" of the benefit/damage estimates as officially accepted in the Netherlands so far.

Benefit estimates and decision making
It is our impression that the damage or benefit studies are not used to trade-off costs and benefits of specific government actions, but their use lies in the *justification* of these actions to other departments and the general public. The need to take actions is explicitly not dependent on monetary assessments of damage or benefits. This impression was confirmed by a responsible officer

in this field in the Department of Environmental Management.

The reason for the limited use of monetary benefit estimates lies in their limited accuracy and reliability. A special problem is the valuation of human health benefits, which is disputed and hardly ever carried out in the Netherlands. At the same time, human health is one of the most important criteria in environmental policy.

To be considered for acceptance into environmental policy, benefit estimates must have a core of "hard" estimates, e.g. forgone repair costs to materials, forgone productivity losses, etc. Willingness-to-pay estimates, especially if measured with the contingent valuation technique, are often much larger than hard estimates but are considered to be less persuasive. As a rule, they are not accepted by other Departments or Ministries.

Opportunities and obstacles for a wider use of benefit estimates

Opportunities
Opportunities for a wider use of benefit assessments in the Netherlands primarily lie in the fact that they can be used to further the acceptance of environmental policy. Dutch environmental policy is formulating long-term environmental goals and periodically updating timetables for reaching these goals. Environmental policy makers feel that it would increase the acceptance of environmental policy if these timetables include estimates of cost and benefits of alternative paths of action in the environmental field.

An opportunity for the use of benefit assessment lies in the recent upsurge of public as well as governmental concern about the environment in general. It can be expected that in this situation larger funds become available for environmental research and therefore also for studies on benefit assessment. In the Netherlands, a publication of the National Research Institute of Health and Environment (RIVM, 1988; Concerns over Tomorrow) certainly contributed to this growing environmental concern. In this publication, long-run (1985–2010) environmental developments, problems and policy options are explored. It must, however, be admitted that the descriptions rather than the monetary assessments triggered the public interest. In the chapter on costs and benefits it is acknowledged that opportunities to estimate benefits are very limited. Costs are estimated at Dfl. 16–30 billion p.a., depending on the strictness of policy. The amount of prevented (sometimes total) damage is an order of magnitude lower. Most benefits are estimated on the basis of forgone production and prevented outlays, not willingness to pay; damage to human health is not monetized. A bolder approach would have resulted in a substantially higher (but less accepted) estimate of benefits. The figures thus, indirectly, indicate the need for more complete and comprehensive estimates, if they are to be used for justification of policy.

A new incentive for benefit estimates will come from the EEC which states in its Single European Act, an amendment to the Treaty of Rome, that "Community environmental policy shall take account of benefits and costs of action or lack of action" (Article 13OR). Guidelines are being drawn up that will contribute to the implementation of this requirement.

There is some indication that assessments become cheaper and more reliable once researchers and research institutes become more experienced in performing benefit assessments. An important development in achieving more efficient assessments – especially in trade-off situations – is the use of computers to guide the assessor. Computer programs designed for this task are called environmental decision support systems. Decision rules used by the system can be based on traditional cost-benefit analysis (CBA) – with efficiency as the sole criterion – but they can also be based on some type of multi-criteria analysis. A decision support system gives the assessor freedom to choose a decision rule, to cope with uncertainties (sensitivity analysis), and to choose criteria on which to base the decision. Decision support systems are tailored to a decision context where no complete agreement exists on objectives, priorities and problem content. This is usually the case with decisions concerning the environment.

Obstacles

Practical obstacles for the use of benefit estimates for policy making include:

• Physical dose-effect relations of environmental measures are not generally known.
• Valuation of human health is a disputed topic; inclusion of monetary benefits of human health is not generally accepted, but neglecting this category can lead to gross under-estimation of potential benefits.

• Most benefit or damage studies estimate *total* damage due to a certain pollution but not differentials. Few studies try to assess the specific form of the damage function.
• One measure (e.g. the abatement of sulphur dioxide emissions) may have several effects (e.g. on health, on forests, on materials). The various estimates of damage to these items may not be well addable due to differences in estimation methods.
• There does not seem to be much confidence in the accuracy and reliability of benefit estimates among Dutch policy makers.
• Because of the bias of Dutch policy makers in favour of relatively hard financial-economic benefits, the total benefits of environmental policy (based on the willingness-to-pay approach) are likely to be grossly under-estimated.
• Pollution often poses uncertain risks in the long run. There is no agreement on the correct discount rate for future benefits. In the Netherlands, there is an official guideline to use one uniform discount rate of 5 per cent for government projects, but this seems rather arbitrary.

Seven cases studies

Introduction

In Table 4.4 a summary is given of the case studies explored in this section. In each case, the Table shows the estimated amount of damage or benefits, the valued objects, the methods used, the costs of the study and some general remarks.

In the selection of cases our first purpose was to obtain a broad variety with respect to:

• policy area (water, air, noise, energy);
• policy use (justification, trade-off);
• success in influencing policy.

During the selection process it became clear that most of the studies performed were mainly used for justification of environmental policy and for awareness building. The studies estimate the damage caused by pollution if no policy change were to occur. Only few studies try to trade-off costs and benefits of a certain policy or try to trade-off alternatives of certain actions or projects. It became clear that, as yet, benefits of regulatory action have never

Table 4.4: Selected cases of benefit assessment

Case	Damage: *10⁶ Dfl. p.a.	Objects valued	Methods used	Costs of study: *10³ Dfl	General remarks
Cultural property (1984)	15–30 10	monuments paper	c	124	Estimates are not based on real dose-effect relations, but on fixed percentage of actual restoration costs
Forests and heather areas (1988)	1,400	forest and heather	a	173	In this estimate, all value elements are included: user, existence, option, bequest
Water quality (1983)	198–556	recreation, commercial fisheries, navigation, drinking water, industrial water use, agriculture	a,b,c	50–60	No loss of consumer surplus estimated, no value elements other than user value. Nature and health effects are not valued
Nuclear energy accident (1988)	14–35*10₉ (lump sum)	energy production, health, agriculture, tourism, evacuation, decontamination	b,c	1,300	Damage probably under-estimated

Case	Damage: *10⁶ Dfl. p.a.*	Objects valued	Methods used	Costs of study: *10³ Dfl*	General remarks
Agriculture (1987)	640	agricultural crops	a	129	Benefits of air pollution reduction would for 2/3 accrue to foreign consumers
Noise reduction (1985)	Dfl. 400,-	per db(A) houses	a	60	No total damage estimate for the Netherlands
Electricity production (1988)		no objects valued in money terms	MCA	127	Multi-criteria analysis of alternative electricity production strategies

Key:
a = based on willingness to pay
b = based on material damage
c = based on costs of compensating measures

been monetarily assessed in the Netherlands. It also became clear that there have been no studies that guided policy, except perhaps indirectly. The final selection of benefit studies therefore reflects the reality of Dutch benefit assessment; most cases are damage studies, justifying policy in a broad sense.

Case study: "Cultural property"

Summary
The objective of a study by Feenstra (1984) was to make a survey of the damage occurring in the Netherlands due to air pollution, focused on acidification damage by sulphur dioxide to monuments, art objects, archives and buildings. In addition, a critical survey was made regarding the possibilities existing for making an economic valuation of the damage observed.

There are more then 41,000 national monuments in the Netherlands, such as castles, church buildings, mills, etc. The damage due to air pollution is taken as a fraction of the annual restoration costs. Annual damage amounted to Dfl. 15–30 million, calculated as 30–50 per cent of annual outdoor restoration outlays. The study notes that the restoration costs actually *spent* may be lower than restoration costs *needed*. An indication of this underspending on restoration is given by the "reservoir" of applications for restoration subsidies. This reservoir amounted to more than Dfl. 800 million in 1984. Assuming that 50 per cent of that restoration need is outdoors and 30–50 per cent is due to air pollution, damage calculated via this reservoir amounts to Dfl. 120–200 million.

Damage to *stained glass windows* can be avoided by application of outer glazing in front of the stained glass. The costs of an experimental scheme in Gouda amounted to Dfl. 4,500 per square metre. For the total 4,400 square metres of stained glass in the Netherlands, damage prevention costs would amount to Dfl. 20 million.

Damage to *carillons*, as calculated from annual restoration costs, amounts to circa 250 thousand guilders per year.

Damage to *textiles* in cultural-historical museums amounts to Dfl. 20 million on the basis of man-years required for restoration.

Deacidification of *paper* in museums, archives and libraries amounts to Dfl. 10 million per year.

Evaluation

The study calculated the damage of air pollution to cultural objects by estimating the fraction of restoration and preservation costs necessitated by the pollution. Estimation problems existed in the quantification of physical damage functions that relate exposure to damage per unit of material exposed; there were also problems of making assessments of the quantity of material exposed per pollution level.

The approach probably leads to an under-estimation of the benefits of air pollution reduction because, in the case of restoration, no valuation is placed on the authenticity of the objects involved. Also, there is no way of knowing whether an optimal rate of prevention and restoration (from a welfare point of view) is applied.

The study attracted much publicity in newspapers and on television; figures from it were published in the Environmental Programme of the Netherlands 1986–90. The study has in many ways contributed to public awareness of the negative effects of acidification on buildings and monuments. In addition, the study made valuable suggestions for improvement in the organization of the archives of the Government Service for the Preservation of Monuments and Historic Buildings.

The costs of the study amounted to *c*. Dfl. 124,000.

Case Study: forests and heather areas

Summary

A study by Van der Linden and Oosterhuis (1988) aimed at estimating the welfare loss for the Dutch population of severe damage to forests and heather, which is assumed will take place in the next decades if the present level of air pollution is not reduced. Forests and heather areas produce both marketable goods (timber) and non-marketable goods (e.g. the presence of a natural environment and recreational opportunities). The method used to assess the value of the potential damage to the non-marketable goods is the contingent valuation method.

A random sample of households was confronted with two conditions:

(1) the present condition in which the damage is still somewhat limited, and

(2) the expected condition of forests in 2010 in the absence of any additional policy (80 per cent of forests severely damaged and 90 per cent of heathers crowded out by grassy vegetation).

The respondents were asked to state their willingness to pay for the preservation of the present condition. On average, respondents were prepared to pay Dfl. 22.83 per household per month. This would amount to Dfl. 1.45 billion per year for the Dutch society as a whole.

The actual willingness to pay was found to be (among other things) dependent on level of income and changes in that income, the number of visits to forests and heather areas, the perceived gravity of the acid rain problem, age, education and social class. The most important non-marketable functions of forests and heather areas were found to be oxygen production/air purification, recreation, the provision of living conditions for plants and animals, and landscape.

Damage to timber production (which is the only substantial private function of Dutch forests) would amount to c. Dfl. 13.1 million per year. This is the estimated value of the difference in timber growth between the two conditions sketched above.

Discounted at an official government discount rate of 5 per cent, the total net present value of the benefits of the conservation of Dutch forests and heather areas by improving ambient air quality would amount to Dfl. 29 billion.

Evaluation
In the approach used, all value elements (user value, existence value, option value, etc.) are included. From a theoretical point of view, willingness to pay is the correct measure with which to value increments in (environmental) goods. There is however much controversy around the question of whether the contingent valuation (CV) method correctly measures the willingness to pay.

The Ministry of the Environment – the sponsor of the study – regards the study as an interesting experiment but does not use its results, in actual policy preparation or otherwise, because the results will not be accepted by other ministries or interested parties. The huge figures produced by this method tend, however, to make the more modest figures of other damage studies more acceptable. Officials in the Ministry of the Environment learned that large benefits can be calculated with this method. Before this study the only available estimate of the damage of air pollution to forests was an estimate of productivity losses in forestry, which amounted to an annual damage of Dfl. 30–50 million (see Table 4.1). This estimate is marginal compared to the willingness to pay estimated in this study. Even if the method and thus the exact magnitude of the benefits remain controversial, it does tend to lend support to increased environmental action.

The cost of the study was Dfl. 173,000, including Dfl. 45,000 for the survey.

Case Study: water quality

Summary

The main purpose of a study by Baan (1983) was to give an overview of potential benefits of a maximum improvement in water quality of Dutch surface waters, related to the type of pollution. To this end, Baan used a classification of potential benefits which was based on earlier American research. Using various methods, the effects of a maximum water-quality improvement were then estimated. We describe the methods used and results obtained per category.

Recreation is divided into boating, swimming and fishing. For *boating* little effect is expected; potential benefits are not estimated. The potential benefits of better *swimming* facilities are valued with market prices of entry to commercial swimming pools. Total entry fees are Dfl. 60 million yearly. The assumption is made that half of the visits to commercial pools will be redirected to surface waters if there is a maximum water quality improvement. Benefits to swimming are thus estimated at Dfl. 30 million per year. However, due to uncertainties, the range of Dfl. 10–50 million per year is presented as benefits of better swimming facilities. The benefits of expected extra *fishing* days are valued with the costs associated with fishing (Dfl. 10–20 per day). The benefits of existing fishing days are valued with the market value of the expected extra or better catch (Dfl. 2–4 per day). The expected increase in number of fishing days due to improved water quality is estimated at 5–15 per cent. The total benefits of improved recreational fishing facilities are valued as Dfl. 100–300 million per year.

The benefits related to the visual aspects – *aesthetics* – of the water-quality improvement are not estimated.

Effects on *ecosystems* (inland and marine waters) are described, not valued.

Benefits to *commercial fisheries* are the expected income gains of fishing due to better quality of fish. The benefits are modestly estimated at D*fl*. 2–4 million per year. Benefits to sea fishing due to a better quality of inflowing river water are not estimated because of uncertainty of the dose-effect relationship.

Benefits to *navigation*, caused by savings in financial outlays for sludge removal, are estimated at D*fl*. 12–42 million per year.

Effects on *public health* can be caused by direct contact with the water (swimming) and by consuming foodstuffs exposed to the water (fish, irrigated crops). Improving the water quality can cause positive effects on health, but there can also be negative ones due to increased water recreation (more drownings and diseases which are not related to pollution, e.g. Weil's disease, skin diseases by parasites). Negative and positive effects are not quantified or valued.

Benefits to the *public water supply* can be caused by less corrosion (not estimated), reduction in outlays for purification (5–10 ct/m3 or D*fl*. 15–30 million per year) and water softening (3 ct/m3 or D*fl*. 6 million per year) and reduction in cost of sludge removal (D*fl*. 2–9 million per year).

Benefits to *industry* can be caused by less corrosion (not estimated), cost saving in purification and water softening (D*fl*. 11 million per year).

Benefits to *agriculture* can be caused by productivity gains in crop production (estimated at D*fl*. 20–60 million per year), fewer problems with water quantity management and (in the long run) better opportunities for agriculture on river forelands.

Benefits to *households* can be caused by reduced corrosion and hardness (not estimated) and a better tasting water. A survey held in 1976 revealed that the consumption per capita of drinking water from surface water is significantly less than consumption of drinking water from groundwater (0.24 against 0.26 1/caput/day). If this difference is valued with the market price of soft drinks, then the total welfare loss due to the inferior taste of surface water can be estimated at D*fl*. 20–30 million per year; these are the benefits of water improvement if, after the quality improvement, the taste of surface water becomes as good as that of groundwater.

Evaluation

In total, the monetary benefits of maximum water improvement of Dutch surface waters amount to Dfl. 198–556 million per year. Not valued were important benefit categories such as nature conservation and public health nor value elements other than use values. No attempt was made in this study to estimate costs of a maximum water-quality improvement policy, so cost and benefits were not compared. Future benefits were not discounted, so no discount rate was chosen. No attempt was made to assess benefits of less than maximum water-quality improvements.

Figures from the study were quoted in the Environmental Programme of the Netherlands 1986–90 and results of the study were discussed in Parliament. The study was the first in a recent series sponsored by the Ministry of the Environment to assess the potential benefits of environmental policy in different areas (water, air, noise, etc.). The objective of the Ministry was to show that environmental policy is worthwhile. The studies were not undertaken to calculate, with the help of economic analysis, the optimum policy in a certain area (e.g. the optimal degree of water quality improvement) but all, including this one, were merely meant as a *justification* for environmental policy.

As this study was the first in a potential series, benefits were estimated rather cautiously or conservatively for easier acceptance. The study proved to be a success because the results were generally well received by other ministries and by society at large. The study thus paved the way for further environmental benefit assessments in the 1980s.

The costs of the study amounted to c, Dfl. 50,000–60,000.

Case Study: A nuclear energy accident

Summary
In this study by Goemans et al. (1988) the economic damage due to an accident in a nuclear power plant in the Netherlands was estimated. A number of scenarios for possible accidents with a newly built 1,000 MWe nuclear power plant were investigated. The cases were specified by (a) the severity of the accident, (b) the location of the plant and, (c) the weather conditions during the accident. Two different sets of intervention values were taken into account, specifying the acceptable level of radioactivity in food and

water and on the ground. Economic damage was calculated for the following impact categories:

(1) loss of the power plant;
(2) public health;
(3) evacuation and relocation of population;
(4) export of agricultural products;
(5) working and living in contaminated regions;
(6) decontamination;
(7) costs of transportation;
(8) incoming foreign tourism.

In general, the conclusion is that the present value of the economic damage could amount to Dfl. 14–17 billion, mainly because of the loss of the power plant, loss of foreign trade and incoming tourism. The damage could amount to a present value of Dfl. 35 billion if the plant were located in a heavily urbanized region. The probability of a small accident is estimated as less than 10^{-6}, the probability of a bigger accident between 10^{-7} and 10^{-8}.

Evaluation
The damage estimation in this study is very conservative. Only financial–economic damage is assessed and no attempt is made to assess the willingness to pay to avoid or the willingness to accept the possibility of a nuclear disaster. The latter approach would probably have yielded much higher estimates. Even within the financial–economic approach, estimates seem rather low; the damage to a house in a contaminated area, for example, is estimated at Dfl. 5,000. The possible great damage to the drinking water supply is mentioned but not valued.

In the Netherlands, nuclear power is a very sensitive political issue; it seems not impossible that the extremely conservative character of the estimated damage is related to this aspect.

The total costs of this study were Dfl. 1.3 million, but only a fraction (unknown) was for the economic assessment.

Case Study: Agriculture

Summary
Air pollution adversely affects agricultural production in the Netherlands. In a study by Van der Eerden, Tonneijck and

Wijnands (1987) the extent of yield reduction and the economic consequences were estimated.

Total yield reduction due to air pollution was 5 per cent in 1983. Of this yield reduction, 3.4 per cent was caused by ozone 1.2 per cent by sulphur dioxide and 0.4 per cent by hydrogen fluoride. Especially sensitive to air pollution are leguminous plants, potatoes and greenhouse-grown pot plants and cut flowers. About 42 per cent of the yield reduction occurred in the province of South-Holland. The relationship between production volume and air pollution level appeared to be non-linear: if air pollution decreases by 50 per cent, production increases by 3.7 per cent; if air pollution increases by 50 per cent, production decreases by 4.8 per cent. In general, air pollution causes relatively little financial damage to Dutch producers since air pollution-induced crop loss is largely compensated for by higher prices. Consumers in particular benefit from a decrease in air pollution. When air pollution is reduced by 50 per cent, the total welfare effect for the Netherlands is Dfl. 133 million p.a. Inclusion of the gains experienced by foreign consumers adds another Dfl. 290 million p.a. to the benefits. Total abatement of ozone, sulphur dioxide and hydrogen fluoride concentrations to background levels would induce annual benefits of Dfl. 208 million to Dutch consumers and Dfl. 432 million to foreign consumers.

Evaluation
In this case, forgone productivity seems a fair method to assess the benefits of air pollution control. Non-user values do not seem to be of any importance in this case. Second-order effects, like a change in cropping pattern after price changes of crops, are not taken into account but it seems hardly possible to do this.

Some doubt can be cast on the welfare effect on consumers abroad of the Dutch productivity gains. It does not seem likely that Dutch supply is the only price-influencing factor on world markets, although, admittedly, for some products it can be very important.

Case Study: Noise reduction

Summary
Oosterhuis and Van der Pligt (1985) have tried to *trade-off* costs and benefits of a concrete regulation, i.e. the costs and benefits

of noise reduction measures resulting from the Dutch Noise Act.
The assessment of benefits was made with the house price method
(hedonic approach). In this method it is assumed that the benefits
of noise reduction will (partly) be expressed in the market value
of affected houses. The authors stress that benefits such as positive
effects on wellbeing, aggression, learning capacity and longterm
effects on health are not totally captured with this approach. From
a welfare-theoretical point of view, value increases in house prices
cannot be taken as benefits of noise reduction, but only as a lower
bound of those benefits.

To assess the benefits of noise reduction measures in practice
(keeping the above-mentioned restrictions in mind), seven cases
were examined where noise reduction measures had been taken.
The formula to assess the estimated increase in house value was:

$$dTV = N \star c \star dG \star V$$

where:

dTV = change in total market value of houses due to measure
N   = number of houses affected (dependent on threshold
        value of noise in dB(A))
dG   = Change in noise level in dB(A)
c   = noise depreciation sensitivity index (NDSI), per centual
        increase in house price due to 1 per cent decrease in
        noise level (dB(A))
V   = market value per house

Because of uncertainties three different values for the threshold
level of noise (65, 60 and 55 dB(A)), and for the NDSI 0.1, 0.4
and 1.0 per cent, are used in the calculations. The NDSI values are
based on American research. Because of difficulties in establishing
the exact house prices (V), three different house prices were used
– Dfl. 50,000, Dfl. 100,000 and Dfl. 150,000. So the expected
increases in house values due to a decrease of noise of 1 dB(A)
(c * V) range from Dfl. 50 to Dfl. 1,500, with a "most likely" value
of Dfl. 400.

In the actual cases, the difference between costs and benefits
of noise reducing measures ranged from a deficit of Dfl. 222 to
Dfl. 9,925 per dwelling. The authors conclude that costs of noise
reducing measures are for a *substantial* part compensated by rising
house prices. Because of the existence of non-monetized benefits,
the authors find no reason to conclude that the costs of noise

reducing measures exceed the (social) benefits.

Evaluation
This study assesses, *ex post facto*, the benefits of a concrete policy measure. Noise is an environmental nuisance that is very likely to affect the actions of economic subjects, because it can be easily observed and taken into account. It is therefore disappointing that the study only arrived at rather weak conclusions in the studied cases.

Because of the application of the Dutch Noise Act, in a great variety of circumstances generalizations of the results of this study are of limited validity. The study was part of a series of reports that evaluated the Noise Act. The evaluation itself was discussed in Parliament, but the cost-benefit side was not discussed separately. Because of the drawbacks of the study mentioned above, the Commission that was responsible for the evaluation did not use the conclusions of the study in its main report.

The cost of the study amounted to Dfl. 60,000.

Case Study: Electricity production

Summary
So far, the cases described consist of evaluation reports which assessed damage and/or benefits. Decision makers can use the results of a report or they can ignore them. Another sort of decision-making tool is not a report but an interactive, computer-based Decision Support System (DSS). A DSS contains the same information as the evaluation report but can be amended by the participants to the decision. This approach is especially useful for decisions where the various participants not only have different objectives and priorities but also different opinions about the problem content. A DSS can thus be used in negotiations about the planned policy.

A DSS was developed (Janssen, 1988) that can be used in the assessment and evaluation of alternative strategies in electricity production. This DSS is used to compare different combinations of energy systems (e.g. combinations of coal, nuclear power and oil) on their environmental effects, in terms of their contribution to acidification, forest damage, etc.

The production mixes evaluated consist of technically feasible combinations of different conversion systems. The impacts of the alternatives on health, forests, etc. were not monetized but were expressed in appraisal scores relating effects to thresholds and damage categories, e.g. "number of people exposed to concentrations of certain pollutants beyond threshold values", "square miles of forest exposed to beyond threshold values of pollutants". Table 4.5 represents a "decision matrix" with three different alternatives on the horizontal axis and the different impact categories on the vertical axis.

Evaluation
If a decision problem is completely structured, that is, if problem content and priorities are agreed upon by all participants to the decision, there is no need for a decision support system. If at the other extreme, no structure can be brought into the problem content and/or the problem solving procedure, decision support is impossible. It is between these extremes that DSS is relevant.

The decision on the best electricity production mix can be described as semi-structured. There is agreement on the type of

Table 4.5:   **Decision matrix of a DSS (expected damage in 2000)**

	Gas	Coal	Nuclear	Dimension
Health	8583	10204	8583	* 1000 habitants
Forest	1021	1152	1141	km^2 pine forest
Water	1270	1328	1270	km^2 water
Heather	692	692	692	km^2 Heath/Dune
Agriculture	1495	2391	2391	km^2 Agriculture
Space Use	57369	65438	179945	ha
Materials	773	1313	1313	* 1000 habitants

The meaning of the figures in the Table is as follows:
- if the "gas" alternative is chosen, 8.6 million Dutch citizens will be exposed to concentrations of pollutants beyond a certain threshold value;
- if the "coal" alternative is chosen, 10.2 million people will be exposed to such concentrations;
- in the "gas" alternative, 1021 square kilometres of Dutch forest will be exposed to concentrations of pollutants beyond threshold value;
- in the "coal" alternative, this will be 1152 square kilometres.

The "gas" alternative scores best in all damage categories, the "coal" alternative has the worst score in all but one – space use – of the categories. The nuclear energy alternative takes the middle position except in the category of space use.

production methods, the type of data, the type of alternatives and the type of appraisal criteria to be included. There is no agreement, however, on the exact specification of all alternatives, the damage categories included, the level-of-effect thresholds, etc. There is even strong disagreement on the relative importance of the various categories.

The strength of the DSS is that more alternatives can be included, alternative impacts can be assessed, technical ratios (e.g. emission factors) can be adapted and priorities of policy objects can be altered. As an example of these possibilities, sensitivity analysis was applied both to priorities of policy issues (acidification, eutrophication, risk, greenhouse effect, (nuclear) waste, photochemical air pollution, visual disturbance) and emission factors. The ranking of the alternatives proved to be very robust, the only change that occurred was that the coal alternative became better than the nuclear alternative if the nitrogen oxide emissions per unit of energy production could be reduced to 28 per cent of current emissions.

DSS can be used for *trade-off* purposes, if monetary estimates of differences in environmental consequences are impossible or too weak and unreliable.

The cost of the study was *c.* Dfl. 127,000.

Conclusions

The following conclusions emerge:

(1) The majority of Dutch benefit studies are not linked to a specified proposal for a policy, regulation or project, but relate to pollution categories (e.g. air pollution, water pollution, acidification) and/or damage categories (e.g. crops, materials, forests).

(2) The use of benefit/damage estimates is for justification of policy and for awareness building rather than for trading-off between costs and benefits of alternative proposals. Due to inaccuracy and bias (generally *under*-estimation of the value of the environment), CBA is not regarded as a particularly useful tool for a trade-off between alternative environmental measures. Decision support systems (see case study, "Electricity production") can be an alternative to CBA as a tool for decision making.

(3) Assessment of environmental damage in physical terms can be as useful (or even more) for public awareness building as monetary assessment; this appeared from a recent publication (RIVM, Concerns over Tomorrow, 1988). Although this publication succeeded in arousing public awareness, subsequent political negotiations on the National Environmental Programme are not progressing smoothly, due to arguments over financing. It thus seems that monetary estimates are needed to convince politicians rather than the public.

(4) There is a (sometimes strong) bias in monetary estimates of environmental damage. This tendency to under-estimate is caused by lack of completeness and comprehensiveness.

(5) Lack of completeness. In the studies, some (possibly important) categories of damage are not evaluated. It is still in practice very difficult to value ecosystems. Valuation of human health is disputed and not generally accepted. In the nuclear power plant case, the damage to the water supply system was not valued, due to lack of knowledge. Valuation of species diversity and ecosystem integrity is disputed on ethical grounds. Nevertheless, during recent years more damage categories have been evaluated than was expected in the 1970s.

(6) Lack of comprehensiveness. For reasons of acceptability, estimates are often restricted to prevented outlays and forgone production. Softer parts of the value (consumers' surplus, non-user values) are often not included.

(7) Softer parts of the value of environmental assets can be estimated by contingent valuation (willingness to pay). The case of forests and heather areas indicates that an estimate based on contingent valuation can be substantially higher than an estimate based on forgone production. A willingness to pay (WTP) approach is expected to yield much higher estimates in the categories of ecosystems, nuisance, recreation, human health, not in the categories of materials and crops. In the case study on cultural property, the valuation method could be seen as social WTP; it is not certain if an approach based on individual WTP would give significant differences. Because of the now low acceptability of the WTP approach and contingent valuation, research is needed into the stability of these methods and into possible

methodological improvements.

(8) Dose-effect relations, derived from the scientific disciplines and used for valuation purposes, are often unreliable and/ or expressed in physical units which are not well suited for economic valuation (e.g. decreased lung functions due to air pollution). Moreover, knowledge on synergism and antagonism is almost completely lacking.

(9) Confidence intervals given in case studies most often have their origin in thin air rather than in statistical analysis.

(10) The described case studies do not allow a firm conclusion on a trend in the costs of benefit studies, but within the Dutch Department of Environmental Management the impression is that costs decrease in time. If this is true, a possible explanation is a learning effect among researchers; but another explanation could be the stricter budgeting by sponsors of the studies.

References

Baan, P.J.A. (1983) *Baten Milieubeleid Water* (Benefits of Environmental Water Policy). (Ministry of Public Housing, Physical Planning and Environmental Management: Leidschendam).

Eerden, L.J. van der, Tonneijck, A.E.G. and Wijnands, J.H.M. (1987) *Economische schade door luchtverontreiniging aan de gewasteelt in Nederland* (Economic Damage by Air Pollution to Crop Production in the Netherlands). (Ministry of Public Housing, Physical Planning and Environmental Management: Leidschendam).

Feenstra, J.F. (1984) *Cultural Property and Air Pollution* (Ministry of Public Housing, Physical Planning and Environmental Management: Leidschendam).

Goemans, T., Schwarz, J.J. et al (1988) *Economische schade van een ongeval met een kerncentrale*. (Economic Damage of an Accident in a Nuclear Plant). Project Herbezinning Kernenergie, SPH-06-13. ('s-Gravenhage).

Hueting, R. (1974) *Nieuwe Schaarste en Economische Groei* (New Scarcity and Economic Growth). (Elsevier: Amsterdam).

Jansen, H.M.A. (concept 1988) *Baten van Milieubeleid* (Benefits of Environmental Policy). (Institute of Environmental Studies: Amsterdam).

James, D.E., Jansen, H.M.A. and Opschoor, J.B. (1978) *Economic Approaches to Environmental Problems*. (Elsevier: Amsterdam).

Jansen, H.M.A., van der Meer, G.J., Opschoor, J.B. and Stapel, J.H.A. (1974) *Een Raming van Schade door Luchtverontreiniging in Nederland in 1970* (Estimate of Damage Caused by Air Pollution in the Netherlands in 1970). (Institute of Environmental Studies: Amsterdam).

Janssen, R. (1988) *Milieu Vergelijking Elektriciteitsopwekking* (Environmental Assessment of Electricity Production). R-88/09. (Institute of Environmental Studies: Amsterdam).

Linden, J.W. van der and Oosterhuis, F.H. (1988) *De Maatschappelijke Waardering voor de Vitaliteit van Bos en Heide* (The Public Valuation of the Vitality of Forest and Heather). (Ministry of Public Housing, Physical Planning and Environmental Management: Leidschendam).

Ministry of Public Housing, Physical Planning and Environmental Management (1985) *Indicatief Meerjarenprogramma Milieubeheer 1986–1990* (Environmental Programme of the Netherlands 1986–1990). ('s-Gravenhage).

OECD (1987) *Project on the Use of Benefit Estimates in Decision Making* (Draft outline). ENV/ECO/87.16.(Paris).

Oosterhuis, F.H. and van der Pligt (1985). *Kosten en baten van de Wet Geluidshinder*. (Cost and Benefits of the Noise Nuisance Law). Commissie Evaluatie Wet Geluidshinder. CW-AS-06.

Opschoor, J.B. (1974) *Economische Waardering van Milieuverontreiniging* (Economic Valuation of Environmental Pollution). (Van Gorcum: Assen/Amsterdam).

Pearce D. and Markandya, A. (1989) *Environmental Policy Benefits: Monetary Valuation*. (OECD: Paris).

RIVM (1988) *Zorgen voor Morgen* (Concerns over Tomorrow). (National Institute for Public Health and Environmental Management: Bilthoven).

Vos, J.B. (1975) *Beoordeling van Projektevaluatiemethoden -en een toepassing van ELEKTRA-M op het Markerwaardprobleem* (Assessment of Project Evaluation Methods – and an Application of ELEKTRA-M on the Problem of the Markerwaard). A no. 13. (Institute of Environmental Studies: Amsterdam).

5 Norway

Ståle Navrud

Introduction

Legislation and guidelines on cost-benefit analysis

In Norway there are no general or special requirements in any Act on performing cost-benefit analysis (CBA) of projects or regulatory actions. However, impact analysis (IA) in general is mentioned in several Acts and/or in the provisions of the Acts. The regulations and provisions concerning IA of these Acts differ with respect to explicit requirements on:

(1) The contents of the IA, which include:
   (a) types of effects analysed (economic, environmental, sociological effects etc.);
   (b) analysis of impacts during the construction period;
   (c) analysis of alternative actions;
   (d) outline plan to be worked out (i.e. evaluation of effects in relation to County Plans, Municipal Master Plans, etc.);
   (e) counter-measures to be analysed (i.e. what measures can reduce/eliminate damages or disadvantages caused by the project)

Other aspects include:
(2) the drawing up of a detailed scheme/programme for the construction of the IA;
(3) stepwise performance of the IA (i.e. preliminary–complete analysis, etc.);
(4) broad co-operation and early participation of all affected interests (i.e. public information about the project, IA submitted for affected interests' opinion etc.);
(5) use of IA in the process of choice of location, choice and

framing of regulations etc.;
(6) IA as a specified document, suited for public presentation and debate;
(7) evaluation of the need for follow up-studies and *ex post factso* evaluation in IA.

Table 5.1 gives a review of all Acts that contain regulations and/or provisions on IA, and how they fulfil these seven requirements for a complete IA. The complete IA is defined as the proposed, general regulation and pertaining, detailed provisions on IA in the Planning and Building Act (Ministry of Environment, 1989). This regulation will, when (or if) it comes into force, make the legislation on IA more consistent, complete and all embracing with respect to its content and use in all sectors of society.

In addition to the eight Acts listed in Table 5.1, the Nature Conservation Act also contains a regulation that requires IA to be carried out for major works, constructions or activities that could cause substantial damage to the natural environment (§2). However, this regulation has not yet come into force.

The review of the eight Acts in Table 5.1 shows that only the Watercourse Regulation Act and the Petroleum Activities Act have a detailed scheme/programme for the construction of the IA (i.e. item 2 in Table 5.1). The Petroleum Activities Act is closest to requiring a CBA of planned projects. The provision to §23 of the Act requires a review of the advantages and disadvantages to other private sectors and public interests to accompany the plans for petroleum extraction. However, the implementation of the regulations of this Act is in an early phase, and so far very few IAs have been completed. Many IAs have been performed for projects pertaining to the Watercourse Regulation Act, but these IAs are more likely to be characterized as environmental impact assessments (EIA) than as CBAs. Although there is no detailed IA scheme or programme in the Road Act and the Establishment Control Act (or in provisions of these Acts), they contain explicit requirements concerning analyses of the economic welfare effects of projects pertaining to these Acts (according to item 1a in Table 5.1). In the other Acts, for example, the Pollution Control Act, there are no such explicit requirements.

The discussion above has concentrated on the content of IA. However, the crucial question is whether these analyses are used

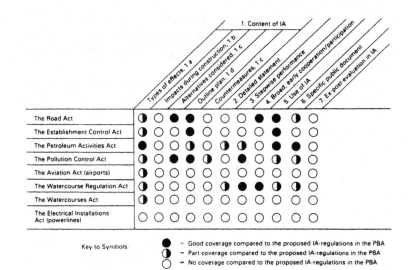

Table 5.1: **Review of regulations on impact analysis (IA) in Norwegian Acts and their provisions, as compared to the proposed general, "complete" IA regulation in the "Planning and Building Act" (PBA).**

in the decision-making process or not. Table 5.1, item 5 "Use of IA" and item 6 "Specific public document" can provide some information in this respect. The Road Act, the Establishment Control Act and the Petroleum Activities Act require the use of IA in the choice and framing of projects/regulations. However, only the Petroleum Activities Act requires IA to be a separate document suitable for public presentation and debate. The two other Acts only require the IA to be part of the background information submitted to the decision makers.

The Watercourse Regulation Act has no specific regulation that says how the IA should be used, although its use in the decision process is emphasized in the Act's requirements concerning the content of the application for concessions to regulate rivers. In the Pollution Control Act the use of IA is not clarified. However, pursuant to §12 of this Act, specific conditions are stated concerning the content of applications for pollution permits. Pursuant to §13 of the Act, anyone planning activities which may lead to significant pollution in a new site or planning major new developments where there is already existing activity, must undertake an IA. Special requirements concerning the content of the IA are given, but there is no specific stipulation that the document should be suitable for public presentation and debate (even though according to §14 the IA is open to public inspection).

This review of the regulations on the content and use of IAs clearly shows that the present legislative basis for IA (and CBA) of projects is weak. However, there are also instructions on carrying out separate analyses of the administrative and economic consequences of public deliberations, drafts of laws, provisions and parliamentary reports and bills. These came in effect in 1982, and were revised in 1985 (Ministry of Consumer Affairs and Government Administration, 1985a). Guidelines for economic IAs according to these instructions (especially concerning provisions) have been prepared by the Ministry of Finance (Ministry of Consumer Affairs and Government Administration, 1985b, p. 125–56). However, a general manual on the CBA of public projects and regulations (called programme analysis) serves as the main guide to these analyses (Ministry of Finance, 1979). The individual ministries and their agencies are responsible for the preparation of the analyses.

In addition, only one public agency (to the author's knowledge) has written its own manual for using CBA to choose priorities among investment projects. The Directorate of Public Roads (DPR) published a new handbook on CBA (Directorate of Public Roads, 1988), which serves as a guide in the preparation of IAs required for planning of roads under the regulations in the Road Act and its pertaining provisions. Transport infrastructure projects also seems to be the only area in Norway where CBA is routinely applied.

Both the general manual and the manual of the DPS recommend verbal description and quantitative analysis (in physical units) of environmental effects. Methods for the economic valuation of environmental effects are barely mentioned. The general manual concludes the three-page discussion on "unpriced" effects in CBA with:

> The Ministry of Finance therefore recommends that the discussion of "unpriced" effects is based on precise verbal descriptions, appropriate figure statements (in physical units), tables reviewing all these effects and ranking of regulations for each of the effects.
>
> (Ministry of Finance, 1979, p. 43)

Likewise, the CBA manual of the DPR says:

In analyses of road projects there is no common unit of measure for all effects. Roughly, the effects can be divided into four groups:

• The effects that we naturally can put a price (in NOK) [Norwegian Kroner] on (e.g. construction-, maintenance- and vehicle-operation costs).
• The effects it is generally usual to express in monetary terms (e.g. time savings and savings in accidents).
• The effects that cannot be valued in monetary terms, but that can be described in physical units (e.g. the road as a barrier, air pollution along roads and in tunnels).
• The effects that cannot be valued in monetary terms, but that can be described verbally (e.g. nature conservation and recreational activities).

It would be best if all effects could be valued by a common unit. As this cannot be done, one has to choose the unit of measure that is most natural for each effect. In some cases, however, it could be of interest to use different units of measure to describe the same effect.

(Directorate of Public Roads, 1988, pp. 15–16)

To compare the different effects, the DPR (1988, pp. 92–3) recommends the construction of tables where all effects of different alternatives are described (measured in different units). This table is used to make a rough screening of alternatives. Then, net present values (NPV) for negative and positive effects are calculated for the remaining alternatives. If the "unpriced" effects of these alternatives do not differ significantly, benefit-cost (BC) ratios are calculated. The final step is to compare information about the unpriced positive and negative effects, with the economic efficiency (NPV and/or BC ratios) of the project. In this process the unpriced effects of each alternative are ranked, and a subjective summation of these ranking numbers is used to rank the alternatives with respect to good/bad unpriced (mainly environmental) effects. A statement or explanation of the importance weights assigned to the different effects of each alternative, an analysis of distributional effects and a sensitivity analysis are also recommended in this final stage of the CBA.

All in all, the guidelines in the manual of the DPR coincide closely with those of the general manual. However, in both these manuals, environmental benefit estimation is a neglected area. As a result of requiring verbal descriptions or quantification in physical terms, environmental effects have been more or less ignored in the recommendations from CBAs carried out with reference to these manuals. In most cases, there is also no detailed EIA, and the treatment of environmental effects is therefore very much dependent on the analyst's own subjective opinion and level of information. This leads to inconsistent evaluation of environmental effects. Wider use of methods for valuation of environmental goods (see e.g. Pearce and Markandya, 1987 for a review of these methods) could make evaluation of such effects and the final recommendations from the CBA less subjective and more consistent.

This review of the legislative basis and governmental guidelines for IA indicates that benefit estimation and CBAs in general play a fairly small role in environmental decision making. However, in practice the situation may be somewhat different. Making detailed studies of selected cases therefore seems to be the best way to find out what role benefit estimates and CBA in general play in environmental decision making.

Cost-benefit analysis (CBA) and Locally Adapted Regulatory Impact Analysis (LARIA) in the environmental decision-making process

The majority of the relatively few complete CBAs carried out by the environmental authorities in Norway have been made by the Department for Pollution Affairs within the Ministry of Environment (MOE), and by the affiliated State Pollution Control Authority (SPCA). These CBAs have mainly been made in connection with the work on general provisions for environmental measures. In addition, there have been a few case studies on controversial environmental regulations imposed on separate firms within the mining industry.

The study by Kartevoll et al. (1979) is an early example of a CBA based on the guidelines in the general manual on programme analysis (Ministry of Finance, 1979). Thus, this CBA study of measures towards use of detergents containing phosphates does not try to value the environmental benefits from countermeasures.

In 1980–81, MOE and SPCA carried out two CBAs, with economic valuation, of the environmental effects of pollution caused by the mining industry. These early attempts at valuation were not based on empirical benefit estimation studies, but rather on qualified guesses accompanied by sensitivity analyses (see Sanderud and Beck, 1980; Strand and Sanderud, 1981). However, the qualified guesses for the reduced recreational value of changes in fish stocks in these studies were based on a theoretical study (Strand, 1980), which was part of an OECD project on the economic effects of different sulphur emission levels in Europe.

In 1981, Jon Strand carried out the first two empirical benefit estimation studies in Norway (Strand, 1981a and 1981b). In 1982, these estimates of the economic value of freshwater fish populations were used in a CBA of an extension of the provision on limits to sulphur content in heating oil. The CBA also covered activities established before 1977 (Ministry of Environment, 1982).

Another example of a CBA using benefit estimates from studies not constructed for that specific purpose, is that carried out by SPCA (1985) on regulatory action governing traffic noise. Later, a CBA containing environmental benefit estimates based upon an empirical study done specifically for this purpose was carried out by SPCA (1986), on provisions for stricter car emissions regulations. These three last mentioned analyses were conducted in accordance with the instructions from the Ministry of Consumer Affairs and Government Administration (1985a).

In addition to these complete CBAs, the environmental authorities have also initiated simplified CBA's on specific environmental issues. These analyses are environmental benefit studies, where the estimated annual benefits from regulations are compared to corresponding annual costs (Hervik et al., 1987; Dahle et al., 1987; Navrud, 1989).

This short review of CBAs carried out by the environmental authorities shows that CBAs of environmental regulations, complete with benefit estimates, are still the exception rather than the rule. Some reasons for this can be found in the decision-making process. Although this process may often be quite complex, the main steps for, for example, a provision pursuant to the Pollution Control Act, are usually as follows.

First, either the SPCA or the MOE suggests that a provision should be issued. Then a project group within the SPCA works out a draft of the provision, together with an analysis of the economic and administrative effects (in accordance with the above-mentioned instructions). Usually this analysis is very simple and is not a complete CBA. The draft of the provision and the CBA are then discussed with the MOE Department of Pollution Affairs before being submitted for other affected departments' opinions. If the provision has pronounced economic and administrative effects, or is expected to raise larger principal questions, the Government should be informed. The Government will then decide whether or not to allow the work to continue. Because most of the provisions on environmental measures have large economic implications, the Ministry of Finance will almost always be one of the affected ministries. The Ministry of Finance recommends in its guidelines on economic IAs (Ministry of Consumer Affairs and Government Administration, 1985a, p. 125–56) that the extent and content of the economic IA should depend on the expected benefits of new knowledge from increased research (e.g. on benefit estimation), and thus be a more complete CBA. Concerning the valuation of environmental benefits, these guidelines state that the large degree of uncertainty in these estimates reduces the decision makers' benefits from the results. In this way the Ministry of Finance discourages attempts at benefit estimation. As a result, the MOE (and the SPCA) in their analyses of provisions describe the environmental benefits in verbal terms and/or physical units, and very seldom try to monetize these benefits.

In the next phase, after consultation with the Ministry of Finance, the MOE decides (based on the comments from other ministries) whether further studies of economic impacts are needed before the proposed provision and the CBA can be submitted for affected interest groups' opinions. Then this material is used by the SPCA to revise the provision and/or the CBA. If there are only minor changes, no new consultations with the other affected ministries have to be made, and the provision is approved by the cabinet minister of the MOE. Final confirmation is made by the King in the cabinet meeting.

This simplified description of the decision-making process for provisions on environmental restrictions indicates that environmental benefit estimates in CBAs are considered by the Ministry of Finance to be of little value, presumably because they lack knowledge of and/or are sceptical about the valuation techniques. Therefore, in their documentation of economic and administrative effects of the provisions, the MOE mostly finds little use in carrying out such valuation studies. In the effort to convince the Ministry of Finance that these provisions are socially economic efficient, verbal statements and physical estimates of the environmental benefits seem to be more effective.

Locally Adapted Regulatory Impact Analysis (LARIA) developed by the State Pollution Control Authority in 1986 can, however, lead to more regular and consistent cost-benefit evaluations in environmental decision making, both at the local and national level. LARIA is a regulatory impact analysis, where benefits of different measures towards local pollution problems are valued according to a set of weights based mainly on previous benefit estimation studies. LARIA aims at giving priority to regulatory actions (both local and nationwide) in those areas of Norway with the greatest pollution problems. Thus, LARIA focuses on the recipient, not on a particular regulation.

This analysis differs from the Regulatory Impact Analysis (RIA) in the USA in that it focuses on the effects of a public policy for the nation as a whole, and in some cases benefit estimation studies of this policy are also carried out (see Fisher, 1984 for an overview and evaluation of the EPA guidelines for RIAs, and Miltz, 1988 for a review of case studies).

The first LARIA was completed in September 1987. This was an analysis of regulatory actions to get further reductions of air pollution in Oslo (SPCA, 1987). In addition to this pilot study, three more analyses have been conducted (reduction of water pollution in the Inner Oslo Fjord, reduction of air pollution and traffic noise in the Sarpsborg/Fredrikstad area and further reduction of water pollution in Lake Mjøsa), and a fifth study has started (reduction of water pollution in the Drammen Fjord). Like the RIA, LARIA is an interdisciplinary, intersectoral analysis of all possible measures, so that these can be considered collectively. All regulatory actions that are used to arrive at a priority ranking are assigned a BC ratio. Total benefits of each regulatory action are calculated using a set of weights for different benefits (e.g. one person no longer living in an area where air pollution exceeds the recommended threshold value for sulphur dioxide (SO_2), nitrogen oxide (NO_2), carbon monoxide (CO) and soot; one person no longer strongly affected by noise; one tonne reduced

SO$_2$ deposition, etc.) plus information about the reduced number of persons affected, the reduced number of tonnes of SO$_2$ and NO$_x$ with respect to acidification, etc. The set of weights is constructed on the basis of expert opinions and previous benefit estimation studies (conducted in Norway and other countries, mainly the USA) that were originally compiled for other purposes. Moreover, the selection of these benefit studies seems rather random, and is not as a result of a systematic review and evaluation of existing studies. This introduces a new type of uncertainty, in addition to the uncertainty about the physical effects of the regulatory actions (dose-response relationships) and the methodological uncertainty of benefit estimation techniques. To reduce this new uncertainty, benefit estimation studies have been conducted in the two LARIAs of reductions in water pollution of the Oslo Fjord (Aarskog, 1988; Heiberg and Hem, 1988), and the Drammen Fjord (Dalgard, 1989). So far none of the conducted LARIAs have been approved by the local authorities. However, the LARIA on further reduction of air pollution in Oslo has been submitted for affected institutions' and interest groups' opinions, and the municipal administration is preparing this case for discussion and decision in the Municipal Executive Board of Oslo.

To conclude, the pollution control institutions of the environmental authorities have initiated much of the work on environmental benefit estimation in Norway. However, researchers at the University of Oslo (Department of Economics), the Agricultural University of Norway (Department of Forest Economics), the Regional University of Møre and Romsdal and the Centre for Industrial Research have played a crucial role in this process. In the last few years, other sections of the environmental authorities (the Directorate of Nature Management, the Department of Natural Resources with the MOE and partly environmental authorities at the county level) have also shown interest in CBA and environmental benefit estimation. At present, the interest in environmental benefit estimation in Norway is growing. However, there still is a great need for information about the usefulness of the benefit estimation techniques in resource allocation, in planning and managerial decisions for decision makers on all levels of environmental management (community, county, nation) and in all sectors of the society.

A Review of Environmental Benefit Estimation Studies in Norway

Pearce and Markandaya (1987) divide the approaches to economic measurement of environmental benefits into two classes: *direct and indirect techniques*. The former considers environmental gains, e.g. improved water or air quality, and seeks directly to measure the money value of those gains through surrogate markets or by experimental techniques. The surrogate market approach looks for a market in which goods or factors of production (especially labour services) are bought and sold, and observes that environmental benefits or costs are frequently attributes of those goods or factors. These techniques include the Hedonic Price Method (HPM), applied to residential housing and labour markets, and the Travel Cost Method (TCM), where the demand for recreational activities is valued through an examination of the costs people incur to enjoy these activities. The experimental approach simulates a market by placing respondents in a position in which they can express their hypothetical valuations of real improvements in the quantity/quality of specific environmental goods. The most popular among these methods is the Contingent Valuation Method (CVM).

The indirect environmental benefit estimation techniques, as defined by Pearce and Markandya (op. cit.), do not seek to measure direct revealed preferences for the environmental good in question. Instead, they calculate a dose-response relationship between pollution and some effect, and only then is some measure of preference for that effect applied. Examples of dose-response relationships analysed in Norway are the corroding effect of air pollution on materials (NIAR, 1981) and the effects of reduced acid deposition on aquatic ecosystems (Munitz et al., 1984; Seip et al., 1986). The former dose-response relationship was utilized to calculate the social costs of corrosion damage in Norway, using market prices (Glomsr¢d and Rosland, 1989) while the latter was utilized in a CVM on social benefits of increased freshwater fish populations due to reduced acid depositions (Navrud, 1988b).

Glomsr¢d and Rosland (1989) give no consideration to the existence value and bequest value of historical buildings and monuments, the values of which could well be far greater than the direct material costs. Navrud (1988b), however, calculates both user and non-user benefits.

Table 5.2 gives a review of the results from both direct and indirect environmental benefit estimation studies, carried out in

Table 5.2: **Review of environmental benefit estimation studies in Norway**

Author(s)	Commodity	Method(s)[1]	Value (in 1989 NOK)[2]
Strand (1981a)	All freshwater fish stocks in Norway	CVM	1600–2550 NOK/person (above 15)/year
Strand (1981b)	Recreational angling for salmon in the River Gaula	TCM	ca 310 NOK/angler/day
Hylland and Strand (1983)	Improved air quality in the Grenland Area	CVM (local and national studies)	• National willingness to pay (WTP): 0.6% of gross income tax as a single payer payment (total benefits = 1013–1773 million NOK) • Local WTP: total benefits = 675 million NOK
Hoffmann (1984)	Airport noise in Bodc	HPM (housing property values)	Ca 1% decrease in market value of housing units per dB increased noise level above 60 dB

Author(s)	Commodity	Method(s)[1]	Value (in 1989 NOK)[2]
Navrud (1984)	Recreational angling for trout in the River Hallingdalselv	TCM	ca 160 NOK/angler/day
Scancke (1984)	Recreational angling for trout in the River Timelv	TCM	Ca 160 NOK/angler/day
Carlsen (1985)	Avoiding reduced Salmon stocks in the River Numedalslågen	CVM (local study)	WTP to avoid: • "some reduction": 157 NOK/household/year (for the 24% of the households that were willing to pay) • "considerable reduction": 325 NOK/household/year (for the 25% of the households that were willing to pay)

Author(s)	Commodity	Method(s)[1]	Value (in 1989 NOK)[2]
Larsen (1985)	Noise from road traffic in Oslo	HPM (housing property values)	0.8% decrease in market value of single-family housing units per 1000 ADT (average daily traffic from the nearest road)
Strand (1985)	Improved air quality from reduced car emissions in Norway (by introducing catalytic converters on private cars)	CVM	1036–2198 NOK/car/year or 630–770 NOK/person (above 15)/year
Amundsen (1987)	Avoiding reduced fish populations in the Oslomarka lakes	CVM	347 NOK/household/year
Dahle et al. (1987)	Preservation of Brown Bear,	CVM	c. 200 NOK/household/year

Author(s)	Commodity	Method(s)[1]	Value (in 1989 NOK)[2]
Heiberg and Hem (1987)	Wolverine and Wolf in Norway Improved water quality in the Kristiansand Fjord	(1) CVM (local and national studies) (2) SMART (local study)	(1) *local WTP:* • 411 NOK/household/ year • 924 NOK/taxpayer as a single payment (total benefits = 27 mill. NOK) *national WTP:* • 635 NOK/taxpayer as a single payment (total benefits = 1448 mill. NOK) (2) *local WTP:* total benefits: = 331–534 mill. NOK
Hervik et al. (1987)	Preservation of water courses from hydro-electric development	CVM	

Author(s)	Commodity	Method(s)[1]	Value (in 1989 NOK)[2]
	(1) Master Plan for water Resources in Norway (2) River Rauma/ Ulvåa		(1) 791–1436 NOK/house hold/year (2) 527–1423 NOK/house hold/year
Heiberg and Hem (1988); Aarskog (1988)	Improved water quality in the Inner Oslo Fjord	(1) CVM (2) SMART (Multiple Criteria Analysis also conducted)	(1) 800 NOK/household/ year (for a 10-year period) (2) 612 NOK/household/ year (for a 10-year period)
Navrud (1988b)	Increased number of lakes and rivers with reproducing fish stocks in southern Norway as a	CVM (local and national studies), based on dose-response functions	c. 370 NOK/household/ year

Author(s)	Commodity	Method(s)[1]	Value (in 1989 NOK)[2]
	result of a 30–70% reduction in sulphur emissions in Europe (or corresponding Norwegian liming actions)		
Navrud (1988c)	Recreational angling for salmon and sea-trout in the River Vikedalselv	(1) TCM (2) CVM	(1) 128–175 NOK/angler/ day (2) 121–172 NOK/angler/ day
Navrud (1988d)	Improved air quality (suspended particles) in Ålvik	CVM	1590 NOK/household/ year
Ulleberg (1988)	Recreational angling for salmon and sea-trout in the River	TCM	219–286 NOK/angler/ day

Author(s)	Commodity	Method(s)[1]	Value (in 1989 NOK)[2]
	Stordalselv		
Sedal (1989)	Recreational moose hunting in the counties of Ystfold and Hedmark	CVM	3,700 NOK/hunter/year
Glomsrcd and Rosland (1989)	Corrosion damages from sulphur dioxide on galvanized steel and paint on steel, wood and stone in Norway	(1) Dose-response function to calculate direct material costs (2) Multi-sectorial macro economic growth model MSG-4 to calculate indirect	(1) 400 mill. NOK/year (2) 130 mill. NOK/year

Author(s)	Commodity	Method(s)[1]	Value (in 1989 NOK)[2]
		losses due to allocation effects	

Notes:
CVM = Contingent Valuation Method
TCM = Travel Cost Method
HPM = Hedonic Price Method
SMART = Simple Multi-attribute Rating Technique (simplified version of Multiple Criteria Analysis, applied to a representative sample of affected households/individuals)
[2] Value in the year of the study corrected by consumers price index.
1 NOK = 0.93 FF = 0.15 US $ = 0.08 £ UK at exchange rates at April 1989

Norway. To the author's best knowledge, twenty studies have been completed so far, and four new studies are in progress (i.e. a CBA on liming of the River Audna with valuation of the increased recreational value of angling, a TCM on the recreational value of angling in the River Drammenselv, a CVM on improved water quality in the Drammen Fjord and a new study on improved air quality in the Grenland Area). The majority of the completed studies have used the CVM. This is probably due to the great versatility of this method. In addition, the method is relatively

Table 5.3:   **Distribution of Norwegian environmental benefit estimation studies on different commodities**

Commodity	Number of completed studies (including studies in progress)	References to studies completed
Air quality	4 (5)	Hylland and Strand (1983); Strand (1985); Navrud (1988d); Clomsrød and Rosland (1989)
Water quality	3 (4)	Heiberg and Hem (1987); Hervik et al. (1987); Heiberg and Hem (1988); Aarskog (1988)
Freshwater fish stocks	9 (11)	Strand (1981a, 1981b); Navrud (1984, 1988b, 1988c); Scanke (1984); Carlsen (1985); Amundsen (1987); Ulleberg (1988)
Wildlife	2 (2)	Dahle et al. (1987); Sœdal (1989)
Noise	2 (2)	Hoffmann (1984); Larsen (1985)
Total:	20 (24)	

easy to use (but also misuse).

Table 5.3 shows that nearly half of the Norwegian benefit studies have been on freshwater fish stocks, while the rest are distributed fairly evenly between air and water quality, wildlife and noise. So far, there have been no studies on, for example, health effects and radiation. Below, some of the studies in Tables 5.2 and 5.3 will be described in more detail.

Five of the nine studies on freshwater fish have used the travel cost method (TCM) to estimate the recreational value (use benefits) of fish stocks in different rivers. The results show that the recreational value per angler per day (RVA) of a good salmon river (River Gaula) is about twice as great as in a good trout river (River Hallingdalselv and River Tinnelv). The RVA of an acidified salmon and sea-trout river (River Vikedalselv) is roughly the same as in the good trout rivers, but significantly smaller than in a comparable salmon and sea-trout river not affected by acid rain (River Stordalselv). In the River Vikedalselv study (Navrud, 1988c), the TCM yielded the same RVA as the Contingent Valuation Method (CVM) used. This increases the reliability of the estimated RVA. To sum up, these results seem consistent and reasonable, since most anglers prefer angling for Atlantic salmon than for other species, and one would expect reduced RVA in acidified rivers with strongly decreased fish stocks. The four remaining valuation studies on fish stocks use the CVM to value quantitative changes. In three of these cases the quantitative change is due to acid depositions (Strand, 1981a; Amundsen, 1987; Navrud, 1988b), while the fourth case is concerned with hydro-power development (Carlsen, 1985). The latter study is an example of how not to use CVM. The commodity specification is very diffuse, only 1/4 of the households had willingness to pay (WTP) larger than zero and the sample size was very small. This is in sharp contrast to the other CVMs on fish stocks. Strand (1981a) estimated the Norwegian population's WTP to avoid extinction of all freshwater fish populations in Norway due to different types of pollution (e.g. acid depositions), while Amundsen (1987) did the same for stocks in the lakes of the forest areas surrounding Oslo. Navrud (1988b) estimated the Norwegian population's WTP for marginal increments in the freshwater fish stocks in Southern Norway due to reduced acid depositions or to liming actions that would yield the same effects. The environmental changes were, as mentioned earlier, calculated from existing dose-response relationships. The total annual benefits from a 30–70 per cent reduction in sulphur emissions in Europe (or corresponding liming actions) which would get back reproducible brown-trout stocks in 567–928 lakes (larger than 5 ha) and "some Atlantic salmon" or "reproducible stocks" in the many rivers in Southern Norway now devoid of salmon, was conservatively estimated to be approximately 565 million 1989-NOK. This value constitutes a very significant part of the welfare improvement to the Norwegian population, obtainable through reductions in long-range transmitted air pollutants. This benefit estimate can also be compared to the annual costs of 400–500 million 1989-NOK for liming the run-off from the entire acidified area in Southern Norway, which corresponds to a 100 per cent reduction in sulphur emissions. This indicates that liming of acidified rivers and lakes in Norway, in anticipation of reductions of long-range transmitted air pollutants, is economically efficient. To construct a national liming plan on how to use the limited liming budget in the most cost-effective way, the Directorate for Nature Management has initiated several CBAs of liming actions in representative rivers and lakes. (Navrud, 1988c is the first part of one of these CBAs.)

Another interesting result from Navrud (1988b) is the large non-user benefit (intrinsic benefit) found. Thus, 76 per cent of the total WTP was due to existence values and bequest values. This shows that one would gravely under-estimate the total benefits of environmental effects by just looking at the user benefits. This result agrees very well with the results from the air-quality studies. Strand (1985) found that 80–87 per cent of the total WTP for improvements in the air quality was due to other reasons than the individuals themselves being affected by air pollution. Intrinsic benefits of the same order of magnitude were also found by Hylland and Strand (1983) and Navrud (1988d). A problem encountered in the first two studies was how to describe the change in air quality so that it could be perceived by the respondents. In the third study (Navrud, 1988d), this was not a problem since it was an *ex post facto* study, and all the respondents had experienced the air quality both before and after the environment regulations had put an end to the large emission of suspended particles from a local ferro-alloy plant. (A more detailed description of Strand (1985) can be found below, p. 166.)

The problems of uncertainty about the effects (due to the lack of dose-response functions) and of how to describe these effects are also encountered in the studies on changes in water quality. Both studies of fjords in urban areas (Heiberg and Hemm, 1987; Heiberg and Hem, 1988 Aarskog, 1988) have this problem. When people can't perceive the commodity for which they are asked to state their WTP, the results become very uncertain. However, the two studies yield values of the same order of magnitude, 400–600 NOK/household/year. Preliminary results from a third fjord study (Dalgard, 1989) are also in the same range. In the third completed water-quality study, concerning people's WTP to obtain the Master Plan for Water Resources (Hervik et al., 1987), the commodity is much easier to specify and the Norwegian population were in general well informed about the effects of this commodity before the study was conducted. (This CVM is described in more detail below.) In the two studies of water-quality improvements in a fjord, both a CBA approach based on a CVM and a simplified version of the Multiple Criteria Analysis (MCA) – called the Simple Multi-attribute Rating Technique (SMART) – were applied to a sample of the individuals affected by the environmental changes. Keeny and Raiffa (1976) and Edwards (1977) give good descriptions of MCA and SMART respectively. In general, the fundamental difference between CBA and MCA lies in the recognition that economic efficiency frequently is not the sole objective of policy. MCA uses mathematical programming techniques to select projects based on objective functions, including weighted goals of decision makers, with explicit consideration of constraints to action and costs. The results, (see Table 5.2) show that the two methods, CVM and SMART, give significantly different results. In the Kristiansand Fjord study, the difference was large (SMART gave a 12–20 times higher estimate than CVM), while the difference in the Oslo Fjord study was quite small (CVM gave a 0.2 times higher estimate than SMART). In addition to these two studies, it should be mentioned that several other studies using MCA have also been performed. These include studies on oil spill combat (Fredrikson et al., 1982), the Master Plan for Water Resources (Wenstyp and Carlsen, 1987), regulatory actions to reduce phosphorus deposition in lakes (Seip et al., 1987), abatement of air pollution in Oslo and health effects of indoor radon exposure (Trynnes and Seip, 1988).

Of the two studies on wildlife in Table 5.3, the simplified CBA on preservation of the wolf, wolverine and brown bear in Norway should be mentioned (Dahle et al., 1987). The total costs associated with preserving these large carnivores had been estimated at approximately 6 1987-NOK/household/year. These costs are mainly due to compensation paid to farmers that had their sheep killed. Due to the harsh conflict between sheep-farming interests and preservation interests, the national CVM permitted both WTP for preservation and WTP for extinction/reduction of the stocks to be stated. The net WTP for preservation was calculated and compared to the costs. The results showed that the net WTP (175 1987-NOK/household/year) clearly exceeded the costs. This study also showed that there was a large degree of consistency between people's attitude towards preservation of the large carnivores and their stated WTP. This increases the reliability of the benefit estimate. However, this study also has a main weakness due to the lack of correspondence with biological data and thereby a somewhat diffuse definition of the good to be valued. The study was financed by the Directorate for Nature Management and was used to support a national plan for management of these species. However, no final decision has yet been reached in this case.

In Norway the Hedonic Price Method (HPM) has only been applied to residential housing prices and noise nuisance (see Hoffmann, 1984; Larsen, 1985). The main reasons for this limited application are the imperfections in the property market, and the difficulties in obtaining the data required. In addition, there are only a few areas in Norway where the pollution problems are so great that people can be expected to perceive local differences in the pollution level, and adjust their behaviour according to this information.

Although the studies described in Table 5.2 vary somewhat in quality, the overall impression is that most of the studies have been performed by a few researchers (or under supervision of these researchers) who have specialized in this field, and this gives a certain guarantee of the quality. This is important, because the benefit estimation techniques, and especially the CVM, are vulnerable to misuse, and low-quality studies may strongly reduce the decision makers' growing confidence in the methods. New empirical studies should also be combined with more methodological research to improve the existing methods (and maybe develop new ones), and thus reduce the uncertainty of the benefit estimates.

To conclude, there have been relatively few empirical benefit estimation studies in Norway. The environmental good most often studied is freshwater fish stocks. This is mainly due to the fact that the extinction of fish stocks by acid rain is one of the greatest environmental problems in Norway. More studies are, however, needed on other environmental goods affected by acid rain, and especially on forest-related environmental goods (see Navrud, 1988a, 1989 for a description of a proposed research programme in this area). In general, it is reasonable to expect an increased demand for studies on air and water pollution, together with effects on health from environmental degradation. This is due to the increased use of LARIA, and a general development towards more use of cost-benefit evaluation as a tool in environmental decision making.

Analysis of Three Selected Case Studies

Criteria for selection of Case Studies

The following three criteria, described by Miltz (1988), were used for selection of case studies:

(1) it should be a worthwhile study;
(2) it should be discussed by decision makers;
(3) the study should preferably incorporate monetized benefits.

Since very few CBAs have been carried out by the environmental authorities in Norway, and only some of these studies include monetized benefits, there are not many studies to choose from. However, to get a *representative* set of these studies, three cases have been selected:

(1) CBA of *provisions* on stricter car emission regulations (SPCA, 1986; Strand, 1985);
(2) "simplified" CBA of the large *national project*: The Master Plan for Water Resources (Hervik et al., 1987);
(3) *Locally Adapted Regulatory Impact Analysis* (LARIA) on further reductions of air pollution in Oslo (SPCA, 1987).

The first two case studies are CBAs with benefit estimates based on new empirical studies, while the LARIA study incorporates benefit estimates from existing empirical studies. Although this last study has not yet been discussed by the decision makers, it has been submitted for the affected interest groups' opinions, and the results from this submission provide interesting information on how the benefit/cost evaluations in this study are perceived. In addition, LARIA is a new, promising approach to benefit/cost evaluations in environmental decision making in Norway. Therefore, this first LARIA was chosen as a case study, in spite of the lack of formal political discussion. With this exception, these case studies, in the author's opinion, fulfil the three above mentioned criteria.

The case studies represent three categories of decision-making issues: (a) provisions; (b) national projects; (c) local regulations. They should provide a broad illumination of the role benefit estimates, when they are available, play in environmental decision making. However, it should be stressed that these studies are not representative of environmental decision making in Norway, since benefit estimates in most cases are not provided.

Case Study: Stricter car emission regulations

Background and decision question
The background for this case study is the environmental authorities' proposal to introduce stricter regulations on emissions of exhaust gases from private cars, in order to reduce detrimental effects to health and environmental damage.

In April 1984, the Ministry of the Environment asked the State Pollution Control Authority carry out a detailed impact analysis of stricter car emission regulations (USA standards) and the use of unleaded gasoline. The analysis was to be completed within the spring of 1985. The deadline for the IA on unleaded petrol was later (August 1984) then was changed to mid-November 1984, due to decisions in many EEC countries to put unleaded gasoline on the market as early as 1985/6. In the summer of 1984, West Germany decided in principle to introduce car emission restrictions on the USA level. (This decision was later withdrawn due to the agreement on less stringent standards within the EEC.) As a response to this rapid international development, the government decided, in December 1984, that in principle Norway would make the regulations governing emissions from private cars more restrictive, bringing them up to the level which applied in the USA. The regulations were scheduled to come into effect at the same time as similar measures were introduced in Sweden, Denmark and West Germany.

The government's decision was based on two NOUs (Norwegian Official Report): NOU 1983:40 on "Air Pollution from Road Traffic" from the inter-ministerial Car Pollution Committee (May 1983), and NOU 1984:5 on "Policy on Private Cars" from the Private Car Committee with representatives from affected interest groups (March 1984). The decision also took into account the damage caused by long-range transboundary pollution, including acidification of water resources and deterioration of forests. The international conventions Norway had signed in this area at that time assumed, for example, that national measures would be introduced to limit nitrogen oxide discharges (and in 1989 Norway signed an international convention on stabilization of NO_x emissions at the 1987 level within 1994). In Norway, the best way to do this was to reduce the emissions from road traffic because the possibilities of reducing NO_x emissions from other sources were limited. In the light of the level of intention which formed the basis of the work in connection with the UN Convention on Long-range Transboundary Air Pollution, the only way for Norway to fulfil expectations as regards NO_x emissions was to introduce the USA standards.

In January 1986, more than half a year after the deadline, SPCA had completed the IA (SPCA, 1986). The main decision question in this analysis was whether or not the social benefits from introducing the USA standards on emissions from private cars exceeded the social costs of this measure. Both costs and benefits were measured in monetary units, and the benefit estimate was based on an empirical study designed for this purpose (Strand, 1985). Distributional effects of different tax systems in connection with the introduction of this measure were also analysed (Hjorthol, 1985). In addition to this complete CBA of the USA standards, a cost-effectiveness analysis of the USA and EEC standards was conducted. It stated that the cost effectiveness of the two measures was approximately the same (120 and 100 g less pollution per NOK of increased costs respectively). It was also documented that USA standards give much greater reductions in air pollution than the EEC standards (440 and 85 kg respectively less pollution per car during its whole lifetime). This means that both the total pollution reduction and total costs are greatest with the introduction of the USA standards. The higher costs were the main reason why the

Ministry of Transport and the affiliated Directorate of Public Roads preferred the EEC standards. In this analysis the SPCA therefore had to convince the transport authorities that the USA standards were worth the higher costs.

SPCA (1986) can be considered as a description of economic and administrative consequences of a provision on introducing the USA standards for car emissions (according to the aforementioned instructions for work on provisions). However, the provision itself was worked out by the Directorate of Public Roads, since it is pursuant to the Road Traffic Act. Although this makes the case study somewhat special, it was chosen because there has been no empirical benefit estimation study on any provisions worked out by the SPCA. In addition, this case study illustrates one of the main problems/challenges in environmental policy in Norway today, i.e. the Pollution Act does not cover the transportation sector. Thus, the environmental authorities' influence on the decisions in this sector of the society is still rather small. However, there are now increasing efforts at trying to incorporate environmental concerns into the decision-making process in all sectors of society, in accordance with the recommendations from the World Commission on Environment and Development (UN, 1987).

Results from the study
The main conclusion of SPCA was:

> Mandatory emission standards of the same level of stringency as the USA standard can be implemented as from the model year 1989 by employing a system of taxes which will not make the cars more expensive to buy, but which will cause an increase in the cost of petrol of approximately 0.20 NOK per litre. This measure will reduce damage to the environment and health in urban areas, as well as road traffic's share of the damage caused by "acid rain". From a cost-benefit point of view, the benefits are assessed as outweighing the costs.
>
> (SPCA, 1986, p. 1)

The conclusions of the CBA in particular were:

> A total evaluation of costs, benefits and distributional effects in connection with the introduction of USA-level emission standards for private cars, tends to indicate that such standards

will be of net benefit to society. The estimates contain a large element of uncertainty, however, particularly as regards the benefits. Certain effects of the measure have not been valued, but these are not so extensive as to alter the conclusions.

The conclusion of the cost-benefit analysis is that the proposed measure will, with a reasonable degree of certainty, be profitable for society.

(SPCA, 1986, Appendix 7)

The benefit estimate in this CBA was based on Strand (1985). Strand designed a sample survey of approximately 2,000 persons among the Norwegian adult population to reveal their maximum willingness to pay (WTP), in the form of taxes and automobile-related costs, for an assumed 50 per cent reduction in the air-pollution level in urban areas. This improved air quality would follow from a requirement that all new cars to be sold in Norway should be equipped with three-way catalytic converters.

Using a Contingent Valuation Method (CVM) Strand found an average, annual maximum WTP of 740–1,570 1985–NOK per car to get the described improvement in air quality. SPCA used the middle estimate of this range, NOK 1,100, to calculate the total annual benefits from more stringent emission standards for new private cars at 1,900 million 1985–NOK. These benefits include:

• reduction in damage to health (e.g. lung cancer, attacks of asthma, allergy and bronchitis, infections of the respiratory system, heart attacks, reduced ability to concentrate);
• the effects of feeling "safer" (due to the smaller probability of becoming sick);
• reduced environmental damage (e.g. fish mortality, damage to vegetation including forests, material damage);
• the smaller probability of general environmental deterioration for this and future generations;
• the decrease in factors negative for well-being (e.g. smell from exhaust gases).

In addition, the international influence which may help to reduce long-range transmitted pollution may increase through Norway's taking the lead as far as environmental measures are concerned.

The benefit estimate of NOK 1,900 million was compared to the real costs of this measure (i.e. fitting all cars with catalytic converters), which was found to be approximately 750 million 1985–NOK per year. NOK 500 million per year are direct costs for actual equipment (the catalytic converters) and NOK 250 million per year is the calculated loss due to a reduced potential for lowering petrol consumption. In addition, there will be some minor cost elements (such as costs of administration, etc.) which are not expected to change the level of real costs stated above. It is emphasized in the report that the method for calculation of the benefits, and therefore the result, contains a large degree of uncertainty. Some of the uncertainty in the benefit estimate is also due to the lack of well-established dose-response functions in this area. However, results from other countries, where somewhat different methods of calculation have been used, were not incompatible with this estimate. SPCA (op. cit.) therefore concluded that the benefits of this regulation exceeded the costs. In addition, the measure was found to have no unfortunate distributional effects between different groups of the population – if the costs were covered (as proposed) by the persons causing the pollution (i.e. the car owners).

In this study, both total costs and benefits of the regulations and how they will be distributed between different interest groups are well documented, and the quality of the study must be characterized as rather high. However, this does not guarantee that the CBA and the benefit estimate would have any influence on the decision to introduce the USA-level emission standards for private cars.

The role of benefit estimation in the decision-making process
In April 1986, the Ministry of Environment submitted the SPCA's analysis for the affected interest groups' opinions. Usually SPCA carries out this "hearing". In this case, however, the MOE thought the SPCA had spent too much time on performing too detailed a CBA, and therefore they did the hearing themselves to make sure that it was completed as quickly as possible. This hurry was due to the rapid international development in the area. A summary of the statements from the hearing was worked out by the MOE in July 1986, and in August of the same year the SPCA gave their comments on these statements. Only four of the 11 ministries and nine organizations/research institutes that had submitted their opinion of SPCA's analysis commented on the cost-benefit evaluations in particular. Most of these comments

concentrated on the benefit estimate. The Ministry of Consumer Affairs and Governmental Administration, for example, noted that the SPCA's IA was an interesting and valuable example on how to analyse benefits and costs of public measures. However, they pointed out that some assumptions and calculations were based on unknown documents and therefore could not be checked, and that the cost-benefit evaluations in general are very uncertain. They especially questioned the value of the CVM survey and the reliability of the benefit estimate. The Motor Trade Organization also was very sceptical about the benefit estimate. In their opinion, the results from three foreign studies SPCA had used to support their estimate showed that the benefits from stricter car emission regulations is considerably lower than the SPCA's estimate of 1,900 million 1985–NOK per year. They demanded much better documentation of the benefits. In addition, they argued that the costs of this measure were under-estimated, in that it was not clear whether or not the introduction of car emission regulations on the USA level in Norway was socially economic-efficient. Therefore they also wanted a more detailed analysis of the EEC standards. The two research institutes that commented on the CBA, pointed out errors in the SPCA's description of health effects from reduced car emissions. In addition to these specific comments, all the organizations for car owners and car dealers and the Ministry of Transport in their conclusions were against the proposal of introducing USA-level car emission regulations. They all doubted that the large costs of this measure were exceeded by the benefits, and that there were more cost-effective measures to reduce pollution from road traffic. These conclusions indirectly also indicate scepticism about the benefit estimate.

In their comments on these statements, the SPCA stressed that the proposed stricter car emission regulations are not solely based on the contingent valuation survey. In addition to the CBA, the SPCA, in their best subjective evaluation of the case, found that expected benefits would outweigh the expected cost. They also state that in most cases their proposals are based on such a subjective evaluation. However, since introduction of stricter car emission regulations had high costs and affected many people, they wanted to use another method to support (or weaken) their subjective judgement. In spite of the uncertainty of the benefit estimate, and the fact that two of the three similar foreign empirical studies indicated smaller benefits (due to omission of effects that should be counted, according to the SPCA), the SPCA concluded that the CBA supported their subjective judgement.

These comments clearly show that the SPCA also has doubts about the value of the benefit estimation study, and found it safer to refer to the "subjective evaluation method". This is probably due to a lack of detailed knowledge about the benefit estimation techniques, and thus they have difficulties in arguing in favour of cost-benefit evaluations.

In the autumn of 1986, the government finally decided that all new private cars from the model year 1989 should have catalytic converters, in order to fulfil the USA standards for car emissions. In their argument with the government in advance of this decision, the MOE did not mention the benefit estimate at all. The description of the health and environmental benefits was based on quantifications in physical units and verbal descriptions. This could be due to the above-mentioned statements from the hearing and the SPCA's comments in this regard.

The MOE felt that the SPCA's CBA came too late, and that there was no need for such a detailed CBA (including benefit estimates) at the time the analysis was presented. The SPCA exceeded the MOE's deadline by more than half a year, and by the time it was completed, the government had one year earlier decided in principle to introduce the USA standards. Ahead of this main decision, the MOE had already had some success in convincing the Ministry of Transport and the government of the large benefits from this measure, without referring to monetary estimates. In this connection, it should be mentioned that the benefit estimation study can hardly be the reason for the SPCA exceeding the deadline, since the survey was done in May and June 1984 and the results were presented in January 1985. This was one year before the SPCA completed the analysis. The cost of the benefit estimation study was approximately 170,000 1989–NOK. (Jon Strand, pers. comm. 1989), and it was financed by the SPCA.

To conclude, the benefit estimate in the CBA on stricter car emission regulations seems to have had no significant influence on the decision to implement this measure. The main reason for this is that the analysis was conducted too late in the decision-making process. In addition, the environmental authorities themselves, when affected interest groups criticized the CBA and the benefit estimation methods, were not able to come up with any good argument for doing benefit estimation studies. Instead of defending the valuation techniques and the conclusion from the CBA, they stated that their decisions were based on the best subjective judgement – and that this was the best decision criteria. Thus, the benefit estimation in this case did not lead to a better appreciation of the benefits.

Case Study: The master plan for water resources

Background and decision question
Since the beginning of this century, the development of water resources in Norway has created a basis for steadily increasing production and use of energy. From 1906 till 1984 the Norwegian authorities, after considering each case individually, had granted a licence permitting regulation of about 500 large or small watercourses. During the same period about 10 proposed projects were refused a licence. In several cases, the authorities' evaluations in connection with the licence had resulted in a reduction in the scope of the project, due to the negative impact on other user interests. This development, however, took place without a co-ordinated plan for the whole country, and conflicts with the other users became progressively greater in the 1970s. It was therefore essential to consider the exploitation of the remaining watercourses within a larger perspective, which also took into account user interests other than those concerned solely with energy. In the Report to the Storting, no. 54 (1979–80) on "Future use and production of energy", the government's suggestion was that in the further planning of hydro-power projects and in the administrative procedures connected with the granting of licences (in accordance with the Watercourse Regulation Act), emphasis should be placed on developing first the watercourses which were the most favourable both economically and from an environmental point of view. Further, in the Proposition to the Storting, no. 130 (1981–82) on "Power Coverage in the 1980s and the Relation to the Master Plan for Water Resources", the government approved the main goal of the Master Plan which was to present to the Storting a proposal for a priority grouping of hydro-power projects for subsequent consideration for a licence. Further, the plan was to provide the basis for taking a standpoint on which watercourses could be used for other purposes. Thus, the Master Plan was neither a protection plan nor a development plan. The work was headed by the Ministry of Environment in collaboration with the Ministry

of Petroleum and Energy, the Norwegian Water Resources and Electricity Board, and other relevant authorities.

When the Master Plan was presented in 1984 it represented a total power potential of 40.9 TWh. Out of the total exploitable hydro-power of 174.3 TWh, 105 TWh had already been developed or was being developed. Of the remaining 28.4 TWh, 17.5 TWh had been protected or was being recommended to be protected through three Protection Plans, and 10.9 TWh had been excluded from the Master Plan in order to ensure adequate power coverage. Otherwise, the Storting would not have been able to reach a final decision on new projects until the Master Plan had been finally discussed. However, since the Storting wanted as many watercourses as possible to be dealt with in the Master Plan, several projects under evaluation for a licence were included in the Plan, and the evaluation procedure postponed for the time being.

The Master Plan was based on 285 reports covering 310 water-courses. These reports were prepared in close collaboration with local planners, the hydro-power developers and the various interest groups. The reports were, in the spring of 1984, sent to counties, municipalities, power companies and local interest organizations for their comments.

In these reports, a total of 16 user interests/topics were studied. These were: hydro-power, nature conservation, outdoor recreation, wildlife, water supply, protection against water pollution, preservation of ancient monuments, agriculture and forestry, reindeer cultivation, prevention of flooding and erosion, transport, formation of ice, climate, mapping and data, and the regional economy. User interests (with the exception of hydro-power, mapping and data, and the regional economy) were classified according to the extent of the consequences if the watercourse was developed, using a scale ranging from -4 for very serious negative impacts to $+4$ for very large positive impacts. After evaluating and weighing the different user interests affected by a project according to this scale, a total evaluation was undertaken. In the Master Plan, the first stage in this process was to sort the projects "technically", where all the user interests had the same weight. In this connection, the projects were sorted into eight impact groups. When a project had been placed in an impact group, each project was evaluated individually. In this evaluation, emphasis was given to the comments received from the different interest groups. Also at this stage, the different interests were weighed against each other. All the projects were also ranked according to the economy of the power plant. The next stage in the process was to weigh the economy of the plant against the impact class. With six economy classes and eight impact classes, there were 48 possible combinations. These 48 possibilities were reduced to 16 priority groups.

Projects with the best power plant economy and the least negative effects on other user interests were placed in the first of the priority groups. When projects were sorted into these groups, emphasis was placed on giving relatively more weight to the economy of the power plant for projects at the top of the priority list and less weight in the case of projects at the bottom of the list. This system of priority groupings meant that more weight was given to undisturbed nature, outdoor life and recreation, for example, as more of the remaining water resources are developed. Other conditions were also taken into account before a project was finally placed in a certain priority group.

Due consideration was given to regional conditions, e.g. whether the hydro-power project was particularly important to ensure an adequate and reliable supply of power. In addition, some larger watercourses were moved further up in the priority ranking. This was due to the fact that large projects with major impacts on other user interests were originally placed far down in the priority grouping; this could have had an unfortunate effect because several smaller projects, taken together, could result in equally serious negative effects as could one large project. Moreover, some projects were given a different place on the list in the light of the comments received when the main report was submitted for affected interest groups' opinions.

Figure 5.1 illustrates the main phases in the process of classification of watercourses described above. Figure 5.2 illustrates the trade-off between degree of conflict and development costs, the adjustment for regional conditions and how the 16 priority groups were divided into three categories. The first category comprises the first five priority groups in the Master Plan (1–5), all of which could be considered for a licence immediately and consecutively in order to cover the energy demand in the years to come. The second category (priority groups 6–8) is considered as a reserve and includes watercourses which may be exploited for power production or for other purposes. The third category (priority groups 9–16) includes watercourses, which on the basis of

Phase of Evaluation   Classification system

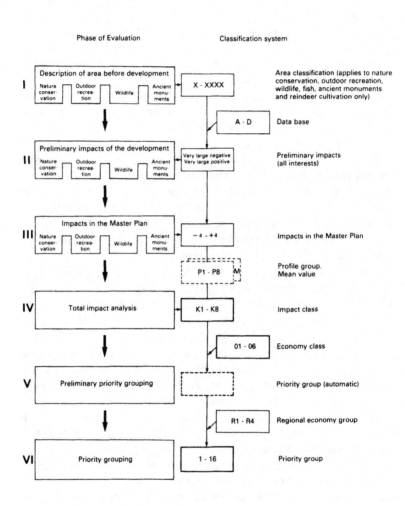

Table 5.4: Classification system in the Master Plan for Water Resources seen in relation to the phase of evaluation of the different projects.
Source: Ministry of Environment (1984)

technical solutions for development considered to date, are not regarded as relevant for development, either because of serious conflicts with other user interests, or because of the high costs involved.

The limit of development of 125 TWh, seen in Figure 5.2, was assumed to be a reasonable illustration of careful hydro-power development in a previous government report on energy. The work on the Master Plan confirmed this, in showing that important conflicts could arise in connection with further power development.

The above-described method for weighing against each other a number of dimensions which are difficult to compare, has many potential errors. First of all, the choice of interest groups evaluated seems somewhat arbitrary. This is especially important since all user interests were given the same weight in the evaluation. Second, the evaluation of each user interest using the aforementioned scale is quite obscure and subjective, and many user interests were evaluated on the basis of non-quantifiable figures. There are also reasons to believe that many user interests were intercorrelated. This should have been taken into consideration. However, a comparison has to be made between these dimensions, and it is better in each case to do this explicitly in the Master Plan than implicitly through the previous individual considerations for a licence and implicit weighing by the government and the Storting. By explicit evaluation, the risk for inconsistent decisions is reduced.

For politicians, another strength of this method is that it is simple and easy to understand. However, due to the criticism of this ranking method, an expert group within the MOE decided to try out another method to find the implicit cost of not undertaking the most economically profitable projects first. The environmental authorities and the developing interests did, however, not agree upon whether the calculated implicit costs of the Master Plan were large or small. To throw more light on this issue, a contingent valuation study was used to measure the Norwegian population's willingness-to-pay (WTP) for the Master Plan. This would be an expression of total benefits from the careful hydro-power development the Master Plan implied. The *decision question* was, through a simple CBA (see Hervik et al., 1987), to see if the benefits of the proposed Master Plan for Water Resources outweighed the implicit costs. Thus, this analysis only considered

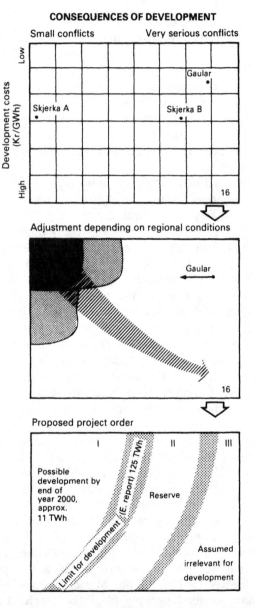

Table 5.5: The trade-off between development costs and environmental damage in classification of projects in the Master Plan for Water Resources.
Source: Ministry of Environment (1984)

whether the proposed plan was socially economic-efficient or not, and did not look at the ranking of different watercourses. This was, however, done by Wenstyp and Carlsen (1987) using a multiple criteria analysis technique. In December 1984 they pointed out some weaknesses of the MOE's method, and in April 1985 their final report was presented. This analysis gave a very different ranking compared to the MOE's method. The MOE was very sceptical about this new approach, but they reconsidered their results in the light of the new information, and supported the new analysis financially.

The results of Wenstyp and Carlsen had, however, no significant effect on the ranking of projects in neither the final framing of the Master Plan (approved by the government in March 1985 and by the Storting in the spring of 1986) nor the first revision of the Plan (approved by the Storting in the autumn of 1988). In the following section only the simplified CBA, containing benefit estimates (Hervik et al., 1987), will be analysed.

Results from the study
The final report on implicit costs of the Master Plan for Water Resources (there was also a pilot study) was presented in 1984, and the corresponding national benefit-estimation studies were carried out in March and April 1985. The simplified CBA, where the calculated costs and benefits were compared, was presented in January 1986 (see Hervik et al. 1987 for an English version), and received wide media coverage.

The implicit costs of the Master Plan were calculated as the difference between the present value of the Plan compared to the economically most profitable development. Implicit costs of several alternative rankings of the projects in the Master Plan were calculated, and sensitivity analyses for different prognoses of demand for energy and prices of alternative energy resources were carried out. The present value of the implicit costs was calculated as an annuity over the project's lifetime, and this amount was divided between all of the 1.55 million households in Norway. The reason for this calculation was to show how much the mean annual electricity bill per household had to increase in order to cover the increased development costs. This estimate could then be compared directly to people's mean annual willingness to pay for an increment in the electricity bill, as calculated from the national CVM.

The implicit-cost approach showed that each household had to be willing to accept an increase in its electricity bill of 100–450 1985–NOK if the Master Plan were to be economically efficient from society's point of view. This corresponded to an increase in the annual electricity bill of an average household of 1–5 per cent. The lowest estimate was based on the high prognosis of both demand and the price of alternative energy resources, while the largest estimate was based on the corresponding low prognosis for these two factors. The calculations were more sensitive to different prognoses of these two factors than to the alternative rankings of projects within the Master Plan. One problem with the implicit cost calculations was that history shows that Norway has never managed to develop projects in the most profitable manner. This gives reason to believe that the implicit costs could be less than the estimates above. The results from the nationwide contingent valuation survey of 2,200 households showed that each household was willing to pay an increase in its annual electricity bill of 500–1000 1985–NOK in order to implement the Master Plan. This indicated that the total benefits of the Master Plan for Water Resources exceeded the total implicit costs. Although the contingent valuation method has many potential sources of error, the benefits are so much larger than the costs that this result must be characterized as robust. The potential error induced by placing people in a hypothetical situation with no payment obligation (i.e. the hypothetical bias) was greatly weakened here by telling the respondents that the results from the project might be used in the political process and that their answers could influence their future electricity bill. In addition, people in general were well informed about the content of the Plan through the wide media coverage at that time, both at the local and national level. Thus, they knew what they were paying for, and this reduced the commodity specification bias that may easily arise in such surveys. Moreover, as mentioned above, the implicit cost may be overstated.

It should also be mentioned that a local contingent valuation survey of 400 households in connection with a specific development project (River Rauma-Ulvåa in Western Norway), was carried out in connection with this study.

The role of benefit estimation in the decision-making process
The report to the Storting, no. 63 (1984–85) on the Master Plan for Water Resources was approved by the government in

March 1985. However, it was not approved by the Storting until the spring of 1986. This meant that the "simplified CBA" of the Master Plan, which was presented in January 1986, came too late to have any influence on the framing of the report to the Storting. However, it was used by the MOE to support their view that the ranking technique they had used was good, and that the Master Plan was profitable from society's point of view. The development interests argued that the benefit estimate could not be trusted since it was based on a hypothetical willingness to pay an increased electricity bill. In addition, they claimed that careful hydro-power development could be achieved without the Master Plan and its high implicit cost.

Thus, the development interests still thought that the implicit costs were too high, in spite of the "evidence" from the benefit estimation study which was designed especially for answering the question of whether the implicit costs were large or small. Although the MOE tried to use it in support of the Master Plan, they were not able to use the benefit estimate effectively in the decision-making process. This seems once again to be mainly due to their general scepticism of and the lack of knowledge about benefit estimation techniques. Thus, it seem likely that non-monetization would not have made any significant difference. However, if the benefit estimate had turned out to be less than the implicit costs, that could have had quite large implications. Although it is difficult to predict what would have happened, it is reasonable to assume that the MOE in this situation would have had greater difficulties in defending their ranking method, especially since the results from the aforementioned multiple criteria analysis also indicated some serious errors in the MOE's method. This could, in turn, have lead to a total revision of the Master Plan. In this way, benefit estimation seems to have played a certain role in the decision-making process. However, this role could have been more significant if the CBA had been performed at an earlier stage in the process and if the MOE (especially the Department of Natural Resources, to which the project group of the Master Plan was affiliated) had been more familiar with benefit estimation techniques. The cost of the benefit estimation study, both the national and the local survey, was approximately 240,000 1989–NOK, and it was financed indirectly (through another research programme) by the MOE (Arild Hervik, pers. comm. 1989). This estimate only included the direct project costs. Labour cost of the project team (corresponding to half a year fulltime employment for one person, i.e. approximately 120,000 1989–NOK) must be added to find the total costs. The MOE did not consider this to be a very costly study, especially not when compared to the total costs of preparing the Master Plan.

Case Study: Further reductions of air pollution in Oslo

Background and decision question

As a step towards the effort to give priority to measures in areas with the largest pollution problems, the SPCA in 1984 invited the municipality of Oslo to co-operate on a study of measures to reduce air pollution in Oslo. Air pollution there can affect the health and well-being of so many people that it was considered necessary to implement further measures to reduce emissions. All measures were to be evaluated, across sector boundaries, and with a time perspective of 10–15 years. Measures requiring authority other than the Pollution Act were also to be considered (e.g. measures in the transport sector). This manner of working was new, and it was therefore necessary to develop the methodology as the work progressed.

A working group was established in the autumn of 1984, including representatives from the SPCA and the involved sectors in the municipality. By June 1985, a project plan for the work had been prepared, specifying the measures to be studied. It was estimated that the project would take 70 man-weeks in Oslo municipality and 50 man-weeks at the SPCA, and that the need for external assistance would cost SPCA 1.3 million 1985–NOK (or about 1.7 million 1989–NOK). The project was to be completed by 31 December, 1986.

The project plan was approved by the SPCA and the Municipal Executive Board in October 1985 and a special project group and a steering group were appointed. The steering group consisted of the directors of the affected sectors within the Oslo municipality (health, traffic and finance), the County Governor of Oslo and Akershus, the Director of the SPCA and another representative of the SPCA. A reference group was appointed in order to develop methods to arrive at a priority ranking. Subsidiary project groups were made responsible for the work of studying several specific measures. The ranking method used was benefit-cost (BC) ratios, based on monetary evaluation of both costs and benefits of the different measures. However, the benefit estimates were based on previous empirical studies and transformed into a weighing scale for different types of benefits. Thus, the monetary benefit estimates were not used directly in the calculation of BC ratios, although they provide the basis for the calculations. (As mentioned earlier, this type of analysis is now called Locally Adapted Regulatory Impact Analysis (LARIA).)

The *decision question* in this first LARIA was which measures to reduce air pollution in Oslo had larger benefits than costs, and which measures had the largest BC ratio. Thus, the socially most profitable extent of the total pollution reduction was not estimated. It was left to the politicians to decide how far down on the priority list they would go. However, a package of all measures with a BC ratio larger than one was recommended by the SPCA. It should be emphasized that the analysis provides a basis for considering all measures in different sectors collectively.

Results from the study
The LARIA of further reductions in air pollution in Oslo (SPCA 1987) was presented in September 1987, nine months behind schedule.

Calculations were carried out on the spread of, and exposure to pollution in order to establish the extent of the pollution problem in Oslo today, and the expected extent in the year 2000. If further measures are not introduced, in addition to those decided already, air pollution in 2000 will lead to a situation where:

• 150–200,000 persons will live or spend time in areas where the air pollution will exceed the recommended threshold values for air quality;
• 250–300,000 persons will be troubled by smell and dust.

These estimates included the effect of more restrictive private car emission regulations, as from 1989. The calculations were also based on assumptions about the development in consumption of heating oil (40–50 per cent increase), sulphur content of light oils (will increase) and traffic (30–40 per cent increase) in the period 1986–2000.

The benefits and costs for a total of 38 measures considered to be relevant were analysed. The following benefits of the measures were calculated in each case:

A *Improved air quality*

- Reduction in the number of persons who live or spend time in areas where the concentration of the following substances exceeds the recommended threshold values for:
  SO_2;
  NO_2;
  suspended particulate matter (soot);
  CO.
- Reduction in the number of persons troubled by:
  smell;
  dust.

B *Other benefits to society*

- Savings to society expressed in NOK:
  reduced noise;
  less corrosion and acidification;
  fewer traffic accidents;
  reduced costs for cars (maintenance costs, costs of tyres, etc.);
  reduced travelling time;
  savings on cost of petrol.

The first step of the analysis was a rough, subjective sorting of all relevant measures into three main groups depending on the extent of emission reductions/increased welfare (large, medium, small) in relation to the costs. Emission reductions were measured in tonnes/year and increased well-being in the number of persons troubled by smell and dust. The measures in group 3 (small benefits per NOK of costs) should then be omitted in further calculations, and it should be considered whether to scale up the measures in group 1 (large benefits per NOK of costs). A simplified form of discounting was performed to correct for the different distribution of benefits over time for different measures, and to obtain comparable annual benefits. Investments and operation costs of the measures were also discounted and distributed as annuities on their lifetime. This rough sorting did, however, not work very well because of difficulties in comparing different benefit components. Therefore, the different measures were ranked with respect to each benefit component, and then divided into groups.

However, this technique also gave a very uncertain division of measures into groups. In order to carry out a more exact ranking, the different benefits had to be compared and aggregated. To

Table 5.6: **SPCA's set of weights to compare different benefits from measures to reduce air pollution in the Sarpsborg/Fredrikstad area**

Benefits from the reduction of the following health and environmental problems by:	*Weight (range of uncertainty)*
● 1 person above the recommended threshold value for:	
SO_2	2.0
NO_2	4.0 (3.6–4.6)
CO	6.0 (5.6–6.6)
Soot	4.4 (4.0–5.0)
● 1 person troubled by dust from the industry	0.3 (0.14–1.00)
● 1 person troubled by smell from the industry	0.4 (0.2–1.4)
● 1 person troubled by dust/ smell from other sources	0.2 (0.1–0,7)
● 1 person "strongly affected" by noise	8.0 (4.0–16.0)
● 1 traffic accident with persons injured	1400.0 (600.0–4000.0)
● 1000 NOK saved costs	1.0 (0.6–6.0)
● 1 tonne SO_2 emitted (with respect to acidification)	2.7 (1.6–6.0)
● 1 tonne NO_x emitted (with respect to acidification)	1.4 (0.6–2.4)

Note: These revised weights are very close to those used in the Oslo study. The weights have been normalized so that 1000 1987-NOK/year have been given the weight 1

Source: Modified after SYVERSEN (1988)

achieve this, the benefits were assigned different weights. This set of weights was based on previous benefit estimation studies, expert opinions and subjective evaluations by the SPCA and MOE. However, since the set of weights was partly based on benefit estimation studies, all benefits can implicitly be assigned a monetary value (see Table 5.4).

The weight of 4.00 for NO_2 exposure in Table 5.4 means that it is considered four times more important to obtain a reduction of one person exposed to NO_x levels above the recommended threshold value (for one year), than it is to reduce the costs by 1000 NOK. In other words, there is willingness to pay 4,000 NOK to have one person less exposed to NO_2 for one year. The other weights in Table 5.4 can be interpreted in the same way.

Based on this set of weights for the benefits and information about the costs, all measures could be assigned a BC ratio and ranked according to this criteria. Sensitivity analyses were carried out to see if the uncertainty in the benefit weights affected the ranking, but the ranking seemed relatively robust. Antagonistic effects of the ranking of the measures were also controlled for. Twenty measures, both nationwide and local ones, were found to have a BC ratio larger than 1, and a package of these measures would solve 90 per cent of Oslo's air pollution problems in the year 2000. Therefore, this package was recommended by the steering group.

The majority of the 20 measures were in the transport and energy sector, and only five of them were nationwide measures. Four out of the five measures with the highest BC ratio were in the transport sector. This illustrates the importance of doing studies of measures across sector boundaries, and of introducing environmental concerns in all sectors of society.

The total costs to society to implement this package of measures were estimated at 780 million 1987-NOK/year. These costs were exceeded by the savings to society (saved fuel costs, fewer traffic accidents, less noise, reduced costs for car maintenance, tyres, etc., reduced travelling time, less corrosion) of 1,380 million 1987-NOK/year. In addition to this annual net benefit of 600 million NOK/year there are the described effects of improved air quality on health, well-being and the environment.

The role of benefit estimation in the decision-making process
This discussion of the role of benefit estimation in the decision-making process cannot at the time of writing (April 1989) be complete, since the LARIA was awaiting approval in principle by the Municipal Executive Board of Oslo at the end of May. However, comments from the "hearing" on this analysis can provide some information.

After the LARIA had been presented in September 1987, it was submitted for affected interest groups' opinions. In November 1988, a working group with representatives from the SPCA and the administration of the Oslo Municipality worked out a summary of comments from the hearing and evaluated them (SPCA, 1988). Then the proposed package of measures was adjusted, based on the results from the hearing. In this process the most controversial measures (the traffic measures) were excluded and partly replaced by less controversial, but also less profitable measures. The revised package contained 17 measures. This new package – the final report (SPCA, 1989) – was submitted to the Executive Board of Oslo, and to the national authorities (due to the national measures within the package).

From the summary of the comments to the SPCA's original package of measures (SPCA, 1988), it can be seen that only a few of the 34 institutions/interest groups commented on the ranking techniques. The health authorities noted that the health benefits were not well documented. However, they did not comment on the indirect monetary evaluation of the health benefits. This was probably due to the fact that the SPCA in their report presented the value of different benefit components only as weights. Thus, they concealed the fact that this set of weights could be interpreted as monetary estimates of the benefits. The Norwegian Petroleum Institute was very positive towards regulatory impact analyses and cost-benefit evaluations in general. However, they questioned the calculations concerning measures in the energy sector. The Labour Union of Economists were critical about the way benefits of improved air quality were measured (i.e. the reduced number of persons above the threshold value) and the calculations of costs. In addition they thought that the proposed package of measures may have been too large. This could have been due to the fact that lower economic growth than assumed in the analysis can be expected, and/or that a complete CBA to find the socially economic most profitable air-quality level in Oslo has not been undertaken. None of the decision-making institutions commented on the ranking method. However, they wanted to replace controversial measures with less controversial ones. Since they at the same time chose less profitable measures, it seems as though the decision makers gave higher priority to avoiding controversy than to economic profit. However, this does not mean that the results of the LARIA will have influence on the decision-making process. Since the ranking method has not been much criticized, the politicians will probably view the results of the LARIA as the scientific truth. Thus, it will be difficult for the political parties to ignore this analysis.

Concerning the monetization of benefits, this was not explicitly mentioned in the report, but "hidden" behind the set of weights. In addition, the benefit estimates of positive health effects, increased well-being and reduced environmental damage were only mentioned verbally when SPCA (1987) stated that the benefits of the proposed package of measures exceeded the corresponding costs. This indicates that the indirect benefit monetization has not and is not going to play a significant role in the decision-making process. However, the weighing of the benefits were crucial in the comparison of the different benefits and thereby for the ranking of the measures. Thus, the LARIA-approach is dependent upon benefit estimation. If the decision-makers are not aware of this, it is very difficult to tell what role benefit estimates have played and will play in the decision-making process.

The total costs of this LARIA were about 1,540,000 1988-NOK and took 156 working weeks. This was about 20 per cent more than originally assumed. The study, counting from when the project plan was prepared, took about 2½ years to complete. In comparison, the LARIAs on air quality in the Sarpsborg/Fredrikstad area and on water quality of Lake Mjøsa were completed in 1½ and 2 years respectively. The costs of these analyses were 1,025,000 1988-NOK/67 working weeks and 1,420,000 1988-NOK/194 working weeks respectively. Thus, the costs of the LARIAs seem to have been relatively constant, but the time they take has been reduced somewhat, probably due to increased experience with performing such analyses. However, the Sarpsborg/Fredrikstad study and the Mjøsa study considered more regulatory measures than the Oslo study; 50,100 and 38 respectively. In addition, the Mjøsa study on water quality demanded more methodological research. This indicates that the costs are also decreasing over time.

From the total cost figures it is not possible to extract the cost of the benefit estimation part. This cost is presumably quite small, since no empirical studies were carried out. This will, however, be necessary in future LARIAs, because of the relatively few existing Norwegian studies, and the potential errors of using findings from these studies in other cases. In addition, empirical studies would substitute for the many expert opinions and subjective evaluations of the existing LARIAs, and thereby reduce the large potential errors of these approaches.

To conclude, LARIA seems to be a promising approach to incorporating benefit estimation into environmental decision making. However, the implicit valuation of benefits, through the use of weights to compare different benefits, should ideally be based on empirical studies designed especially for this purpose. When this is not possible, due to financial or time constraints, the benefit estimates should be based on the best existing studies, and not, like now, on more or less randomly chosen studies and a large degree of subjective evaluation. Moreover, the decision makers should be made aware of the monetization of benefits inherent in the benefit weights. It is still too early to say anything certain about the role of benefit estimation of these analyses in the decision-making process.

Obstacles to Wider Use of Environmental Benefit Estimates and how to Overcome Them

In this section, possible obstacles to wider use of benefit estimates will be identified. Solutions as to how to overcome these obstacles are also provided. This discussion is based on analyses of the case studies, and comments from practitioners of benefit estimation studies and from executive officers within the environmental decision-making system. Five main categories of potential obstacles have been identified:

(1) Cost and time constraints
(2) Methodological problems
(3) Information and communication problems
(4) Administrative constraints
(5) Political constraints.

Cost and time constraints

So far the costs and duration of the benefit estimation studies seem to have been no general constraint to wider use of these techniques. The project officers within the MOE and SPCA did not view this as an important constraint, as far as the completed studies were concerned. However, the expected value to decision makers of the additional information from benefit estimation has been evaluated, and found to be less than the costs in many cases, e.g. projects with small environmental effects and/or environmental measures with small costs. As a result, simplified cost-benefit evaluations without monetary benefit estimates have been conducted. This subjective evaluation is, however, based on the environmental authorities' perception of the valuation techniques, especially how they view the reliability of the results, and the probability of the assessment becoming the focus of controversy.

Although the costs of benefit estimation studies in LARIAs and CBAs in general so far have been moderate, the costs of the LARIAs, in particular, will increase if many empirical benefit estimation studies are carried out in each new case. An increased number of Norwegian benefit estimation studies will, however, be necessary to increase the reliability of the LARIA as a decision-making tool. Also, the many simplified CBAs should become more sophisticated, and this implies increased costs and duration of the studies. Over time, the need for new empirical benefit estimation studies will stabilize (because findings from the increasing number of Norwegian studies can be generalized to a certain extent), and so also will the costs of LARIAs and CBAs. However, this will, at least temporarily, lead to more costly and time-consuming analyses, even though valuation procedures will be more reliable.

The benefits of a more extensive and reliable analysis probably exceed the costs. An analysis of 15 American RIAs associated with Executive Order 12291 (that requires CBAs to be performed for regulations) provides an example of the potential benefits of more extensive use of these techniques. EPA (1987) found that the studies, which cost US$10 million to produce, resulted in modifications to regulations with an estimated net benefit of about US$10 billion (EPA, 1987). This clearly shows that more extensive cost-benefit evaluations may themselves have a very high benefit/cost-ratio.

In general, the time it takes to complete the analysis should be kept to a minimum, since decisions often have to be made quickly. Moreover, the case studies on the "Master Plan for Water Resources" and on "Air Pollution in Oslo" clearly show the importance of timing of studies. For the analyses to have any influence in the decision-making process, they have to be conducted in an early phase.

Methodological problems

Methodological problems seem to be one of the basic and most important obstacles to wider use of benefit estimates. This is due to several factors: unclear basic underlying physical relationships; difficulties in connecting expected physical damage on the affected environmental resources to the quality features of the resource that consumers would more readily be able to value; and technical problems of the valuation methods. The technical issues that often are the focus of controversy include concerns about: (a) consistency between economic theory and human behaviour; (b) validity of methodological assumptions; (c) adequacy of experimental design; (d) clarity and validity of interpretation; (e) appropriateness of generalization; and (f) adequacy of economic measures to include and represent all dimensions of human concern. These different categories of methodological problems lead to a considerable degree of uncertainty in the benefit estimates. However, this uncertainty can in many cases be drastically reduced by investing time and money in developing better dose–response relationships, and conducting more comprehensive empirical stuies. These studies should include checks for the potential biases of the valuation technique in question, and use several valuation techniques on the same commodity if possible. In this way, empirical studies could be combined with methodological research, which will increase the general reliability of these techniques.

The most promising approach for determining public willingness to pay for many environmental goods seems to be the Contingent Valuation Method (CVM). Mitchell and Carson (1989) comprehensively examine the American experience with CVM. They conclude that contingent valuation, if carefully used so as to avoid potential sources of error and bias, may succeed when other methods may fail. They also provide systematic guidelines for practitioners of the method to obtain reliable and valid benefit estimates.

However, studies on behaviour in actual markets for environmental goods, such as auctions of fishing and hunting licenses (e.g. Bishop and Heberlein, 1979) and people's donations to environmental organizations (e.g. Samples et al., 1986), and performing laboratory experimental economics to contingent valuation of public goods (e.g. Coursey and Schultze, 1986), are also important to check the validity of the benefit estimates. It should also be emphasized that interdisciplinary co-operation will be crucial in extending existing approaches and developing new ones, and thereby reducing the controversy about benefit estimation (see Peterson et al., 1988).

Information and communication problems

Maybe more important than the actual methodological problems in benefit estimation is the decision makers' information level and perception of these methods. Here, it is important to distinguish between decision makers at different levels. First, we have the project officers, within the MOE or affiliated institutions, to whom the researchers report their results. The project officers are in most cases economists, with a certain knowledge about benefit estimation techniques. However, the case studies show that they do not know the techniques well enough to defend them effectively against the often unjustified criticism from affected interest groups, and also from colleagues in other disciplines (especially natural scientists) within their own institution. Ethical concerns combined with scepticism about the neo-classical micro-economic theory, which is the foundation of CBA and benefit estimation, are the most important reasons for this critique. The critique often goes like this: "It is not possible to put a price tag on the environment because nature has its own value independent of individual preference. A healthy environment is a human right and not a commodity that can be bought and sold in a market". In this connection it should be noted that the SPCA finds it much easier to argue in favour of the LARIA, which they have largely developed themselves, than defend the benefit estimate in the CBA of stricter car emission regulations. This may, however, also be due to the fact that monetization of benefits is disguised as a set of weights in the LARIA, and this was not readily perceived by others.

It also seems to be of great importance for the administrative leader of the institution in question to have knowledge about and be interested in benefit estimation techniques. The same can be said about the government and politicians in general. Increased information to decision makers on all levels about the methods and their potential areas of application therefore seems appropriate. Although both the MOE and SPCA have arranged courses in CBA and environmental economics for their employees, the information about valuation techniques has been very limited. This is partly because there are very few practitioners in this area in Norway. However, the researchers would also benefit both from educating the decision makers in valuation techniques in such courses, and from communicating results from specific case studies in a way understandable to decisionmakers and adapted to their needs.

It is also important to increase the level of information about environmental benefit estimation in other sectors/ministries, e.g. the transport sector and the Ministry of Finance. The information about the valuation methods should not conceal the many potential errors of the valuation techniques, and the limits of the techniques should be clearly stated. However, it should be emphasized that benefit estimation will make implicit valuations explicit, and thus is a tool to make management of environmental quality and natural resources less subjective and more consistent.

Administrative constraints

The lack of descriptions of valuation techniques in the administrative guidelines on CBAs (see above, Introduction) discourages environmental benefit estimation in all sectors of society. These guidelines should therefore be revised to include descriptions of valuation methods and guidelines on how to use the methods. Moreover, the legislative basis for CBA should be strengthened. This would signal to decision makers that CBA should be an important part of their decision support. Moreover, benefit estimation would become more "legitimate".

Another administrative constraint is that there are relatively few economists in the environmental agencies. More economists, trained in environmental and resource economics in general and benefit estimation in particular, should be employed. This would greatly reduce the information and communication problems related to environmental benefit estimates. During the last few years the MOE has hired some new economists, mainly through the increased funding of Norwegian environmental policy from taxes. A similar process can not be seen in the SPCA and the Directorate for Nature Management. Thus, there are still too few economists trained especially in environmental and resource economics within the environmental agencies. In general, there are also very few Norwegian researchers who are highly qualified in the use of benefit estimation techniques. Therefore, international contacts and collaboration in this field are very important.

Political constraints

The experience from the case studies indicates that the politicians often give higher priority to avoiding controversy than to economic efficiency. This is partly due to corrections for unfortunate distributional or equity effects, but it also reflects the power structure of society. However, there has been an increased use of the market mechanism in the public sector in Norway, and all the political parties now, in principle, agree on increased "pricing" of environmental goods by using taxes. In this way, the pollutors must pay the total, social costs of their actions. This is also in accordance with the recommendations from a report to the Storting, no. 46 (1988–89) on "Environment and Development: the Norwegian Follow-up of the Report from the World Commission", chapter 7.2. To find the correct level of taxes in economic theory, one has to know the socially optimal level of pollution, which again is based on knowledge about abatement costs and the monetary value of damage from pollution. In addition, cost-benefit evaluations of all the possible measures must be carried out to find the most cost-effective package of measures to reach this optimal pollution level. This clearly points in the direction of increased demand for benefit estimation in defining both the goals for the environmental policy and the measures for getting there. LARIA will be a well-adapted approach to accomplishing the latter task, while an iteration process of comprehensive benefits estimation studies can be an important aid in defining the goals.

All in all, it seems as though the political constraints to wider use of benefit estimation are in the process of being removed, and that environmental benefit estimation will play an increasingly important role in top-level decision making in the future.

Conclusions and Recommendations

In this chapter the use of benefit estimation in environmental decision-making in Norway is discussed. The discussion is based on a review of the legislative basis and the administrative guidelines for cost-benefit analysis (CBA), a review of all Norwegian empirical benefit estimation studies and a more detailed analysis of what role some of these studies have played in the decision-making process. Obstacles to wider use of benefit estimation are identified, and solutions to overcoming these obstacles are provided.

In Norway there is a weak legislative basis for impact analysis (IA) in general, and no regulations or provisions explicitly mention CBA. However, there are some general, administrative instructions concerning analyses of economic and administrative effects of regulations, provisions, and reports to the Storting (Parliament). Moreover, there is a manual on performing CBA of governmental projects/policies and regulations (called "Programme Analysis"). This manual does not describe the existing benefit estimation techniques, and recommends that environmental effects are described verbally and/or are quantified in physical terms. Therefore, there have been few attempts at performing CBAs of environmental regulations and other projects with environmental effects. The only sector of society where CBA is used regularly, and which has its own CBA manual, is the transport sector. However, according to this manual, the environmental effects of transport infrastructure projects should not be monetized. Thus, CBAs, complete with benefit estimates, are still the exception rather than the rule in environmental decision making. However, when benefit estimates were available, they were useful in providing support for decisions but did not play a crucial role in the decision-making process, according to the reviewed case studies on stricter car emissions regulations and the national plan for undeveloped water resources.

However, in the last few years there has been an increasing interest in CBA and benefit estimation, especially among the pollution control authorities. This has lead to the development of the Locally Adapted Regulatory Impact Analysis (LARIA).

LARIA is an interdisciplinary, inter-sectoral regulatory impact analysis of all potential measures directed towards a local pollution problem. Thus, the analysis focuses on the recipient, not on a particular regulation. All the measures are assigned a benefit-cost (BC) ratio. While the costs are quite easy to calculate, the benefits are valued according to a set of weights for different benefit components. These weights can be assigned a monetary value, since they are partly based on previous benefit estimation studies. Since there are only 20 such studies in Norway, foreign studies, mainly American, have also been used for this purpose. In order to increase the reliability of this approach, *more empirical benefit estimation studies* in Norway are needed. In addition, more research on the *transferability of benefit estimates* from one area to another, both within a country and between countries, should be performed. Increased research on physical dose–response relationships (damage functions) and technical problems of the valuation methods are also needed. In spite of the uncertainty of the present LARIAs, LARIA is a promising approach to more regular and consistent treatment of environmental benefit in decision making. However, more comprehensive CBAs and benefit estimation studies are needed as aids to define the goals of environmental policy.

The main obstacles to wider use of these techniques seem to be methodological problems and sceptisism about the valuation techniques, often due to information and communication problems. However, financial, time, administrative and political constraints may also limit their use. To overcome the first-mentioned, most important obstacles, a Norwegian *research programme on environmental benefit estimation* should be established. The task of this programme would be to improve the existing valuation techniques and check the large non-use benefits found in previous studies, mainly through doing more empirical studies. In addition, the programme should focus on how to increase the general information about CBA and environmental benefit estimation in all sectors of society, and how to communicate the results of empirical studies to the decision makers on all levels in a more effective way. The research will be interdisciplinary and directed towards decision makers' needs. International collaboration will be very important, especially on the methodological side, and should therefore be developed further.

To conclude, increased use of the market mechanisms in environmental policy (and thereby "pricing" of environmental goods) as recommended in the recent report to the Storting, no. 46 (1988–9) on "Environment and Development: the Norwegian Follow-up of the Report from the World Commission", will increase the demand for CBA approaches and benefit estimation. It is, therefore, important to be prepared for this development. The proposed research programme will be a crucial element in this respect, and in getting better informed decisions in environmental policy making.

References

Aarskog, E.M. (1988) "Willingness-to-pay for cleaning up the Inner Oslo Fjord". (In Norwegian). M.Sc. thesis. Department of Economics, University of Oslo. Report No. 871013–2, March 1988, 42 pp. (Centre for Industrial Research).

Amundsen, B-T. (1987) "Recreational value of the fish population in Oslomarka". (In Norwegian). M.Sc. thesis, Department of Forest Economics, Agricultural University of Norway, 89 pp.

Bishop, R. and Heberlein T.A. (1979) "Measuring values of extramarket goods: are indirect measures biased?" *American Journal of Agricultural Economics*, 61: 926–30.

Carlsen, A.J. (1985) "Economic valuation of hydroelectric power production and salmon fishing". In Carlsen, A.J. (ed.) (1987) *Proceedings. UNESCO Symposium on Decision Making in Water Resources Planning*, May 5–7, 1986, Oslo, 173–82.

Coursey, D.L. and Schultze W.D. (1986) "The application of laboratory experimental economics to contingent valuation of public goods". *Public Choice*, 49: 47–68.

Dahle, L., Solberg B. and Sydal D.P. (1987) "Attitudes towards and willingness-to-pay for Brown Bear, Wolverine and Wolf in Norway". (In Norwegian). Report No. 5/1987. Department of Forest Economics, Agricultural University of Norway, 114 pp.

Dalgard, M. (1989) "Willingness-to-pay for regulatory actions towards water pollution in the Drammen Fjord". (Preliminary title; in Norwegian). M. Sc. thesis, Department of Economics, University of Oslo. Report from the Centre for Industrial Research, forthcoming.

Directorate of Public Roads (1988) *Impact Analysis*. (In Norwegian). Handbook No. 140 from the National Road Administration, 121 pp.

Edwards, E. (1977) "Use of multi-attribute utility measurement for social decision making". In Bell, P.E., Keeny R.L. and Raiffa, H.F. (eds.) *Conflicting objectives in decisions, International Institute for Applied Systems Analysis*. (John Wiley and Sons: New York).

EPA (1987) *EPA's Use of Benefit Cost Analysis; 1981–1986*. EPA-230–05–87–028. (Environmental Protection Agency (EPA): Washington D.C.).

Fisher, A. (1984) "An overview and evaluation of EPA's guidelines for conducting Regulatory Impact Analyses". In Smith, V.K. (ed.)

Environmental Policy under Reagan's Executive Order, 99–118. (University of North Carolina Press: Chapel Hill).

Fredrikson, G.W., Ibrekk, H., Johannesen, K.I., Kveseth, K., Seip, H.M. and Wenstyp, F. (1982) "Oil spill combat: damage assessment using multi-attribute utility analysis". Report No. 82–02 25–1, 66 pp. (centre for Industrial Research).

Glomsǿrd, S. and Rosland A. (1989) "Air pollution and material damages: social costs". (In Norwegian). Report No. 88/31, 70 pp. (Central Bureau of Statistics: Oslo-Kongsvinger).

Heiberg, A. and Hem, K-G. (1987) "Use of formal methods in evaluating countermeasures to coastal water pollution. A case study of the Kristiansand Fjord, Southern Norway". Centre for Industrial Research, 29 pp. Forthcoming in Seip, H.M. and Heiberg, A. (eds.) (1989) *Risk Management of Chemicals in the Environment*. (Plenum Press: London).

Heiberg, A. and Hem, K-G. (1988) "Regulatory Impact Analysis for Inner Oslo Fjord. A comparison of three different methods". (In Norwegian). Report 88 0105–1, September 1988, 67 pp. (Centre for Industrial Research).

Hervik, A., Risnes M., and Strand, J. (1987) "Implicit costs and willingness-to-pay for development of water resources". In Carlsen, A.J. (ed.): *Proceedings. UNESCO Symposium on Decision Making in Water Resources Planning*, May 5–7, 1986, Oslo. 195–202. (Also published in Norwegian in the journal *Sosialckonomen*, No. 3, 1985, 3–6 and No. 1, 1986, 2–7, and in several special reports).

Hjorthol, R. (1985) "Distributional effects of stricter car emission regulations". (In Norwegian, English summary). Project report, June 1985, 44 pp. (Institute of Transport Economics).

Hoffmann, J.V. (1984) "Air traffic noise and the value of housing properties – 1984." (In Norwegian). Working paper, 42 pp. (Institute of Transport Economics).

Hylland, A. and Strand J. (1983) "Valuation of reduced air pollution in the Grenland area". (In Norwegian). Memo No. 12–83, 135 pp. (Department of Economics, University of Oslo).

Kartevoll, T., Granli G. and Otterstad, B. (1979) "Programme analysis of measures towards use of detergents containing phosphates". (In Norwegian). Report from a working group, February 20, 1979, Report No. T-503. (Ministry of Environment).

Keeney, R.L. and Raiffa, H.F. (1976) *Decisions with multiple objectives: Preferences and value trade-offs*. (John Wiley and Sons: New York).

Larsen, O.I. (1985) "Road traffic and the value of housing properties. (In Norwegian, English Summary). Project Report, July 1985, 26 pp. (Institute of Transport Economics).

Lerstang, T. (1987) "Requirements for impact analysis in the Planning and Building Act – the relationship to special acts". (In Norwegian). Appendix 1 in Ministry of Environment (1989), 19 pp. (Norwegian Institute for Urban and Regional Research).

Miltz D. (1988) The use of benefit estimation in environmental decision making. Organization of Economic Co-opertion and Development (OECD), Environment Directorate, Report ENV/ECO/-88.8, 46 pp.

Ministry of Consumer Affairs and Governmental Administration (1985a) "Rules for the work on public deliberations, acts, provisions and reports/bills to the Storting". (In Norwegian). (Regelverksinstruksen). Given by royal resolution, August 30, 1985.

Ministry of Consumer Affairs and Governmental Administration (1985b) Handbook in Reform Work. (In Norwegian). Report P-712, 164 pp.

Ministry of Environment (1982) "Summing up the work on social costs and benefits of extending the sulphur provisions to take effect for existing activities also". (In Norwegian). Note from the Department of Pollution Affairs, Ministry of Environment, November 11, 1982, 22 pp.

Ministry of Environment (1984) "The Master Plan for Water Resources". Report No. T-613, 28 pp. (Ministry of Environment).

Ministry of Environment (1989) "Act on changes in the 'Planning and Building Act'. Regulations on impact analyses". (In Norwegian). Ot.prp. No.XX (1988–89), 76 pp. + appendixes.

Ministry of Finance (1979) "Programme analysis. A guide to performing programme analyses". (In Norwegian). Report R-504, 169 pp. (Tanum-Norli: Oslo).

Mitchel, R.C. and Carson, R.T. (1989) *Using Surveys to Value Public Goods: the Contingent Valuation Method. Resources for the Future.* 482 pp. (Washington D.C.).

Munitz, F.P., Seip, H.M. and Sevaldrud L.H. (1984) "Relationship between fish populations and pH for lakes in Southernmost Norway". *Water, Air & Soil Pollution*, 23: 97–113.

Navrud, S. (1984) "Economic evaluation of recreational fishing in the River Hallingdalselv". (In Norwegian, English summary). M.Sc. thesis, Agricultural University of Norway. Published in the Norwegian Water Resources and Electricity Board's report series, "Biotopjusteringsprosjektet – Terskelprosjektet", Information No. 26 (1987), 121 pp.

Navrud, S. (1988a) "Valuing public goods affected by acid rain in the Nordic countries". (In Norwegian, English summary). Environmental Report No. 4:1988, 110 pp. (Nordic Council of Ministers: Copenhagen).

Navrud, S. (1988b) "Estimating social benefits of environmental improvements from reduced acid depositions: A Contingent Valuation survey". In Folmer, H. and van Ierland, E. (eds.) (1989) *Valuation Methods and Policy Making in Environmental Economics*. Studies in Environmental Science 36, pp. 69–102. (Elsevier: Amsterdam).

Navrud, S. (1988c) "Recreational value of atlantic salmon and sea-trout angling in the River Vikedalselv in 1987 – before regular liming". (In Norwegian, English summary). Report, 108 pp. (Directorate for Nature Management).

Navrud, S. (1988d) "Distributional effects of environmental regulations in the ferro-alloy industries. Case: Bj¢lvefossen A/S". (In Norwegian, English summary). Report T-712, 71 pp. (Ministry of Environment).

Navrud, S. (1989) "Forest decline in Norway: valuation of impacts on environmental goods". *Scandinavian Forest Economics*, No. 30, 167–78.

NIAR (1981) Effects on atmospheric corrosion costs of regulations on lower sulphur content in heating oil". (In Norwegian). Report No. OR 17/81. (Norwegian Institute for Air Research (NIAR)).

Pearce, D. and Markandya, A. (1987) "The benefits of environmental policies. An appraisal of the economic value of environmental improvement and the economic cost of environmental damage". Report ENV/ECO/97.3, 155 pp. (Organization for Economic Co-operation and Development (OECD), Environment Directorate).

Peterson, G.L., Driver B.L. and Gregory R. (1988) *Amenity Resource Valuation. Integrating Economics with Other Disciplines.* 260 pp. (Venture Publishing Inc: Pennsylvania).

Samples, K.C., Gowen, M.M. and Dixon, J.A. (1986) "The validity of the Contingent Valuation Method for estimating non-use components of preservation values for unique natural resources". 15 pp. Paper presented at the 1986 Annual Meeting of the American Economics Association.

Sanderud, P. and Beck, P.Å. (1980) "A social economic evaluation of the two deposition alternatives for mining wastes from Titania A/S". (In Norwegian). Report, December 12, 63 pp. (Ministry of Environment).

Scancke, E. (1984) "Economic valuation of the recreational fishing in the River Tinnelv". (In Norwegian). M.Sc. thesis. Department of Economics, University of Oslo.

Seip, H.M., Christophersen, N. and Rustad, S. (1986) "Changes in streamwater chemistry and fishery status following reduced sulphur deposition. Tentative predictions based on the Birkenes model". Proceedings from "Workshop on Reversibility of Acidification", Grimstad, Norway, June 9–11, 1986, 177–84. (Comission of European Communities).

Seip, K.L., Ibrekk H. and Wenstyp, F. (1987) "Multiattribute analysis of the impact on society of phosphorus abatement measures". *Water Resources Research*, 23, 5: 755–64.

SPCA (1985) "Proposal for a programme on regulatory actions towards traffic noise". (In Norwegian). Report, May 1985, 42 pp. (State Pollution Control Authority (SPCA)).

SPCA (1986) "Emission regulations for private cars. Proposals to introduce more regulations in order to reduce the health and environmental effects. Evaluation of the consequences of the proposal". Report, January 1986, 63 pp. (State Pollution Control Authority (SPCA)).

SPCA (1987) "Further reduction of air pollution in Oslo. Proposals for measures which will give a more healthy and pleasant environment". Report, August 1987, 23 pp. (State Pollution Control Authority (SPCA)).

SPCA (1988) "Further reductions of the air pollution in Oslo. Summary of what should be changed in the proposal submitted for interests' groups opinion, based on the received comments". (In Norwegian). Mimeo, November 11, 1988, 32 pp. (State Pollution Control Authority (SPCA)).

SPCA (1989) "Less air pollution and improved urban environment in Oslo. Proposed measures after the hearing". (In Norwegian). Final report, 20 pp. (State Pollution Control Authority (SPCA)).

Strand, J. (1980) "Evaluation of changes in recreational value as a consequence of acidification of freshwater bodies in Norway". Report, revised version, Oct. 3, 1980, 49 pp. (Ministry of Environment).

Strand, J. (1981a) "Valuation of freshwater fish populations as a public good in Norway". (In Norwegian, English summary). Working paper, Department of Economics, University of Oslo, 91 pp.

Strand, J. (1981b) "Valuing benefits from recreational fishing in the River Gaula". (In Norwegian). Memo. Nov. 18, 1981, Department of Economics, University of Oslo, 91 pp. English version: "Valuing benefits of recreational fishing in Norway: the Gaula case". In Carlsen, A.J. (ed.) (1987) *Proceedings. UNESCO Symposium on Decision Making in Water Resources Planning*, May 5–7, 1986, Oslo, 245–78.

Strand, J. (1985) "Valuing reduced air pollution from automobiles in Norway". (In Norwegian). Memo No. 1–85, Department of Economics, University of Oslo, 89 pp. (For a shorter version in English, see: "The Value of a Catalytic Converter requirement for Norwegian automobiles: a Contingent Valuation study". Mimeo, Department of Economics, University of Oslo, 32 pp.)

Strand, J. and Sanderud, P. (1981) "Pollution from 'Grong Gruver' – a cost-benefit analysis". (In Norwegian). Report, revised February 2, 1981. (Ministry of Environment).

Sydal, D.P. (1989) "The recreational value of moose hunting in Norway: towards modelling optimal population density". In Mattson, L. and Sydal, D.P. (eds.) "Multiple use of forests – economics and policy". Proceedings of a conference held in Oslo, Norway, May 1988. *Scandinavian Forest Economics*, No. 30, 62–78.

Syversen, T. (1988) "Weighing of different benefits". (In Norwegian). Mimeo of January 4, 1988, 9 pp. (State Pollution Control Authority (SPCA)).

Trynnes, D.H. and Seip, H.M. (1988) "Decision making in control of air pollutants posing health effects". Mimeo. (Centre for Industrial Research).

Ulleberg, M. (1988) The recreational value of fishing for atlantic salmon (Salmo salar) and sea trout (Salmo trutta) in the River Stordalselv in 1987". (In Norwegian). M.Sc. thesis. Department of Forest Economics, Agricultural University of Norway, 55 pp.

UN (1987) *Our Common Future. United Nations World Commission of Environment and Development*, (Oxford University Press).

Wenstyp, F.E. and Carlsen, A.J. (1987) "Ranking hydro-electric power station projects with multicriteria decision analysis". In Carlson, A.J. (ed.): *Proceedings. UNESCO Symposium on Decision Making in Water Resources Planning*, May 5–7, 1986, Oslo, 423–35.

6 The United Kingdom

Anil Markandya, David Pearce and R. Kerry Turner

Introduction: the Decision-Making Framework

Environmental economics research in the last two decades has greatly extended the range of techniques available for the monetary evaluation of environmental damages and benefits. Extensive surveys of both the theory and practice are to be found in Pearce and Markandya (1989), Johansson (1987), Bentkover, Covello and Mumpower (1986), Kneese (1984) and Freeman (1979, 1982). Surveys specific to particular environmental media are to be found in Smith and Desvousges (1986) and Feenberg and Mills (1980) for water quality Halvorsen and Ruby (1981) for air pollution, and Wilman (1984) for beach pollution. Specific techniques have been extensively studied. The contingent valuation method (CVM), which relies on direct eliciting of values by questioning respondents, has been evaluated in depth by Cummings, Brookshire and Schulze (1986).

It seems fair to say that benefit estimation (or its obverse, damage estimation) has been most extensively developed and applied in the nited States. In large part this reflects the existence of legislation in the USA which requires specific forms of assessment for new regulations. Notable among these are the requirement for regulatory impact assessments (RIAs) under Presidential Executive Order 12291 of 1981 which explicitly requires benefit assessments (see EPA, 1987; Smith, 1984); environmental impact assessments (EIAs) under the National Environmental Policy Act (NEPA) of 1969; and "resource damage" estimates under the Comprehensive Environmental Response, Compensation and Liability Act of 1980 (CERCLA).

In contrast, the United Kingdom does not have a tradition of using EIA for development projects, nor does it have a mandatory requirement for benefit assessments to be undertaken for new regulations. In July 1988, the UK formally complied with the European Economic Community Directive on Environmental Impact Assessment. Under the Directive certain projects, listed in an Annex I, must be subject to an EIA (In brief, these are oil refineries, large power stations, radioactive waste storage facilities, iron and steel works, asbestos extracting/processing, chemical installations, roads, railway lines, airports, ports and inland waterways and hazardous waste installations.) Other projects, listed in an Annex II, are also subject to EIAs if they are thought to have significant environmental impacts. Assessment must relate to impacts on humans, flora and fauna; soil, water, air and climate; and material assets and cultural heritage. The EEC Directive does not, however, require any form of benefits or damage assessment in the sense of monetary evaluations. In principle, such assessments would probably fit the overall requirements for the type of information that a developer must supply. These include, for example, "a description of the likely significant effects on the environment" (Haigh, 1987). In general, however, it seems unlikely that EIAs will typically encompass monetary benefit estimation, whereas such a feature is fairly commonplace in the EIAs produced in the USA.

The initial impression – that benefit estimation is an unusual feature of decision-making in the UK – is not however a correct one. In general terms, cost-benefit analysis (CBA) has been extensively used in various areas of public expenditure, ranging from health and education to power stations and transport. For a detailed survey see Colvin (1985) and for an appraisal see Walshe (1987). But the extent to which *environmental effects* have been valued is much more limited. If environmental effects are construed to include such things as valuations of accidents, then, in the area of *transport policy* there has been a long tradition of attempts to measure intangible costs and benefits in money terms. Below (p. 228), we discuss in detail UK procedures for the "valuation of life". The main benefits of road investment, time savings, have similarly been the subject of extensive research and use by both the UK Department of Transport (the Ministry responsible for public trunk road investment) and local authorities. The explanation for the standard adoption of cost-benefit approaches in road investment are self-evident: public roads do not generate revenues and hence their priority ranking depends on the evaluation of non-monetary benefits. These approaches are detailed in a formal modelling procedure – COBA – which computes the net present value of road investments.[1] But environmental factors are still only included in such appraisals in terms of non-monetary indicators – e.g. area of land taken, noise and vibration, visual intrusion and community severance.

While cost-benefit techniques have perhaps been advanced the furthest in the transport sector, there exist numerous benefit studies in other public and quasi-public sector activities. The existence of these studies is explained by the way in which the UK Treasury, as the "purse-holder" of government, manages expenditures by various agencies. Since 1981 the UK government has set *cash plans* for the following three years, and within these plans there are *cash limits* to programmes. Each spending Ministry is thus subject to a budget set in cash terms. In turn, there are various public and quasi-public agencies which answer to particular Ministries and whose expenditure frequently requires supplements from central government sources – so-called "grants in aid". The Treasury exercises financial control on these agencies by agreeing with the relevant Ministry what a particular agency's grant level should be. Thus, an agency X requiring grant-in-aid will seek the approval of its "parent", Ministry Y, which in turn will agree with the Treasury what the aid level will be. This sets the agency's external financial limit (EFL). Such grants tend to be agreed on an annual basis, with a planning figure set for two further years. This somewhat short-term planning horizon has obvious disadvantages for agencies that need to plan over longer-term periods, but the time horizons are in turn set by the Public Expenditure Survey (PES) system applied to all government expenditure.

The significance of this chain of controls is that both the parent Ministry and the Treasury apply economic criteria to the expenditure plans, and included in those criteria are *benefit-cost appraisals*. Thus the Ministry and the Treasury might expect to see the particular development expenditure by X subjected to a net present value or benefit-cost ratio test. Guidance is provided by the Treasury to government departments on how to appraise investments through a Green Booklet (UK Treasury, 1984). In general, the guidance is to adopt discounted cash flow approaches. In respect of intangible costs and benefits the Treasury advises:

Many costs and benefits are measured directly in money terms;

for example, savings in expenditure on resources, and sales revenues. Where they are not (examples are travel time saved, noise and other forms of pollution, and broad managerial or political factors) costs and benefits can sometimes still sensibly be given money values, often by analysing people's actual behaviour and declared or revealed preferences. These imputed money values can be used in the appraisal as if they were actual cash flows. Other factors which cannot be valued should be listed, and quantified as far as practicable, making it clear that they are additional factors to be taken into account. It can sometimes be helpful to calculate the value which such factors would have to take for the net present value of a scheme to turn positive or negative . . .

Account sometimes needs to be taken of the value which individuals may place now on the possibility of using a service or visiting an attractive area even when they do not currently use the service or make visits.[1]

(UK Treasury, 1984, paras. 33 and 34).

As we shall see, an agency seeking Ministry and Treasury approval for a particular capital project may also have to present a further economic case if it is seeking funds from the European Economic Community. Here the emphasis is likely to be on the *regional* benefits and this is more likely to require demonstration of the employment effects and the dynamic development effects than costs and benefits in the sense being discussed here. In summary, a spending agency seeking approval for a capital project could find itself presenting a case at three levels: a purely financial one based on revenues and costs to the agency; a regional impact study (if EEC or other regionally-focused agencies are involved in funding) and a national cost-benefit study. It is the national evaluation that could involve the monetary valuation of environmental damage or benefit.

How far environmental impacts are subject to monetary estimation thus tends to be influenced by the expectations and guidance offered by the Treasury. It seems fair to say that, until recently, environmental impacts were acknowledged by all concerned, but were not generally the subject of monetary evaluation. In very recent years, however, some benefit estimation techniques have been acknowledged by the Treasury and the result has been the emergence of benefit estimation as one of the techniques for furthering the use of cost-benefit principles in evaluating development expenditures. In the case studies that follow, we illustrate both the kinds of benefit estimation that have resulted from this public expenditure control, and the more established benefit estimation in the planning of the UK transport sector.

Some UK Ministries have their own appraisal manuals. In no case, however, do they encompass guidance on the monetary valuation of environmental impacts. Monetary evaluation is, of course, not the only way of securing a proper role for environmental dimensions in project planning. Environmental Impact Assessment (EIA) seeks to do this and there are other means of reflecting environmental values in decision-making.

The UK Overseas Development Administration has several relevant documents on project appraisal. A user-friendly approach to project planning in general is given in its 1973 guide, *Planning Development Projects* (Bridger and Winpenny, 1983). However, this contains nothing on environmental issues. A 1988 guide has sections on environmental evaluation which are taken from a publication originally produced for the Asian Development Bank (Mac Arthur, 1988; Dixon et al., 1986, 1988). The ODA has also issued a *Manual of Environmental Appraisal* but this does not address the issue of valuing environmental impacts (ODA, 1989). It seems fair to say therefore that current ODA procedures do not directly address the issue of how to evaluate environmental impacts in terms of either monetary valuation or some "importance indicators". The ODA work does, however, address the issues of integrating environmental concerns into project appraisal. The valuation issue is now being addressed in an additional guidelines/manual document (Winpenny, forthcoming).

The UK Department of Transport has a computerized approach to investment appraisal – COBA.[2] This enables a standard programme to be adapted to local conditions in terms of the relevant parameters, e.g. traffic flows, so that benefits or costs are produced for time values, operating costs and accidents. These benefits and/or costs are then fed into a comparison with the construction and running costs of the road. Accident valuations are based on a standard "value of life", currently £500,000.[3] and a standard value for non-fatal injuries. The Department's approach to environmental valuation is interesting. Monetary evaluation is explicitly rejected but environmental impacts are carefully listed and measured. This reflects the original advice of the Advisory Committee on Trunk Road Assessment Leitch Committee, 1977) to the effect that monetary evaluation was infeasible but that environmental impacts clearly mattered. The Standing Advisory Committee on Trunk Road Assessment (SATRA) has apparently considered the evidence on monetary evaluation on a number of occasions since. The House of Commons Committee of Public Accounts has expressed doubts about the alleged difficulties of monetary evaluation of environmental damage (House of Commons, 1988–9). Thus it not clear what exactly the status of such valuation is at present.

Six Case Studies

The following sections provide six "cameo" studies of situations in which benefit or damage estimation has been assessed. In each case the context is very briefly described. This is followed by a discussion of the techniques used and the results obtained. The role of benefit/damage estimation in actual decision making is then discussed.

The case studies are:

(1)   The urban environmental benefits of improving a derelict canal in Glasgow
(2)   A valuation of the drainage functions of inland waterways
(3)   Valuing the benefits of sewage disposal
(4)   The evaluation of a coastal defence scheme for Aldeburgh
(5)   Valuing the environmental benefits of afforestation, and the benefits of afforestation for economic security purposes
(6)   The "valuation of a human life" in transport planning.

Restoring a derelict canal

The Forth and Clyde Canal was opened in 1790 to link Glasgow in Scotland with the Atlantic and North Sea. By 1962 commercial traffic had failed to generate sufficient traffic to justify maintaining the canal. The need to provide permanent road bridges at several points had also become very pressing. The canal was accordingly downgraded to "remainder" status, being maintained by the British Waterways Board (BWB) at the statutory level to serve drainage functions only. The resulting dereliction of the canal produced an unsightly environmental hazard in the centre of a major city. Several deaths resulted from children playing near the unmaintained edges, while the canal was generally dirty and unaesthetic. This decline of the canal occurred at the same time as urban decay was increasing around the canal. By the mid-1980s, especially with explicit government policies of revitalizing inner-city areas, the case for reviewing the status of the canal was timely. Particular features of the canal that lent themselves to the reappraisal included the proximity of buildings of historical and architectural interest; the rapid emergence of a demand for dwellings near to waterways (as with London's Docklands); and the desperate needs of the Glasgow area for investment to secure employment.

In the light of these circumstances the BWB commissioned several studies to evaluate the gains to be obtained from upgrading the canal to a level where it could take leisure traffic. Regional and district authorities were involved, as was the Scottish Development Agency which has special functions within Scotland in respect of development projects. Glasgow is within a designated UK Development Area and is thus eligible for EEC regional assistance through the European Regional Development Fund (ERDF). Detailed analyses by consultants produced the base data from which further evaluations were to be made. Interestingly, early submissions of the appraisal to the UK Department of the Environment (the BWB's parent ministry) were not in the form deemed acceptable by the Department. It was then made clear (1986) that BWB and its associated sponsors needed to present three appraisals:

- a financial appraisal showing how the canal restoration would impact on BWB's finances;
- a regional appraisal suited to the requirements of the ERDF;
- a national cost-benefit appraisal.

The BWB subsequently set out the case in the required format and in 1987 the development was approved by the Department of the Environment and the UK Treasury. The overall appraisals are summarized in Button and Pearce [1989]. Although we concentrate on the national cost-benefit case, the financial analysis is as important in convincing the parent ministry and the UK Treasury of the value of the project. The CBA was concerned with the national gains and losses from the investment. The options considered were:

- to do nothing i.e. leave the canal in its remainder status;
- to make some improvements for safety reasons but not to upgrade for navigation;
- to upgrade the canal (or most of it) for full navigation.

The interest for current purposes is in the efforts made in the cost-benefit study to evaluate environmental gains. The theory of hedonic pricing suggests that the local property market will tend to capture environmental benefits through increases in house prices. The extent to which house prices rise *because* of environmental improvement can be considered as a first approximation of the willingness to pay for environmental amenity. (Strictly, what is required is a further stage of analysis to obtain a marginal willingness-to-pay estimate based on a demand curve. But most hedonic studies do not proceed to this second stage. See Pearce and Markandya (1989). In the survey work for the cost-benefit study, efforts were made to estimate what was known as "property uplift", i.e. the effect of the canal restoration on property prices in the surrounding area. While house price rises might also be construed as a reflection of expected future income growth in the area, the technique used in the cost-benefit study was to ask estate agents (agents for buying and selling property) what the price uplift would be because of the canal improvement. The responses suggested that the values obtained related to environmental improvement rather than expected income generation. Accordingly, the price increases were used as measures of the value of environmental improvement to the residents. Other environmental values could not be measured in money terms, notably the "option" and "existence" values from having a pleasant amenity within potential walking or commuting distance.

Table 6.1 summarizes the main result and shows the extent to which the environmental benefits influenced the cost-benefit outcome. The net gains from full restoration of the canal have to be measured as the difference between the do nothing option – which imposes *costs* on the nation – and the net benefits of the restoration. Thus, the net gains from the canal restoration are shown as some £11.2 million in 1986 prices. Of this sum, about £0.52 million was accounted for by measured environmental benefits due to property

Table 6.1:   **Glasgow Canal: costs and benefits**

	NPV (£million) 1986 prices	Environmental benefits
"Do Nothing" option	− 5.638	−
"Full Restoration"	+ 5.568	+0.517
Differential net benefits	+11.206	

Source: Button and Peace [1989]

price appreciation, i.e. just under 5 per cent of the *differential* net benefits, or 10 per cent of the benefits of the restoration considered on its own.[4]

The Glasgow case study shows that environmental benefits can comprise a significant proportion of the net national benefits of undertaking canal restoration. It seems fair to say that had the benefits been left without a monetary valuation, the decision reached by the Department of the Environment and the UK Treasury would not have been affected. That is, the recreational and output gains to the nation from the restoration were more than sufficient to justify the scheme. Nonetheless, it is of significance that the environmental valuations were implicitly accepted by the relevant Ministries, showing that benefit estimation techniques have been given legitimate status in UK investment appraisal.

Valuing the Drainage Functions of Inland Waterways

Britain's waterways (canals) form an important part of the country's water and effluent drainage system. These functions are covered by various agreements and by custom and usage over the last two hundred years. The discharges include surface rainwater and stormwater via rivers, streams etc; surface water from agricultural, recreational and other private land; surface water from roads and motorways; stormwater and sewage from local authorities, and some effluent from sewage works. That is, the canals act as drains for the above discharges. If the canals did not exist, the water discharged from the various sources would have to be "managed" somehow. Moreover, canals act as receivers of peak discharges and retain the capacity to deal with abnormal floods. As

it happens, while canals serve this drainage function, the drainage
is itself of no particular benefit to the main functions of canals,
namely, to provide recreational cruising and, to a very limited
extent now, commercial navigation. This is because the discharges
arrive in the canals when least needed.

It is widely acknowledged that the drainage function has economic value. Thus:

> closing a canal altogether would entail a considerable capital cost
> to provide an alternative means of drainage. (Monopolies and
> Mergers Commission, 1987).

Yet the BWB, which manages UK waterways, is not able to
exploit this economic function. That is, the BWB is providing
a drainage function for which it cannot charge according to the
statutes under which it operates. Were it able to do so, it would
be of benefit to its own financial status (see case study 1) which
depends on obtaining revenues from licenses, mooring fees etc, and
on grant-in-aid from central government. The drainage function is
in fact just one function which the BWB provides without securing
corresponding revenue. The general public use of waterways and
waterside paths for picnicking or walking are also not subject to
charges, in this case because of the sheer complexity of devising
efficient charging mechanisms. Moreover, the BWB is required to
achieve a "performance target" financially which is to break even,
taking one year with another. Out of an income of some £60 million
in the year to end-March 1986, the BWB received some £42 million
as grant-in-aid; that is, the BWB is heavily dependent upon central
government assistance for its financial viability.

It is this financial background which explains the interest in the
benefits which the BWB's waterways network provides and for
which it receives no income. The policy implications are twofold.
If charging mechanisms could be devised, the BWB might be able
to secure a higher proportion of its required income directly,
reducing its dependence on central government aid. Alternatively,
central government might recognize the non-monetary benefits and
seek to adjust the BWB's grant-in-aid, providing more financial
freedom for it to invest in income-generating activities out of its
own funds. It is clear that estimating the value of the non-monetary
benefits would assist dialogue with government, with the eventual
aim of further improving the water-based amenities of the UK.

Similarly, UK government policy is quite explicit in seeking to make agencies such as the BWB less reliant on central government funds, in keeping with its market-based philosophy.

How might the drainage functions of the waterways be valued? According to benefit estimation theory, the ideal approach would be to identify the beneficiaries of the free drainage functions and seek out their willingness to pay for them. In turn, this willingness to pay should reflect the beneficial effects of drainage on agricultural output, on the quality of road transport surfaces, on the costs of housing development (since sites would otherwise have to be especially drained), on the avoided costs of effluent control and flood control. In practice, such a benefit estimation study would be an immense and expensive undertaking. The BWB sought a short cut by looking at the replacement costs that the drainage beneficiaries would incur if the waterway drainage function was hypothetically removed. This approach is not ideal for an obvious reason. In using a replacement cost to value the benefit of drainage it is implicitly being assumed that the existing drainage system is optimal. Put another way, it is being assumed that if the function was removed then each and every part of it would have to be replaced by the people currently benefitting from the free service. If, in fact, some beneficiaries are not willing to replace the drainage system, this would indicate that the costs (to them) exceed the benefits of the drainage. Using replacement costs will then overstate benefits. However, economic theory also teaches us that those who would seek to replace the drainage function will tend to value that function more highly than the cost they will incur in making the replacement. (This is the phenomenon of "consumer surplus" which, in this case arises because the demand curve for the drainage function can be assumed to slope downward.) It is possible, then, that the overstatement is balanced out by the understatement of consumer surplus.

Engineering assessments of replacement costs for a sample of waterways were made in the mid-1970s. Consultants to the BWB converted the relevant values to 1988 prices and made adjustments for the fact that the official government discount rate in the mid-1970s was 10 per cent, whereas it is currently 5 per cent (both figures in real terms). Some urban networks comprise significant distances of canal and these are shown separately in Table 6.2 which summarizes the resulting costs of replacing the drainage functions currently being provided by the waterway network.

Table 6.2: **Approximate replacement costs for the drainage functions of UK canals**

Canal	(£million, 1988 prices, present values)
Birmingham Canal System	174
Leeds/Liverpool System	33
Other urban canals	59
Rural canals	75
Total	341

Expressed as an annuity (using the official 5 per cent discount rate) this amounts to some £20 million per annum. Put another way, the waterways system generates drainage benefits of some £20 million per annum. If we recall that the BWB's income in 1985–6 was some £60 million, it is clear that the drainage benefits, if they could be appropriated by charging, would comprise a significant proportion of its income.

The calculations shown here are only illustrative in that the numbers have no official status. They do illustrate a simple technique of benefit estimation, although it is one that needs to be used very cautiously because of its lack of rigorous relationship to an ideal benefit measure based on willingness to pay.

Appraising sewerage schemes

While it was known that sewer flooding, sewer collapse repair and the pollution of watercourses by sewage was becoming an increasing problem for the Regional Water Authorities (RWAs) in the UK, little data existed on the magnitude and significance of the social costs involved. In 1985 the UK Water Research Centre (WRC) was contracted by the Department of the Environment (DoE) to examine the potential for development and use of simple user-oriented techniques for evaluating the social costs of sewer flooding, sewer collapse/repair and the pollution of watercourses. Consultants were engaged to evaluate the costs and to consider investment appraisal procedures within the water authorities. In particular, research was directed at estimating and evaluating the social benefits consequent upon the alleviation of flooding from sewers, the reduction of the risk of sewer collapse and the improvement of the quality of rivers and watercourses. The social benefits (damage costs avoided) of improved sewer system performance were categorized as follows:

- damage to property;
- damage to other utilities' equipment;
- damage to contents of property;
- stress and disruption;
- loss of amenity;
- river water-quality improvement;
- health risks;
- loss of memorabilia;
- evacuation costs.

It was recognized that the monetary valuation of some of the categories of benefits would be problematic, given the current state-of-the-art in economic valuation methods and techniques. Nevertheless, it was argued that cost-benefit analysis (CBA) was required in order to supplement the existing technical/engineering approach conventionally adopted by water authorities. This latter approach was formalized in the Water Authorities Association/ Water Research Centre (WAA/WRC) Sewerage Rehabilitation Manual (SRM), first published in 1984. The SRM contains advice on the most cost-effective ways to design comprehensive integrated upgrading schemes for complete sewered catchments. However, the SRM stops short of an economic benefits assessment and is limited to the scientific, engineering and construction cost aspects of sewer construction/rehabilitation.

In the past, the RWAs and their sewerage agents have relied to some extent either on a centralized capital allocation between service sectors, or on a rank order of individual schemes. In the former approach, the allocation of funds to each type of service was governed by observed need, customer preference, or Board policy. Individual schemes were only compared with others in the same service area. In the latter approach, the allocation of funds to each sector was determined by the aggregate of rank-ordered schemes included within it. Individual scheme rank ordering was based on a points/weighting system related to, for example, the number of properties benefitting from reduced flood risk. No monetary valuation of the total scheme benefits was, however, undertaken. A number of official reports on the water industry (or elements of it) in the early 1980s recommended that CBA would provide an economic efficiency framework within which RWAs could better assess the consistency of their scheme priorities and consequent investment expenditure. The Water Research Centre and the Flood Hazard Research Centre (WRC/FHRC) study, *Investment Appraisal For Sewerage Schemes: The Assessment of Social Costs*, applies just such a cost-benefit methodology to the issue of the social benefits associated with improved sewer-system performance. Since RWAs are required by statute and other obligations to provide some minimum, and not necessarily well-defined levels of service, there will be circumstances in which the appropriate economic investment rule will be cost minimization. More generally, however, RWAs are expected to have regard to the net social benefits produced by their assets, hence the appeal of the cost-benefit methodology.

The WRC/FHRC have compiled a User Manual, aimed mainly at engineers and planners closely involved in sewerage project appraisal. This document details the cost-benefit methodology and standard data requirements for the assessment of the social benefits of improved sewer-system performance. It is intended that the cost-benefit analysis manual be used in conjunction with computer program packages dealing with sewer-system performance, esti-mated pollution loading due to storm sewage overflows and a river-impact model.

Benefits estimation methods and results
In order to determine the economic benefits involved, the WRC/FHRC study compares the benefits connected with the alleviation of sewer operational difficulties with a base-line "do nothing" option. The improvement benefits are the reduction in social costs (flooding, odours, water-quality degradation, etc.) connected with a given improvement scheme compared to the base-line option. Three benefits arising through three categories of improvement were assessed:

(1) benefits of flood alleviation;
(2) benefits from reducing the risk of disruption from sewer rehabilitation or collapse;
(3) benefits of water-quality improvement.

Benefits of flood alleviation

The benefits from reducing the risk of flooding by sewage were taken to be the expected value of the losses that would otherwise occur. Standard data tables were provided covering direct damages to property and its contents; indirect or consequential losses, such as traffic disruption and loss of industrial productivity (based on previous research by the FHRC); and non-monetary impacts on households, such as disruption, stress, health effects and loss of memorabilia. The benefits were estimated by calculating the likely losses from each of a range of floods of different return periods. This allowed the quantification of an anticipated average reduction in losses. The present value of the stream of losses over the scheme-life was computed via standard discounting procedures.

In addition to data obtained via literature review/desk study, an analysis of existing survey data from nearly 400 interviews with flood victims was undertaken. In total, a further 450 households were interviewed during the main survey undertaken as part of the WRC/FHRC social costs of sewerage project. Two problems were experienced with flood-victim sample selection. UK records of sewage flooding are incomplete and so it was not possible to select a random sample from the population that had been flooded. Second, surveys in some areas in which flooding was a highly contentious topic would have introduced unacceptable levels of bias. The results were incorporated into standard data tables presented in the User Manual. The tables allow the benefits of flood alleviation to be evaluated for a variety of land uses and types of property. The present value of protecting the average house which floods at present on average once every two years is estimated to be £15,000 for protection up to a 20-year return period event; for a typical small shop, the present value calculated on the same basis is £24,000.

Benefits of reduced risk of disruption from sewer collapse

There are social benefits to be gained from works which reduce the risk of disruption resulting from sewer collapse. A rehabilitated or replaced sewer will carry a lower risk of collapse than that associated with the original sewer. Possible costs resulting from collapse include:

- costs of repair to other utilities;
- costs of restoring the road structure, building or other structures affected;

- cost of utility outages caused by damage to both the sewer and also other utilities;
- costs of traffic disruption (travel costs for a typical urban road network);
- costs to local business arising from reduced access to properties. Water authorities are legally obliged to pay compensation for business losses resulting from sewer works. So the cost of business disruption was taken to be the financial losses to the firms (official gross margins);
- any flood damage that may occur as a result of the sewer breach.

Each year of the scheme-life, there will be a reduced expected present value of collapse costs. As a first approximation, the present value is given by:

$$\sum_{t=0}^{t=n} \frac{(Po - Pr)}{(1 + r)^t}$$

where
Po = probability of original sewer collapse
P_r = probability of replaced sewer collapse
r = discount rate
and Po > Pr.

Actual collapse costs are not, however, uniform along the entire length of pipe. They vary according to the above-ground context, i.e. road junction or playing field, etc. A weighted mean estimate of the benefits was therefore used, based upon the costs resulting from collapse at typical points along the relevant pipe length.

Benefits from improved water quality
Social benefits (in terms of improved water quality) are likely where discharges to watercourses, either through storm-sewage overflows or from sewage treatment works outfalls, are reduced and/or treated to a higher standard. The benefits of water-quality improvement arise either through increased possibilities for use of the river corridor, or increased value of existing uses. The study found that for the average watercourse, most of the benefits are in the form of increased recreational user benefits and non-

use benefits (bequest and existence value increases). It was also concluded that the contingent valuation method was probably the only feasible economic valuation method available to estimate such recreational, amenity and non-use benefits of improved water quality.

The magnitude of recreational user benefits will depend on the total recreational usage and the degree to which individual users relate recreational value to water quality. User benefits will also be constrained by the degree to which users are able to actually perceive higher standards of water quality. Consequently, an Index of Perceived Water Quality was constructed on the basis of survey results, which related to biochemical water-quality indices. It was hypothesized that casual visitors to a river corridor could base their judgements of perceived water quality upon the presence or absence of biota and "expert judgement" assessments. The following perceived water-quality classes were identified:

• good enough water for birds, (e.g. swans, coots, ducks, etc.) to use the water (equivalent to official river class 3);
• good enough to support dragonflies and many fish (including trout) and to allow many different types of plants to grow both in the water and on the edge (equivalent to official river class 2);
• good enough for safe paddling or swimming by children (equivalent to official river class 1).

A preliminary survey of some 300 river-corridor users, stratified by purpose of visit, was undertaken to collect the perceived water-quality information and other recreational attraction data. The survey also revealed that the UK public seems to attach a high importance to water-quality improvement investment on the grounds of intrinsic environmental benefits (i.e. to conserve the environment for its own sake).

Because of data constraints it was decided to consider only the gains to existing recreational users from water improvements, and not to consider the benefits from additional visitors. Three categories of beneficiaries were identified: (a) river-corridor users; (b) users who also live in close proximity to the river corridor; and (c) individuals who do not live in close proximity to the river corridor and do not use the river amenity but nevertheless potentially gain non-use value from water-quality improvement. On pragmatic grounds, the study concentrated its survey analysis on three general types of river corridor: town centres, local park sites and "honeypots" (sites such as country parks drawing on a wider circle of users); and on two types of water quality and river-corridor quality: good and bad. Four honeypot sites were surveyed, two town centre sites and six local park sites, only one of which was in the good water-quality/bad corridor-quality category. The majority of sites were located in regions with the most problems with water quality (i.e. Midlands and North of England).

Contingent valuation survey results, based on interview surveys with around a thousand river-corridor users, indicated that the average household would be willing to pay an additional £6 per annum (in water rates) for further water-quality improvements. The typical present value of the benefits from improving the water quality from an existing level, equivalent to class 3 rivers, up to a level where it will support diversity of fish and plant populations is £450,000 for a country park and £90,000 for a local park site. The results are highly dependent on accurate visitation rate estimates and the User Manual provides guidance on the formulation and use of site-specific visit forecasts. The survey method and payment vehicle chosen were both designed to produce "conservative" lower bound monetary estimates.

Currently, the social benefits assessment methods contained in the manual are meant to be applied only to any non-agricultural point source of discharge on non-tidal rivers. The manual has been targeted specifically at water authority engineers and planners dealing with sewer-improvement investment programmes. The manual may be used during the early planning or preliminary scheme design stage of project appraisal. In this capacity, it can serve as a gross screening device for the assessment of the general economic viability (efficiency) of candidate projects. At the more detailed single project ranking and design stage, results from the gross screening stage can be improved/updated again by reference to the manual. The manual methods are intended to be simple and user-friendly, allowing a balanced compromise between detail and ease of use.

Benefits assessment for the Aldeburgh Sea-defence scheme

In May 1988 the then Regional Water Authority (Anglian Water) instructed consultants to carry out an economic benefits assessment for a proposed Sea Defence Scheme at Aldeburgh, Suffolk. The area at risk was protected by a main sea wall which was reaching the end of its effective lifetime. Overall responsibility for sea-defence scheme investment is held by the Ministry of Agriculture, Fisheries and Food (MAFF). Regional Water Authorities were able to apply to MAFF for capital grant aid for such schemes. The granting of such central government funds was and is dependent on both MAFF and UK Treasury approval. The approval process requires the production of detailed scheme plans and a supporting economic CBA. The candidate scheme, in this case a new sea wall and supporting works, must yield a positive net present value if it is to qualify for grant aid. The consultants were initially instructed to evaluate, as far as was practicable, all urban, agricultural, environmental and recreational benefits likely to be produced by the sea defence scheme. Subsequently, the EAG terms of reference were widened to encompass the computation of a full CBA for the scheme, utilizing sensitivity analysis.

The consultants' report produced in response to the water authority's instructions dealt with the appraisal of two engineering options:

- a "do nothing" option;
- a full capital works scheme.

The do nothing option would result in increasing costs over time due to both flood damage and changes in the current patterns of erosion and accretion. In order to evaluate the impact of allowing the in-place sea wall (which by 1988 was showing visible signs of significant deterioration) to fail, two flood risk/erosion scenarios were considered. Scenario A dealt with a timescale of risk judged to be "most likely" in the consulting engineers' reports. It assumed a gradual failure of the sea and river defences. Scenario B assumed a "worst case" sequence of events, in which both the sea wall and some river flood walls fail completely and at approximately the same time, due to unusually severe meteorological conditions. These two scenarios result in different scheme benefits profiles over time.

In benefits assessment studies undertaken for UK government grant-aid purposes, the norm has been to count only national economic efficiency impacts (see Introduction to this chapter). On this basis, the scheme was assumed to generate national economic benefits in terms of flooding/erosion damage costs avoided. Any financial losses suffered locally, and which could be offset by counterbalancing gains elsewhere within the nation, were not counted in the analysis. For the purposes of this sea-defence scheme context, the following types of local losses were deemed to also represent national losses:

(1) when a resource cost is involved in the transferral of business and/or recreational activity between one firm and another or between one locality and another;
(2) when, because of local disruption, customers/recreationists transfer their activity to other less satisfactory suppliers/ services/amenities;
(3) when some informal recreational opportunities enjoyed by a defined local population are being lost.

A conservative approach to benefits estimation and valuation was adopted throughout the analysis. The aim was to establish *minimum value benefit estimates* in order to facilitate the grant-aid approval process. The study identified the following categories of benefits:

(1) *Expected property damage costs avoided*
In cases where flooding under the do nothing option would be relatively infrequent, damages were assessed using standard, national UK depth-damage function data. These data were adjusted by the relevant post-breach flood risk factor to give the expected average annual damage costs. In cases where flooding would be so frequent (i.e. annually or every two years) as to make the property uninhabitable, the loss in use was taken to be the property's market value.

(2) *Agricultural output losses avoided*
On all the lower lying marsh agricultural areas, the relevant economic loss was taken to be the forgone enterprise (crop/ grazing regime) net margin. Net margins were then adjusted to reflect their estimated economic value, in line with the MAFF direction on intervention pricing and the implied producer subsidy equivalent. Some of the higher ground supports irrigated crops dependent on water abstraction points located on the marsh, and therefore at risk from saline flooding. For those enterprises with an alternative source of irrigation water, the only loss involved is the potential

extra cost of using this alternative. If no viable alternative source of irrigation water is available, then the economic damage costs which would be avoided by the implementation of the proposed sea-defence scheme would be equivalent to the difference between adjusted enterprise gross margins with irrigation and substitute crop adjusted gross margins without irrigation.

(3) *Recreational/amenity losses avoided*
The local coastline is a defined Heritage Coast and attracts significant numbers of tourists from outside the locality. Local residents also make use of Orford quay and the sea wall at Aldeburgh for informal recreation activities (walking, picnicking, etc). Three types of recreationist were identified: local informal recreationists, day-trippers from outside the local area, and holiday makers from outside the local area. A questionnaire survey was undertaken in order to derive visitor valuations of the recreation experience.

Local users were asked to express their willingness-to-pay for the maintenance of the existing recreational asset via a contingent valuation technique. *Non-local visitors* were asked indirectly about the uniqueness of the coastal asset at Aldeburgh and Orford. This was assessed via a question which asked them to name an equivalent alternative recreation location. All non-locals who were unable to give such an alternative site were assumed to regard Aldeburgh/Orford as possessing some uniqueness. This group was then asked to value its recreational experience using the contingent valuation technique. Non-locals who were able to name an equivalent alternative recreation location were not asked directly to value their Aldeburgh/Orford recreation experience. As this group did not feel that the study area was unique, it was assumed that this category of damage cost avoided did not represent a potential national economic benefit. Real economic resource costs were, however, still found to be present because the diversion of these recreation users away from Aldeburgh/Orford and to alternative sites resulted in extra net travel costs (distance and time costs).

A conservative approach to the estimation of the recreation benefits was taken in this study. The payment vehicle chosen (for the willingness-to-pay question) was extra annual rates and taxes. Although a number of contingent valuation studies have argued that this type of payment vehicle biases results downward, it was utilized in this study because of its "realism" property. This is the mechanism through which people would actually have had to pay for extra sea defences in the UK. A minimum estimate only of the extra travel costs (based on distance costs) was also utilized. Finally, the contingent valuation method was restricted to the estimation of use value and therefore ignored all non-use values which other studies have shown to be significant.

Results for the recreation use survey indicated that local users (households) were prepared to pay an average of around £15 p.a. extra to retain the existing recreation experience. Non-local users without alternative sites were found to be willing to pay £18.78 per group p.a.. Non-local users with alternative sites had, on average, to travel extra distances. The annual extra cost to the nation amounted to some £186,137 (distance costs only).

The rivers Aide and Ore provide extensive opportunities for sailing and there are clubs located at both Aldeburgh and Orford. The Landmark Trust also has an interest in the locality, having fully restored the early 19th-century Martello Tower, situated on the sea wall at Slaughden. Both the tower and sailing facilities were deemed to be at risk if a breach in the sea wall developed. The Landmark Trust provided an estimate of the costs which would be involved in the purchase of a derelict Martello Tower elsewhere (there is a fixed stock of such towers) and its restoration. This purchase and restoration cost was taken to be the proxy measure for the tower's damage-cost avoided.

Representatives of various sailing and dingy clubs, both in Aldeburgh and Orford, as well as elsewhere on the East Coast of England, were approached to establish whether or not there were any similar facilities in the region which would not be affected by a breach of the sea wall. It became apparent that equivalent alternative facilities did not exist locally. In the sailing club case, the measure of damage-costs avoided was represented by the approximate costs associated with the relocation of the majority of the sailing/dinghy facilities to a new, safer site further upstream.

(4) Environmental losses avoided
Some of the marshland area at risk from saline inundation has been entered by the landowners into the government's environmentally sensitive area (ESA) conservation scheme. The designation of the area implies the existence of valuable environmental assets (landscape and ecology) which society wishes to see conserved.

The payments to farmers under the ESA scheme in this sense were taken to represent an approximate per hectare social value. This approximate public preference value would be lost if the marshland in question was lost due to permanent or frequent saline inundation.

The Nature Conservancy Council (NCC) already owns some land in the study area and has indicated a willingness to pay for an extended acreage. It was therefore assumed in the report that, via the NCC, society is prepared to pay for the conservation of the designated area and value the land at the market price. If that land is lost or radically changed because of the sea-wall breach, the environmental conservation value will be significantly reduced or lost altogether.

The Royal Society for the Protection of Birds (RSPB) also has a reserve in the study area. The RSPB would have to incur a net increase in reserve management costs due to physical changes in a post-breach situation.

The net present value of the scheme was computed, assuming a project time horizon of 50 years and a discount rate of 5 per cent. Sensitivity analysis was employed and a total of ten cases were tested, differentiated in terms of flooding scenario, timing of benefits streams and value of individual components of the aggregate scheme benefit. All ten cases produced positive net present values, ranging from a low of £+0.01 million to a high of £+9.51 million.

After completion of the cost-benefit study, Anglian Water submitted the full scheme proposals to MAFF in 1989 for grant-aid approval. Approval in terms of scheme outline permission was granted in early 1989. The water authority was then given the go-ahead to produce detailed scheme plans in order to qualify for full permission and grant aid. As part of this second-stage approval process, MAFF have insisted on the production of an Environmental Impact Statement based on a full environmental assessment of the likely significant scheme impacts. The study will follow the UK Land Drainage Statutory Instrument Guidelines, as laid down under the terms of the EEC Environmental Impact Assessment Directive, which became operational in July 1988.

The Aldeburgh Sea Defence Scheme Report contained some benefits assessment methods (e.g. contingent valuation and social preference valuation of environmental and recreational assets) which had never previously been used in a scheme analysis supporting a grant-aid application. Because of this situation every effort was made to test the scheme's economic viability, utilizing as conservative an estimate of economic benefits as was feasible. The granting of scheme outline permission by MAFF and the UK Treasury has therefore to be seen as an acceptance in principle of some of the newer methods of environmental benefits valuation. Full scheme permission is still conditional on an "acceptable" environmental impact situation. The EIA process will involve two parallel stages: a technical assessment of the likely landscape, ecological etc. effects (in non-monetary terms) of the proposed scheme; and a consultation process with all interested parties (conservation bodies, local authorities, etc). Suggested scheme modifications and ameliorative measures that arise during the consultation process will all be considered before the final scheme design is sent to government for final approval.

Valuing the environmental benefits of forests

The Forestry Commission in the UK is responsible for around 900,000 hectares of estate in the country, producing almost 3 million cubic metres of timber. Commission land is used for commercial recreational facilities to the extent of 20,000 visitor-weeks a year, and for non-commercial facilities (nature walks, picnics, etc.) to the extent of 24 million visits a year (National Audit Office, 1986). Its annual budget is currently around £150 million, of which it recovers £120 million through its commercial activities. This leaves a gap of £30 million that has to be filled by a government grant. Of this, £7 million or 23 per cent is earmarked for conservation and recreation development.

Thus it is explicitly recognized that forestry activities have benefits that cannot be captured through the market place and that merit some government subsidy. On the production of timber, this subsidy is argued partly on the grounds that long gestation projects suffer a bias because market-based discount rates are too high compared to social rates, and partly on the grounds that forestry has a "security" aspect. The latter implies that government policy should take account of the possible costs of an embargo or of a change in the available supplies for other reasons (Markandya and Pearce, 1989a). On the recreational side, benefits are clearly perceived to flow from the non-commercial use described above, but it is not clear to what extent *additional* forestry projects add to such benefits. In total, these considerations are incorporated in the valuation procedure for forestry projects by requiring a lower rate of return than that required for other government-supported projects – a minimum rate of return of 3 per cent against a rate of 5 per cent for UK public sector investment as a whole.

As far as the non-commercial benefits of forestry are concerned, the following questions of policy arise:

- Should more or less be spent on conservation and recreation development?
- How should the conservation and recreation development budget be allocated amongst the 70 forest districts?
- What kind of activities are most beneficial as far as the recreational users are concerned – trails, maps, lookout posts, picnic spots, etc?

The answers to all these questions will depend on what the perceived benefits of the non-commercial aspects are and how they are derived. Until recently, the only research on which the non-commercial benefits could be calculated was a Treasury study undertaken in 1972 (HM Treasury, 1972). This attempted to value the recreational benefits from three forestry activities: new planting, replanting and the management of existing estates. It recognized the concept of willingness to pay as the appropriate one for valuing such benefits but it did not have enough empirical data to carry out any detailed estimates of the willingness to pay. However, some estimates were derived for day visits, based on a sample survey carried out in 1968, that estimated the annual number of visits to various sites. Although such information is useful, it is inadequate to apply any of the established methods for recreational valuation that are now in use (Pearce and Markandya, 1989). Nevertheless, it is worth noting that the study derived a total value for *all* recreational use (day visits, campers, shooting and fishing) of £1.32 million in 1968 prices. In 1989 prices, that would be worth about £8.2 million.

In 1987 a study of user benefits of forest recreation and wildlife was undertaken by Willis et al. (1988) at the request of the Forestry Commission. It examined six forests (Clatteringshaws, Dalby, Grizedale, Hamsterley, Symonds Yat and Thetford) and applied a travel-cost model to estimate the benefits of recreational use within them. A sample survey of visitors to each site was conducted, using 1,780 questionnaires, representing 5,721 visitors. The exercise yielded the following results:

- Consumer surplus varied from £2.51 for a visit at Thetford to £1.26 at Grizedale, with a weighted average of £1.90;
- Extrapolating these values to obtain aggregate estimates for the Forestry Commission estate as a whole yielded a range of between £14.4 and £45.6 million a year. Even the minimum of this range is higher than the Treasury study quoted above, and is 50 per cent higher than the figure used by the National Audit Office in its Forestry Commission Review (1986);
- Of the identified uses of forest land, the willingness to pay for its use broke down as follows: 36 per cent for wildlife, 34 per cent for landscape, 16 per cent for information or museum facilities, and 14 per cent for recreation; with little variation from site to site.

The Forestry Commission sees this as a useful exercise and plans to extend it in the future. One plan is to extend the analysis to another eight sites chosen on the basis of a cluster analysis. This should help to improve the extrapolated estimates of benefits, as well as identifying more closely those that yielded the greatest benefits. A second plan, related to the last point, is to use the results to appraise investments in recreation in greater detail. A third is to begin to estimate option and existence values for forestry land. Such values are excluded from the estimates derived so far and would necessitate the use of contingent valuation techniques. Finally, there is a longterm desire to be able to produce "value of recreation" figures on an annual basis. These would be made available to the National Audit Office and would be a response to the Public Accounts Committee's recommendation that such benefits be quantified where possible.

The valuation of human life in transport planning

In the UK the Department of Transport is responsible for the evaluation of major road investments and it undertakes these using a full cost-benefit approach, referred to as the COBA model. Within this approach, the two items that have to be valued from non-market data are the time savings generated by a project and the change in accidents that are associated with it. Accidents are classified into fatal and non-fatal and estimates are made of the expected change in the number of each, as well as the types of non-fatal injuries that are likely to arise. It is interesting to note that all schemes valued through the COBA method involve accident *reductions* and so in every case a benefit item has to be estimated.

Until 1988 the Department valued the benefits of accident reductions through what is known as the human capital approach. This calculated the gross value of the lost output and then estimated the costs of medical treatment, ambulance services, police, insurance administration and damage to vehicles and property. In addition, a notional sum was added for the pain, grief and suffering caused to the injured and his or her friends and relatives. By this method a figure of £284,000 at 1988 prices was estimated as the average value of a life, so that if a scheme could be shown to reduce fatalities by say, ten, per year then a figure of £2.84 million was included as the benefits flowing from the project. A similar figure was calculated for injuries, which were classified as serious and slight.

It was widely felt that this method was unsatisfactory, essentially because it was not based on the individual valuation of the risk. The criticism that the method reduced human beings to the value of their output was, to some extent, mitigated by including an item for "pain, grief and suffering" but it was clear that the amount attached to this item was arbitrary. In response to this situation, the Department of Transport funded some work in the UK on the valuation of accidents, measuring the willingness to pay via the contingent valuation approach (Jones-Lee et al., 1985) and subsequently undertook a survey within the Department of the literature on the value of human life (Dalvi, 1988).

The work of Jones-Lee and his colleagues came up with an estimate of the value of life of around £1.8 million. There were many difficulties in carrying out this study, notably in overcoming the hypothetical nature of the choices, the subjective perception of probabilities and the perception of some of the "external" benefits of accident reduction (e.g. reduced police and ambulance services, health expenditures). Nevertheless, the results were fairly consistent within the study and in comparison with other studies: the average value of life was estimated at £1.8 million, with a median value of approximately £1 million, both in 1987 prices.

Dalvi (1988) reviewed this study, along with many others based on hedonic wage methods, and came to the conclusion that the range of estimates was quite wide, even when restricted to the more reliable studies. Variations can arise because of the nature of the risk being considered, the question of whether it is voluntary or not, the method of estimation used and the sample of people being analysed (Pearce and Markandya, 1989). Nevertheless, the range of reliable estimates are in the same order of magnitude as in the Jones-Lee study, with the mean being close to the latter. In view of this evidence, Dalvi concluded that Jones-Lee's estimate could be used as the working basis for revaluing fatality costs. However, he concluded that a sudden jump from the (then) present value of £284,000 to the kind of figure suggested by Jones-Lee would be too large to take at one time. "Such a (high) figure would probably change the present relationship between time savings and accident benefits and would relatively downgrade the priority given to faster traffic movement and congestion benefits as opposed to safety of life and limb" (Dalvi, 1988, p. 34).

Therefore, Dalvi suggested taking a value of £500,000 for the value of life in future studies. This proposal was discussed with experts in the field and it was agreed that it would be a desirable step, at least in the first instance.

As a result of taking a higher value of life, the proportion of benefits accounted for by reductions in accidents has gone up from around 14 per cent to around 19 per cent. The implication is that more roads will be built and that more schemes that have a specific safety feature will pass the COBA model test. Jones-Lee has recently estimated that the increased valuation will result in a saving of 300 lives a year at an incremental cost of approximately 6 per cent of the annual budget for road building and improvement (Jones-Lee, 1989). However, he does not indicate how he arrives at these estimates.

In addition to influencing the Department of Transport's road programme, the changes valuation will also affect the activities of local authorities. Standards for local authorities' roads are set by the Department of Transport but there is discretion at the local level on how much is spent on road building and improvement. Where there has been a run of accidents, the higher valuation of life will generate higher overall net benefits for a safety scheme and will therefore provide stronger arguments for more discretionary local authority funds for the project. In particular, schemes involving safety fencing, skid-resistant surfacing and bridge design are likely to benefit.

Although this is regarded as a move in the right direction,

there are a number of areas of safety in transport that need further consideration. Within the road transport area, there is the question of the valuation of non-fatal accidents. These are still valued on the old "lost output plus pain, grief and suffering" basis. The Department of Transport is currently commissioning research proposals to obtain a valuation for non-fatal injuries on a similar basis to that for fatal injuries.

Even more important perhaps, is the need to extend accident valuation to other modes of transport, notably rail, London Underground and ferries. In none of these are Investments at present appraised on a social cost-benefit basis that includes the benefits of accident prevention. British Rail's appraisal procedures, for example, are focused on narrow financial considerations alone. Given the spate of serious accidents in these areas recently in the UK, the response has been to set up a public inquiry, which will make recommendations regarding safety. However, the costs and benefits of the proposed measures are not estimated and it is unlikely that this method results in an efficient allocation of resources to safety within these modes.

Conclusions

Although benefit estimation is practised in the United Kingdom, it is currently used on an *ad hoc* basis. No legislation exists to mandate CBA, but there is some probability that the EEC Directive on Environmental Impact Assessment will evolve to include benefit estimation. The approach tends to be viewed with suspicion in some government circles. This scepticism reflects a number of factors.

First, the historical experience of benefit estimation in the UK is not good. Considerable popular antipathy was generated by the studies of the Commission of Inquiry into London's Third Airport in 1969–71 (the Roskill Commission). The Commission attempted measures of the money value of noise nuisance and, at one stage, produced a value for an historic Norman church based on fire insurance premia. The eventual overturn of the Commission's recommendation for an inland site for the airport tended to brand the Commission's cost-benefit work as over-technocratic. It is perhaps significant that London's actual third airport *is* inland.

Second, it is clear that economists in the public service in the UK have limited expertise in environmental economics generally and benefit estimation in particular. This reflects the lack of a "forcing" agent, such as legislation requiring cost-benefit approaches (as in the USA), and the general absence of university training in environmental economics.

Third, some agencies report having made efforts to secure monetary valuations but found them unsatisfactory. In general, however, these reported attempts are not made public and it is not possible to evaluate them.

It is also clear that the ethos has changed in very recent years. As the costs of environmental protection grow there is a much wider recognition that "value for money" considerations require some attempt at benefit estimation. The focus on cost-effectiveness also reflects general concern about efficiency in government expenditure. Popular reaction to proposals in an officially commissioned report in 1989, which urged greater benefit estimation, suggests also that more and more people see the need to engage in at least some monetary valuation.[5]

Overall then, benefit estimation has quietly increased in the UK after the hostility towards cost-benefit in the 1970s. It now looks set to play a much more significant role in decision making in the UK.

Notes

1   Interestingly, these brief statements imply quite an extensive acknowledgement of benefit estimation principles. The reference to actual behaviour and declared and revealed preferences makes it clear that both surrogate markets (e.g. hedonic prices from property markets) and hypothetical markets (contingent valuation) could qualify. The use of "what if" valuations – i.e. finding what the value would be for an NPV to become positive or negative – is widely used in actual cost-benefit studies. The "what if" value is then compared to some intuitive appraisal of what the benefits might be. Finally, the last sentence quite explicitly encompasses the concept of option value (but not existence value). For discussions of all these concepts see Pearce and Markandya (1989).

2   The current Department of Transport programme and accompanying manual, known as COBA, is currently in its 9th version.
3   This is an increase from the previous sum of £252,000 and reflects a review of the procedures in 1988 which concluded that values should be based on willingness-to-pay measures.
4   It might be thought that because the "do nothing" option imposes environmental costs (unsightliness, hazard, smell, etc) there should be a negative item for environment under the do nothing option. However, the property price changes are relative to the existing state of the canal, so that the recorded gain should account for the initial damage. Accident benefits are not shown, but were estimated to comprise a reduction from 1.4 deaths per annum to 0.3 deaths per annum, the same number as is found on other restored urban waterways. The gain of approximately one life per annum was valued in Button and Pearce (1989) at £252,000, the value used by the UK Department of Transport until recently. The new value of £500,000 is discussed on p. 228ff.
5   The report in question was commissioned by the Department of the Environment from the London Environmental Economics Centre. It originally appeared as a limited circulation document entitled *Sustainable Development* and then as a published work (see Pearce, Markandya and Barbier (1989). It was the subject of enormous press and media coverage in the UK.

References

Bentkover J., Covello, V. and Mumpower, J. (1986) *Benefits Assessment: The State of the Art.* (Reidel: Dordrecht).

Button, K. and Pearce, D.W. (1989) "Infrastructure restoration as a tool for stimulating urban renewal – the Glasgow Canal", *Urban Studies.* (Forthcoming).

Colvin, P. (1985) *The Economic Ideal in British Government.* (Manchester University Press: Manchester).

Cummings, R., Brookshire, D. and Schulze, W. (1986) *Valuing Environmental Goods.* (Rowman and Allenheld: Totowa).

Dalvi, M.Q. (1988) *The Value of Life and Safety: A Search for a Consensus Estimate.* (Department of Transport: London).

Dixon, J. et al. (1986) *Economic Analysis of the Environmental Impacts of Development Projects.* (Asian Development Bank: Manila). Now revised and updated, 1988, (Earthscan: London).

Dobbie, C.H. (1985) *Aldeburgh Sea Defences: Part 1 Report*, Vols 1-3. (C.H. Dobbie and Partners, Consulting Engineers: Croydon, Surrey).

Dobbie, C.H. (1986) *Alderburgh Sea Defences: The "Do-Nothing" Alternative*. (C.H. Dobbie and Partners, Consulting Engineers: Croydon, Surrey).

EPA (US Environmental Protection Agency) (1987) *EPA's Use of Benefit Cost Analysis 1981-1986*, EPA 230-05-87-028. (EPA: Washington, DC).

Feenberg, D. and Mills, E. (1980) *Measuring the Benefits of Water Pollution Abatement*. (Academic Press: New York).

Freeman, A.M. (1979) *The Benefits of Environmental Improvement*. (Johns Hopkins University Press: Baltimore).

Freeman, A.M. (1982) *Air and Water Pollution Control*. (John Wiley: New York).

Haigh, N. (1987) *EEC Environmental Policy and Britain*. (Longman: London).

Halvorsen, R. and Ruby, M. (1981) *Benefit-Cost Analysis of Air Pollution Control*. (D.C. Heath: Lexington).

House of Commons (1988-9). House of Commons Committee of Public Accounts, 15th Report, *Road Planning*, Session 1988/89, HOC Paper 101.

House of Lords, Select Committee On Science and Technology (1982) *The Water Industry*, Volumes 1 and 2, (December). (HMSO: London).

Johansson, P.O. (1987) *The Economic Theory and Measurement of Environmental Benefits*. (Cambridge University Press: Cambridge).

Jones-Lee, M.W. et al. (1985) "The value of safety: results of a national sample survey", *Economic Journal*, 95, pp. 49-72.

Jones-Lee, M.W. (1989) "Why British Rail must learn to place a calculated value on life", *The Independent*, Thursday, March 9.

Kneese, A. (1984) *Measuring the Benefits of Clean Air and Water* Resources for the Future. (Washington, DC).

Leitch Committe (1977). Report of the Advisory Committee on Trunk Road Assessment. (HMSO: London).

Mac Arthur, J. (1988) *Appraisal of Projects in Developing Countries: A Guide for Economists* (third version). (ODA: London).

Markandya, A. and Pearce D.W. (1989a) "Economic security arguments for afforestation", Department of Economics, University College of London, *mimeo*, 1989.

Monopolies and Mergers Commission (1981), Severn-Trent Water Authority, East Worcestershire Waterworks Company. *A Report on Water Services by the Authority and the Companies*, (June). (HMSO: London).

Monopolies and Mergers Commission [1982], Anglian Water, North West Water. *A Report on the Sewerage Functions of the Two Authorities*, (November). (HMSO: London).

Monopolies and Mergers Commission [1984], Yorkshire Water Authority, *A Report on the Water Services Provided by the Authority*, (December). (HMSO: London).

Monopolies and Mergers Commission (1987) *British Waterways Board*, Cm 124. (HMSO: London).

National Audit Office (1986) *Review of National Forestry Commission Objectives and Achievements*. (HMSO: London).

ODA (1989) *Manual of Environmental Appraisal*. (ODA: London).

Pearce, D.W. and Markandya, A. (1989) *Environmental Policy Benefits: Monetary Evaluation*. (OECD: Paris).

Pearce, D.W., Markandya, A. and Barbier, E. (1989) *Blueprint for a Green Economy*, (Earthscan: London).

Smith, V.K. (1984) *Environmental Policy Under Reagan's Executive Order*, (University of North Carolina Press: Chapel Hill).

Smith, V.K. and Desvousges, W. (1986) *Measuring Water Quality Benefits* (Kluwer-Nijhof: Boston).

Suleman, M.S. et al. (1988) "Potential flood damage data: a major update". (Flood Hazard Research Centre, Middlesex Polytechnic: Queensway, Enfield, Middlesex).

Turner, R.K. and Brooke, J.S. (1988) *A Benefits Assessment for the Aldeburgh Sea Defence Scheme*. Environmental Appraisal Group Report. (School of Environmental Sciences, University of East Anglia: Norwich).

HM Treasury (1972) *Forestry in Great Britain*. (HMSO: London).

UK Treasury (1984) *Investment Appraisal in the Public Sector: A Technical Guide for Government Departments*. (HM Treasury: London).

Water Research Centre and Flood Hazard Research Centre (1989) *Investment Appraisal For Sewage Schemes: The Assessment of Social Costs*, Project Report. (Water Research Centre: Swindon).

Water Research Centre and Coopers and Lybrand Associates (1989) *Review of Investment Appraisal Techniques in the Water Industry*, (Water Research Centre: Swindon).

Water Authorities Association/Water Research Centre (1986) *Sewerage Rehabilitation Manual*, 2nd Edition, April. (Water Research Centre: Swindon).

Willis, K.G., Benson, J.F. and Whitby M.C. (1988) *Values of User Benefits of Forest Recreation and Wildlife*. (Forestry Commission: Edinburgh).

Winpenny, J. (forthcoming) *Guide to Economic Evaluation of Environmental Effects* (provisional title, in process).

7 The United States

Maryann Froehlich, Drusilla J.C. Hufford and Nancy H. Hammett

Introduction

The use of benefits estimates in environmental decision making has received increased attention in the United States over the past two decades. Environmental benefits have been estimated for a number of purposes, and major strides have been made in the theory and practice of environmental benefits assessment. For example, "Environmental Impact Statements" (EIS) are required for many construction projects and other activities, and much of the early development of benefits measurement methodologies involved the evaluation of individual projects. Since the early 1970s, the use of some type of formal benefit-cost and economic impact analyses has been required to support Federal environmental regulations. Environmental benefits estimates have also been developed as part of more general policy studies.

This chapter describes the use of benefits estimates by the US Environmental Protection Agency (EPA). We focus primarily on the use of environmental benefits estimates to evaluate and justify new regulations. We address in particular the degree to which environmental benefits estimates have actually influenced decision making, and the factors that contribute to greater or less reliance on such estimates.

The first section describes the current Federal requirements for cost-benefit analysis (CBA), both in Presidential Executive Orders and in various environmental statutes. The second section provides a brief overview of benefits estimation by the EPA. We then look in more detail at the use of benefits estimates in the development of four specific US EPA regulations. The final section summarizes some of the barriers to greater use of benefits assessments in environmental decision making, as revealed by these case studies and by the authors' general experience with EPA's rule making.

Estimating the benefits of environmental regulations has received increased attention in the United States. In addition, benefits estimates serve a range of purposes in US environmental decision making. At one extreme, benefits estimates are the sole driving force behind a decision. In other cases, benefits estimates may be one of several factors that influence the debate and decision on regulatory alternatives. The case studies presented here provide examples of the range of uses of benefits estimates in the US. These case studies illustrate problems and conditions that contribute to greater or less reliance by decision makers on benefits estimates.

A number of factors have limited the use of benefits estimates as the sole justification for environmental decisions. These include methodological problems that affect the credibility of the estimates, legislative standards that preclude consideration of cost-benefit criteria, and lack of consensus about the role efficiency and other criteria should play in the design of environment regulations. However, the reader should not be misled. Benefits estimates are widely used in US environmental regulation. Additionally, while environmental decisions may not always be made solely on the basis of net benefits, benefits estimates have a strong influence in stimulating awareness of the costs and gains to be made by environmental decisions, and often play a major role in influencing the choice among competing regulatory alternatives.

Legislative and Executive Requirements for Benefits Analysis

Benefits analysis is required for a variety of Federal actions. First, the National Environmental Policy Act of 1969 as amended (NEPA), and the regulations implementing NEPA, require analysis of environmental impacts for major Federal actions, including rule makings, programme decisions and specific projects. Agencies must either prepare an Environmental Assessment supporting a "finding of no significant impact" or must prepare an Environmental Impact Statement (EIS). The EIS must describe significant impacts on the human environment and identify alternative actions that would minimize adverse environmental impacts. Thus, analysis of adverse environmental impacts is required for a wide range of Federal actions.

Second, Federal agencies are required by Presidential Executive

Order to assess the costs and benefits of major regulations. For environmental regulations, the analysis of benefits requires evaluation of environmental improvements resulting from the regulation. As described below, the cost-benefit decision criteria established by the Executive Order sometimes conflict with the decision criteria for regulations established by the relevant legislation authorizing particular environmental regulations.

Third, environmental legislation sometimes requires that the EPA prepare studies of particular environmental problems, which may involve environmental benefit or damage estimates. For example, Congress has required the EPA to prepare studies of risks from disposal of mining and other specific wastes, and of risks from the discharge of hazardous wastes to public waste-water treatment facilities, under the provisions of the Resource Conservation and Recovery Act. Beyond these occasional requests for studies by Congress, there are no formal Federal requirements for benefits assessments to set overall policy direction or to guide the allocation of Federal expenditures among environmental and other programmes.

This chapter focuses on the use of environmental benefits estimates in the second application listed above – the design and justification of specific Federal environmental regulations. The US EPA issues regulations to implement the provisions of a large number of statutes enacted by the Congress. The decision criteria to be used by the Agency in designing regulations, and hence the emphasis placed by the Agency on benefits estimates and other factors, vary depending on the statute involved. In addition, the EPA and other Federal regulatory agencies must comply with Executive Orders issued by the President that require certain analyses and specify decision criteria. These two influences on the EPA's decision making are described below.

Presidential Executive Orders

Formal requirements for cost, economic impact and benefits analyses to support regulation have steadily increased as a result of a series of Presidential Executive Orders. Executive Order 12291, issued by President Reagan in 1981, requires that a Regulatory Impact Analysis (RIA) be prepared for every major rule, and directs agencies to select a regulatory approach that maximizes "net benefits to society" to the extent permitted by law. This was the first Executive Order to make explicit a "net benefits" criterion for regulation.

A major rule is defined as any regulation that is likely to result in (a) an annual effect on the economy of US $100 million or more; (b) a major increase in costs or prices; or, (c) significant adverse effects on competition, employment, investment, productivity, innovation, or the international competitive position of US firms. Therefore, the Order requires formal analysis of costs and benefits for rules that are expected to impose significant costs or economic impacts.

Each RIA must include:

• a description of the potential benefits of the rule, including any beneficial effects that cannot be quantified in monetary terms, and the identification of those likely to receive the benefits;
• a description of the potential costs of the rule, including any adverse effects that cannot be quantified in monetary terms, and the identification of those likely to bear the costs;
• a determination of the potential net benefits of the rule, including an evaluation of effects that cannot be quantified in monetary terms;
• a description of alternative approaches that could achieve substantially the same regulatory goal at lower cost, together with an analysis of the potential benefits and costs and a brief explanation of the legal reasons why such alternatives, if proposed, could not be adopted;
• unless covered by the description required [in the previous provision], an explanation of any reason why the rule cannot be based on the requirements set forth in Section 2 of this Order.

(Presidential Executive Order 12291, 1981)

Section 2 of the Order provides that "Regulatory objectives shall be chosen to maximize the net benefits to society" and that "Regulatory action shall not be undertaken unless the potential benefits to society for the regulation outweigh the potential costs to society". The Order recognizes that a "maximize net benefits" decision criterion may conflict with the provisions of certain environmental statutes, and therefore provides that regulations be crafted to maximize net benefits "to the extent permitted by law". Where regulatory approaches that do not provide the highest net benefits are selected, the RIA must describe the legal constraints that influenced the Agency's choice of the selected approach.

Executive Order 12291 therefore places a heavy emphasis on measuring and comparing costs and benefits in developing regulations. It establishes maximum net benefits as the major decision criterion, unless specific statutes impose different decision criteria. It requires that all potential benefits and costs of a rule be considered, whether or not they can be quantified in monetary terms. Because the alternative with the greatest net benefits must be identified, the Executive Order implicitly requires that a range of regulatory alternatives be considered and that benefits and costs be estimated for each alternative.

Both the Office of Management and Budget, which oversees compliance with the Executive Order, and the EPA have issued guidelines for compliance with the Order. Both sets of guidelines contain an explicit call for estimating the benefits, costs and net benefits of a range of regulatory alternatives. The EPA's guidelines provide explicit direction on how to value benefits of reduced mortality and morbidity, on choice of discount rates, and on other methodological issues, as well as describing what the RIA must contain.

Statutory decision criteria

Despite the strong emphasis on cost and benefit analysis in the Executive Orders governing regulation, the use of such analysis in actual regulatory decision making varies widely. This variability is due in part to differences in the decision criteria established in different statutes. The following describes the criteria for decision-making established in four of the major statutes implemented by the EPA, as examples.

Clean Air Act

The Clean Air Act mandates a number of different types of regulations, and the decision-making criteria specified in the legislation differ somewhat among them. For example, the EPA is directed to base primary National Ambient Air Quality Standards (NAAQS) on air-quality criteria that reflect public health effects, and to provide for a margin of safety. The legislation does not provide for considering the costs of achieving the NAAQS in setting these standards. The criteria for National Emission Standards for Hazardous Air Pollutants (NESHAPs) are also based on achieving an ample margin of safety to protect the public health. By contrast, the EPA is required to consider cost-effectiveness but not the benefits of improved air quality when issuing emissions performance standards for new stationary sources. In another case – regulations on motor vehicle fuels and fuel additives to prevent impairment of emission controls – the EPA is directed to consider cost-benefit comparisons explicitly.

Clean Water Act

The Clean Water Act establishes rule-making criteria for effluent limitations that are heavily influenced by the performance of available treatment technologies. Cost-effectiveness and economic feasibility are considered in establishing technology-based effluent-limitation guidelines. More stringent water-quality-based limitations may be imposed for specific facilities where necessary to meet state water-quality standards. These water-quality standards are risk-based; therefore, more stringent standards may be established based on risk factors, but requirements less stringent than those achieved by the "Best Practicable Technology" cannot be based on a finding that the monetized benefits of water-quality improvement are low relative to costs.

Toxic Substances Control Act
The Toxic Substances Control Act (TSCA) authorizes the EPA to prohibit, restrict, or regulate the manufacture, processing, distribution, use or disposal of any substance that presents an unreasonable risk of injury to health or the environment. The Act authorizes the EPA to develop rules "to the extent necessary to protect adequately against such risk using the least burdensome requirements . . .". TSCA also requires that the EPA consider and publish its conclusions on health and environmental benefits, the economic value of the substances in use, and the economic consequences of the rule. TSCA therefore does not establish cost-benefit comparisons as an explicit decision criterion for determining how stringent rules should be, but, at a minimum, requires evaluation of cost-effectiveness by requiring the imposition of the "least burdensome requirements".

Resource Conservation and Recovery Act
The Resource Conservation and Recovery Act (RCRA) provides for regulation of the treatment, storage and disposal of wastes.

The Act covers both hazardous and non-hazardous wastes. RCRA emphasizes protection of human health and the environment as a rule-making criterion. No mention is made in the Act of costs or economic impacts as a consideration in rule making. The EPA has interpreted the RCRA language as precluding use of cost-benefit comparisons in determining what levels of protection should be provided. However, the EPA is able to consider costs and economic impacts in choosing the most cost-effective method for achieving the required degree of protection.

Overview of the EPA's Benefits Assessments

Although not required to by any legislative or executive mandate, the EPA has performed some environmental benefits studies designed to provide broad policy-making guidance. For example, in 1987, EPA's Office of Policy, Planning and Evaluation performed a study (called the "Unfinished Business" study) which assessed the relative importance of various environmental problems. (EPA, OPPE, 1987). This study was based on the findings of various work groups assigned to rank sources of environmental contamination based on different measures of environmental damages, such as human health and ecological effects. The study involved largely subjective ranking – no attempt was made to develop monetized estimates of the damages attributed to different sources. Nonetheless, this study provides valuable insight into areas where the current allocation of the EPA's efforts might be modified to better reflect the relative seriousness of different environmental problems.

The most common application of benefits assessment by the EPA involves analyses of the benefits of specific regulations as part of Regulatory Impact Analyses. Although RIAs – and hence benefits analysis – have been performed for numerous rules, the scope and quality of the benefits analyses in these RIAs has varied widely.

A review of 15 RIAs performed by the EPA between 1981 and 1986 (EPA, OPA, 1987) found that only six of the 15 RIAs addressed by the study presented a complete analysis of monetized benefits and net benefits. The 1987 study notes that many rule makings were improved by the analysis of benefits and costs, even where benefits were not monetized and net benefits calculated. The 1987 review nonetheless reveals that the formal use of monetized benefits and net benefits measures has been limited in past EPA rule makings.

The EPA's benefits analyses in RIAs have generally involved predicting specific environmental or human health damages by predicting environmental releases, the fate and transport of contaminants in various environmental media, human exposure and resulting health effects and, in some cases, other environmental effects such as materials damage or loss of drinking-water sources. Only a limited number of RIAs have included monetary estimates of environmental benefits. The methods used in these cases to value environmental benefits are often thought to understate true benefits, because they do not include non-use values of environmental resources and often exclude important components of use value as well.

The EPA's benefits analyses have tended to focus most heavily on human health effects, and have given less attention to ecological benefits such as reduced damage to aquatic life and vegetation, loss of habitat, or contamination of wetlands. The EPA Office of Policy Analysis made a study of the use of ecological benefits measures in EPA's "Superfund" (contaminated site clean-up) and RCRA (waste management) programmes. (EPA, OPA, 1989). The study considered ecological evaluations performed both for specific Superfund and RCRA sites and, in general, policy and regulatory studies. The use of ecological assessments for specific Superfund sites has been increasing in recent years. For the most part, however, the use of ecological criteria to select Superfund sites for remediation, to select remediation methods, or to assess Superfund or RCRA policies has been limited. The OPA study listed the following as barriers to greater use of ecological benefits analysis:

• lack of Agency policy and guidance on the extent to which ecological data should be gathered and considered;
• need for guidance on what levels of ecological effects are unacceptable;
• lack of criteria for predicting ecological impacts for many toxic compounds.

Research and methodology development is particularly needed on analysing threats to terrestrial ecosystems and threats from contaminated sediments.

Approaches advocated by economists to provide fuller measures of environmental benefits – such as contingent valuation (CV) – have found only limited application in EPA's decision making. CV measures have had their greatest use in valuing natural resources, where option, bequest and existence values not captured by traditional benefit measures may constitute a large portion of benefits. Mitchell and Carson (1989) identify over 100 studies that have applied CV methods. However, in only a few cases have CV measures been used to evaluate specific regulations.

One widely reported use of CV survey techniques by the EPA involved estimates of the benefits of improved visibility from reduction of sulphur emissions. (EPA, OAR, 1988). CV estimates of visibility benefits suggested that improved visibility was an important benefit of improved controls on sulphur emissions. The CV studies were criticized, however, because survey respondents may have included perceived health benefits as well as visibility benefits in their value estimates, and because respondents may have overstated their willingness to pay when asked to value a single category of environmental improvement in isolation.

Research on the CV methodology has continued, and approaches have been developed to address some of the problems with past CV estimates. To date, however, the limited use of CV estimates to support policy decision appears to reflect:

● widespread scepticism about the validity of survey "willingness-to-pay" responses;
● the substantial cost of performing such surveys.

In addition, the more traditional approach – predicting and valuing specific environmental endpoints using quantitative risk modelling – may appeal to policy makers for reasons that outweigh limitations in the accuracy of the resulting benefits measures. Policy makers gain insight into the source and nature of contamination from this explicit risk modelling approach, which provides guidance in designing regulations. Given limited budgets for regulatory analysis, accurate aggregate estimates of regulatory benefits may be viewed by policy makers as less important than the insight into the source of the environmental problems provided by the traditional EPA approach to benefits estimation.

In the next section, we describe four specific applications of benefits analysis to support EPA's rule makings. These case studies illustrate the variations in EPA's use of benefits assessments in regulatory decision making, and provide useful insights into the practical difficulties encountered in performing such studies and the conditions that promote use of such estimates in decision making.

Case Studies: EPA's Use of Benefits Estimates in Rule Making

To illustrate the problems and constraints affecting use of benefits estimates, we describe the use of benefits estimates in four past or ongoing EPA rule makings, dealing with lead in gasoline, land disposal, sewage sludge and landfilling.

The regulation of lead in gasoline is widely viewed as a "success" in the use of benefits estimates and cost-benefit comparisons in rule making. In contrast, little use was made of benefits analysis or cost-benefit comparisons in the development of restrictions on the land disposal of hazardous wastes. Recently proposed regulations on the management of waste-water treatment sludge and on the operation of municipal solid-waste landfills represent intermediate cases. While comparisons of monetized benefits and costs were not developed for the sludge rule, analysis of physical measures of benefits did influence the design of the rule. In addition, the sludge rule involved extensive use of new risk-assessment methodologies, and reaction to the rule in the coming months will provide an interesting test of the public's reaction to the use of risk-assessment techniques to support environmental rule making. The RIA for the proposed municipal solid-waste landfill rule showed that costs substantially outweigh estimated benefits, even though the RIA included measures of economic losses due to groundwater contamination as well as estimates of human health effects. This finding has motivated efforts to reduce the costs imposed by this rule, by considering greater use of risk-based performance standards.

Restrictions on lead in gasoline

Purpose of the rule
The Clean Air Act authorizes the EPA to control fuel additives if they cause emissions that endanger public health or welfare, or if they impair the performance of emission control devices installed on vehicles to control other emissions. The EPA began limiting the levels of lead in gasoline 1973, and revised its standards in

1982. After the 1982 rule was issued, continued study of the health effects of lead suggested that the risks were higher than had been previously estimated. In addition, the use of leaded gasoline was not declining as expected because of widespread "misfueling" (use of leaded gasoline in cars designed for unleaded fuel). Lead emissions contribute to elevated levels of lead in blood, causing a variety of health effects and learning impairments. Lead also damages pollution control catalysts, resulting in increased emissions of hydrocarbons (HC), nitrogen oxides (NO^x) and carbon monoxide (CO).

Based on the growing evidence that low blood-lead levels are harmful and on the evidence of misfueling, the EPA decided in 1984 to consider further reductions in the amount of lead allowed in gasoline. In March 1984, the EPA proposed to reduce allowed lead limits in leaded gasoline from 1.10 to 0.10 grams per leaded gallon (gplg). After further analysis of costs, benefits and regulatory options, the EPA issued rules requiring a phased reduction to the 0.10 gplg level by January 1, 1986, and then a total ban on leaded gasoline by 1988. Responding to the concerns of the agricultural community, the Agency did not proceed with the ban, because of the potential for engine damage in older engines (designed for leaded gasoline) when used at the high loads and speeds typical of agricultural equipment.

Policy options
The RIA for the final rule considered a number of potential regulatory approaches. These included:

● making no change in the existing requirements;
● increasing education efforts to discourage misfueling;
● increased enforcement of the current rules;
● use of marketable permits;
● charges on gasoline based on its lead content;
● alternative phasedown schedules for uniform lead limits.

Role of benefits analyses in decision making
Formal estimates of costs and benefits played a major role in EPA's decision to reduce allowed levels of lead in gasoline. This rule is widely viewed as one of the Agency's most successful applications of cost-benefit analysis to support regulatory decision-making.

The EPA made a concerted effort to develop reliable estimates of both the costs and the benefits of the proposed rule. First, it updated and used an existing linear programming model of refinery economics to assess the feasibility and costs of complying with the rule. The cost analysis assumed that refineries continued to produce the same octane mix in gasoline, and analysed the steps that would be taken to meet the mandated limits on lead. Use of an economic decision model, rather than the more common reliance on assumed responses and engineering costs, allowed the EPA to predict use of new technology as the cost of octane increased. A more simplistic approach would have overstated the costs of the rule. Actual costs of the rule still turned out lower than expected, both because of the hugely successful banking programme as a way to phase in the requirements, and because of the reduction in fuel costs as the cost of crude oil declined.

Second, the EPA estimated both direct and indirect benefits of the rule. The reliability of these benefits estimates varied, based on the reliability of the underlying evidence on health effects and on the relationship between emissions and exposures. The benefits estimates for adult white male blood pressure were excluded from the final comparison of costs and benefits since the evidence had not been peer-reviewed. The remaining benefits still resulted in substantial net benefits, however. The RIA estimated net benefits for the period 1985–92 of US $6.7 billion.

Estimating the benefits of this rule required innovative use of a variety of methodologies and data sources. What follows is a brief description of the major components of the benefits analysis. To estimate the direct exposure effects of reduced lead levels, the EPA performed a regression analysis to assess the relationship between levels of lead in gasoline and blood-lead levels. The availability of data on blood-lead levels and on lead levels in gasoline, over time, allowed the EPA to estimate this relationship directly, which avoided the need for complicated and uncertain modelling of emissions, fate and transport, exposure and uptake. Blood-lead levels showed a strong relationship to lead levels in the previous months' gasoline sales. For children, the EPA calculated the probability of experiencing blood-lead levels above the Center for Disease Control's screening standard of 25–30 ug/dl. The EPA then assumed that children with blood-lead levels above this level would be treated to reduce lead in the blood, and used estimates of the costs of treatment to calculate avoided medical costs attributable to the rule. These benefits were valued at US $155 million in 1986.

The same estimates of changes in children's blood-lead levels were used to calculate the benefits of avoiding the need for compensatory education for children experiencing learning difficulties due to lead exposure. To avoid double counting, the EPA assumed that all children with blood levels above the 25–30 ug/dl threshold were treated and that none of the children with lower lead levels would be treated. Therefore, the benefits of avoided compensatory education were developed only for children with the lower blood-lead levels.

The EPA also calculated the indirect effects of the rule on emissions of hydrocarbons, nitrogen oxides and ozone. The RIA assumed that a rise in the price of leaded gasoline prompted by the rule would eliminate misfueling and hence damage to pollution-control equipment. Two alternative methods were used to calculate the benefits of avoided damages to vehicle pollution controls. First, the EPA assumed that the benefits equalled the costs of replacing the damaged pollution-control devices – a total of US $35 million in 1986. Second, the EPA calculated the value of crop damages and lost work days due to respiratory effects that would be avoided if misfueling were eliminated. This calculation relied on rough estimates of how changes in emissions from misfueled cars would affect ambient air quality and exposures. The EPA relied on existing studies of the effects of ozone on crop loss and on respiratory function. The avoided crop losses were valued at market crop prices, and standard estimates of willingness to pay to avoid minor morbidity effects were used to value avoided respiratory effects. The two direct measures combined amounted to between US $103 and US $305 million in 1986 benefits. The EPA used an average of the results of the first and second approaches to calculate the aggregate benefits of the rule.

Finally, the EPA calculated savings from reduced vehicle maintenance. Scavengers are generally added to leaded gasoline to remove lead from cylinders. These scavengers contribute to corrosion. Previous studies showed that avoiding the need to add these scavengers substantially extended the life of exhaust systems and reduced the frequency of oil changes. The EPA estimated the savings in vehicle maintenance to be US $933 million in 1986. This benefit alone was sufficient to offset the estimated costs of the rule. In addition, estimated benefits of US $190 million in 1986 were attributed to fuel savings, due to production of higher density fuels prompted by the rule.

The EPA calculated but did not include in the final benefits estimates the effect of the rule on adult blood-pressure levels. The Agency excluded these benefits because the evidence on the effects of lead on blood pressure was relatively recent and had not completed peer review. These effects would be included in any current analysis of lead health effects.

The cost-benefit results presented in this RIA clearly supported lowering the allowed levels of lead in gasoline. The results might have supported reducing the allowed level to zero. However, concerns about increased engine wear for older cars and farm equipment prompted the EPA to propose the 0.10 gplg level instead. In addition, it proposed to impose the requirement in two phases, to avoid disruption of refinery operations.

Several factors seem to have contributed to the successful use of benefits estimates and cost-benefit analysis in this rule making.

First and foremost, the EPA made the effort to prepare complete and credible estimates of both benefits and costs. In doing so, it was able to draw on a substantial and growing literature on the health and environmental effects of lead and ozone, and was able to use data on gasoline and blood levels to estimate the relationship between the two statistically, rather than relying on complex and uncertain environmental modelling.

Second, the results of the study provided very clear support for lowering allowed lead levels. The benefits clearly outweighed the costs, even if portions of the benefits estimates were believed to be unreliable.

Third, the Clean Air Act provisions authorizing regulation of gasoline additives specifically call for use of cost-benefit comparisons in designing standards.

Finally, the EPA's analysis may have had a greater role here than in other rule makings because of the relative lack of outside pressure for the Agency to act. At the time, there was no organized effort among its major constituencies to reduce gasoline lead levels further. The action was initiated by the EPA, based primarily on its review of recent evidence on lead health effects and the extent of misfueling. More typically, its rules are developed in an atmosphere of great outside pressure to act – perhaps in the form of new legislation from Congress or court suits brought by environmental groups and others. Where there is substantial outside pressure to act, the RIA is frequently viewed as supporting reduced stringency and therefore draws fire from the advocates of more stringent regulation. In the case of lead in gasoline, the RIA clearly promoted increased stringency in the absence of any external mandate to tighten restrictions. Relying on the results of RIAs may be viewed by EPA decision makers and others as more politically acceptable when the analysis supports more stringent rather than more lenient regulatory action than is being proposed by parties outside the Agency.

Land disposal restrictions

Purpose of the rule
The 1984 Hazardous and Solid Waste Amendments (HWSA), amending the Resource Conservation and Recovery Act (RCRA), required the EPA to issue regulations restricting the land disposal of hazardous wastes. This provision of HWSA reflected concerns about the longterm safety of land-based disposal practices, even where facilities comply fully with RCRA design and operating standards, and a strong preference for treatment over land disposal. The legislation established a strict schedule for completing these rules. Certain solvent wastes and wastes containing dioxins were to be restricted first, and then a list of liquid wastes already banned from land disposal in the state of California. Finally, the EPA was to establish a schedule for reviewing and issuing restrictions for all remaining hazardous wastes.

If the EPA failed to meet the deadlines established in the legislation, land disposal restrictions specified in the rule would automatically take effect. In general, land disposal would simply be banned if the EPA did not meet the deadlines, therefore, it has been under substantial pressure to issue a series of land disposal restrictions under a tight schedule.

In general, the objective for the land disposal restrictions was the same as for RCRA in general: to protect human health and the environment. As noted earlier, RCRA does not provide for any balancing of costs and benefits. The HWSA required that land disposal be prohibited for a waste, unless the EPA determined that prohibiting land disposal is not required to protect human health and the environment for as long as the waste remains hazardous. In evaluating potential risks from land disposal, the Agency was directed to consider:

(a) the long-term uncertainties associated with land disposal;
(b) the goal of managing hazardous waste in an appropriate manner in the first instance; and
(c) the persistence, toxicity, mobility, and propensity to bioaccumulate of such hazardous wastes and their toxic constituents."

(RCRA Section 3004 (d))

The Agency was authorized to set standards for treatment that would allow land disposal after treatment of wastes that would otherwise be banned from land disposal.

Policy options
To develop the land disposal restrictions, the EPA had to decide what wastes could be land disposed, with or without prior treatment, and what wastes would be banned from land disposal.

The EPA began the development of the land disposal restrictions rules by proposing an explicit risk-based procedure to be applied for each waste. Under this approach, a waste would be banned from land disposal if it failed a test that was designed to measure potential human health risks due to contamination of drinking water. Specifically, the EPA "back-calculated" the allowed levels of specific toxic compounds in leachate from a waste, starting with an allowable human health risk at the point of exposure. The back-calculation required the EPA to:

• choose allowable health risk levels;
• calculate the levels of toxic compounds in drinking water that would not exceed those risk levels;
• determine what levels in leachate from land disposal would achieve those allowed levels at the drinking-water well, using groundwater fate and transport modelling.

Generators of wastes would then be required to test their waste to see if it would generate a leachate that contained any of the toxic compounds at levels that exceeded the allowed health-based levels, using a test procedure specified in the rule. If the waste failed the test, it would have to be treated prior to land disposal. Any residuals from the treatment would have to pass the leachate test before they could be land disposed. If no treatment technology would produce residuals that passed the leachate test, land disposal of residuals that are no more hazardous than residuals from the "best demonstrated available technology" would be allowed.

The EPA's initial approach therefore relied heavily on explicit calculations of potential human health risk. Technology performance determined requirements only where no available treatment was sufficient to reduce risks to the target levels. Designing the rules required the use of complex and uncertain methodologies for predicting release, fate, transport, exposure, and health effect of toxic compounds.

The EPA described its proposed approach to Congress in oversight hearings. The approach was heavily criticized by both Congress and environmental groups. Critics argued that it did not respond to Congress's strong preference for treatment over land disposal. A major focus of the criticism was the reliability of the methods used to calculate risks.

As a result of the strong negative reaction, the EPA decided to use an entirely different approach to establishing land disposal restrictions. The Agency based restrictions on the capabilities of available treatment technologies, rather than on calculations of potential human health risk. That is, wastes would be banned from land disposal unless they passed a leachate test that would be achieved by the best demonstrated available technology for treating that waste. Some wastes – those that produced a leachate that was no more toxic than leachate produced by a best technology-treated waste – could be land disposed without prior treatment. Wastes that failed this test would have to be treated, and the residuals from treatment would have to pass the test before they could be land disposed.

This new approach required the equivalent of the best available treatment, regardless of the risk posed by the untreated waste. Under this approach, wastes that posed virtually no health risk if land disposed without prior treatment might nonetheless be required to undergo treatment before being land disposed. In addition, some wastes that presented significant risks when land disposed might in theory not be banned from land disposal – if the available treatment technologies were not capable of reducing contaminant levels to acceptable levels. On the face of it, this approach would seem to be less cost-beneficial than the initial approach proposed by the EPA, because the requirements were less closely linked to risks from land disposal. The next section discusses the role of benefits estimates and cost-benefit considerations in the outcome of this rule making.

Role of benefits analyses in decision making
The land disposal restrictions rules represent an extreme among the cases described in this paper. Formal benefits analysis played virtually no role in determining the outcome of the rule making. This case provides a useful illustration of conditions that limit the use of benefits analysis in rule making. This case also illustrates many of the difficult methodological problems that arise in estimating the benefits of certain rules.

The EPA prepared RIAs for each group of land disposal restrictions rules. The first RIA to be completed was the analysis of restrictions on solvent wastes. This RIA compared three regulatory alternatives – the initial risk-based approach, the final technology-based approach, and an outright ban on land disposal of all solvent wastes and residuals from the treatment of solvents.

The benefits analysis in this solvents RIA used standard EPA approaches for predicting reductions in human health risks from consumption of contaminated groundwater. However, it did not calculate aggregate reductions in health effects for the three regulatory alternatives. Two major problems prevented the development of explicit benefits estimates for each alternative.

First, the Agency had estimates of the quantities of solvent wastes managed in land disposal facilities in the baseline, but did not have any information on the composition of those solvent wastes. The RIA simply assumed that all solvent wastes would have to be treated before being land disposed. Distinctions between the risk-based and the technology-based approaches could not be made because the waste characterization information which was needed to predict how much waste would require treatment under each approach was not available.

Second, the Agency did not have information on the characteristics of the land disposal facilities affected by the rule. Specifically, no data were available on the characteristics of the location that would affect potential release and transport of toxics in groundwater, such as net precipitation and groundwater velocity. Neither did the EPA have information on the numbers of people drinking potentially contaminated groundwater at these sites, or on the location of drinking-water wells around the sites. Predicted human health risks are highly sensitive to such location-specific factors, and the range of predicted benefits could be huge, depending on the assumptions made about site-specific characteristics. Without some information on the distribution of affected sites by these characteristics, the EPA did not feel it was valid to estimate aggregate benefits from the proposed rule.

Lack of information on waste and site characteristics has hindered analysis of benefits for many hazardous-waste rules. Since the completion of the solvents RIA, the EPA has taken a number of steps to improve its database on hazardous wastes and hazardous-waste facilities. Even so, the Agency still has to make a number of assumptions about site characteristics, extent of exposure, and waste characteristics in its benefits analyses for RCRA rules. Predicted benefits are usually highly sensitive to these assumptions, which tends to reduce the credibility of benefits estimates for RCRA rules.

In addition, there are substantial technical difficulties with modelling the release and transport of toxic compounds in the sub-surface, which continue to plague analyses of benefits due to reduced groundwater contamination. A detailed discussion of these modelling difficulties is beyond the scope of this chapter. The following, however, are examples of the methodological difficulties the EPA has faced in predicting risks from groundwater contamination:

- lack of reliable methods for predicting how disposal of wastes with specific characteristics contributes to contamination of leachate;
- poor understanding of how toxic compounds are altered in the sub-surface – e.g. through degradation of organics or speciation of metals – and how those alterations affect the toxicity and mobility of these compounds;
- lack of information on the health effects of many potentially toxic compounds found in hazardous wastes.

The benefits analyses prepared by the EPA to accompany the initial land disposal restrictions were therefore limited by severe data gaps, and did not provide measures of aggregate benefits for either the proposed rule or for alternative rules. The RIA did discuss the likely differences in relative costs and benefits among the alternatives in concept, however. The RIA pointed out that the risk-based approach was inherently less likely to over-regulate waste posing low baseline risks. The RIA also presented an example calculation of costs per health case avoided for a site where the reductions in risks would be relatively great. This calculation suggested that, unless a substantial number of people were exposed at the site or the benefits not quantified in the analysis were very large, the cost per cancer case avoided was likely to exceed US$10 million.

It is not clear whether more reliable and complete benefits estimates and cost-benefit comparisons would have altered the Agency's decisions about the design of the land disposal restrictions. The reaction of Congress and other groups to the EPA's initial proposal, however, suggests that cost-benefit considerations played little role in shaping the final rule.

While it is difficult to say with certainty what motivated Congressional reaction to the EPA's initial proposal, a distrust of risk-assessment tools was certainly a major factor. The Congressional hearings focused on the assumptions used by the EPA in back-calculating risk-based restrictions levels. For example, experts in groundwater fate and transport modelling argued that the EPA's models ignored the potential for rapid movement of toxic compounds in fractured rock. The models used by the Agency had assumed a homogeneous, unfractured sub-surface environment. Its choice of assumptions about land disposal facility characteristics was also criticized. For example, critics argued that at a significant number of real facilities, drinking-water wells were closer to land disposal units than the EPA's modelling had assumed.

In addition to concerns about specific risk-assessment methodologies and assumptions, the criticism of the EPA's risk-based approach reflected a more general distrust of land disposal and a preference for treatment. This strong preference for more costly treatment does not appear to be cost-beneficial for many types of wastes, based on the levels of baseline risks usually estimated in the EPA's analysis of risks from land disposal of toxic wastes. Nonetheless, Congress has shown a strong and continuing preference for treatment that permanently reduces the toxicity of wastes over containment in land disposal facilities, despite differences in the cost of waste management that are often significant.

There may be several reasons for this apparent conflict between the low estimated benefits of land disposal regulations and the apparent public desire, as reflected by Congress, to reduce land disposal of toxic wastes to a minimum. Some argue that Congress and the public exaggerate the dangers of land disposal, and would be less likely to restrict land disposal if they truly understood the benefits and costs of such restrictions. Others suggest that the EPA's past analyses of the benefits of regulating land disposal have not adequately measured benefits. These critics argue that the focus on human health risks is too limited, and that benefits analyses should consider ecological risks, welfare effects and resource damages as well. As described earlier, the EPA has not made as much progress in developing methods for assessing environmental benefits as it has for human health benefits. It may be that the environmental benefits of land disposal regulations are substantial and that improving our assessment of such benefits would clarify the real benefits of these regulations.

Finally, the political emphasis on limiting land disposal may reflect a high degree of risk aversion, given the nature of risks from land disposal. Leaching of toxics from land disposal facilities may occur many generations in the future, and is difficult to detect. The risks from drinking water contaminated with leachate vary greatly across facilities, depending on the nature of groundwater collection and treatment, the movement of groundwater and the location of drinking-water wells. Risks may be very limited at most facilities, but very high at a few facilities. Some of the facility characteristics that determine potential risks – such as fractures in the sub-surface – are difficult or impossible to observe. Damages to resources such as groundwater are often extremely costly to reverse, and if not reversed can persist, in some cases, for hundreds of years. It may be that the public is willing to incur high costs to reduce risks that are less detectable, avoidable, and reversible or that affect future generations.

The EPA's benefits analyses typically rely on point estimates of risk reductions, using best estimate or worst case assumptions about baseline risks. The degree of uncertainty about baseline risks and the reductions achieved by regulations is given limited attention at best. Development of better methods for measuring and expressing uncertainty and the effects of inter-generational transfers of risk might help to explain the apparent discrepancy between the political willingness to bear high costs to reduce different types of risk and the estimated benefits of those risk reductions.

In summary, the land disposal restrictions rule represents a relative "failure" in the use of benefits estimates to guide rule making. This is not to say that the approach favoured by Congress and chosen by the EPA was inappropriate. Rather, this case illustrates some of the methodological difficulties with developing credible benefits estimates for hazardous-wastes rules. This case also shows the effects of legislative criteria that do not consider cost-benefit comparisons in limiting the use of benefits estimates.

The EPA continues to make progress in its ability to measure the benefits of such rules, by collecting better data on the affected sites and wastes and by working on methods for estimating benefits other than human health risk reductions. Even with such improvements in the measure of benefits for hazardous-waste rules, however, it is likely that the benefits of such rules will often not outweigh their costs, given the relatively limited numbers of people exposed to hazardous-waste releases. Certainly, hazardous-waste rules are not likely to show the positive net benefits estimated for the lead-in-gasoline rule, for example. The limited role of benefits estimates to date in the design of hazardous-waste regulations therefore focuses attention on two fundamental issues:

(1) Should the RCRA be revised to allow greater consideration of cost-benefit comparisons in designing hazardous waste regulations?
(2) Do traditional cost-benefit analyses capture all aspects of reductions in risk that are valued by the public? Should greater attention be paid to the characteristics of risks – such as uncertainty, risk distribution, or inter-generational effects – to measure benefits accurately?

Regulations governing disposal and uses of sewage sludge

Purpose of the rule
Section 405 of the Clean Water Act as amended in 1987 requires that the EPA regulate the use and disposal of sludge produced by waste-water treatment works. Sludge produced by the treatment of waste waters may contain a variety of chemical and biological constituents, depending on the composition of the waste water and the type of treatment involved. Typical constituents include volatile organics, nutrients, disease-causing pathogens, heavy metals and toxic organics. The Act requires that the EPA identify toxic pollutants in sludge that may adversely affect public health

or the environment, specify management standards and establish numerical limits for each of the pollutants. These standards must be adequate to protect public health and the environment from any reasonably anticipated adverse effects of the pollutants.

In 1989, the EPA proposed regulations governing five conventional practices for sludge use and disposal: incineration; landfilling in sludge-only monofills; land application; distribution and marketing of sludge; and management in surface impoundments. Ocean disposal had been banned by Congress, and co-disposal of sludge with other wastes in municipal landfills will be addressed in forthcoming rules under RCRA.

Policy options
The proposed rules and the major alternatives considered all consist of two components. First, the rules set numerical limits on pollutants in sludge that depend on the type of management selected for the sludge. Treatment facilities may have to clean up their influent, improve their treatment efficiencies, or select different uses or management methods to meet these standards. The limits are based on evaluations of risk in each practice for each pollutant in sludge, based on analysis of a large number of exposure pathways. The proposed rule is similar in concept then to the approach initially proposed by the EPA for the land disposal restrictions programme, in that it back-calculates allowed pollutant levels in wastes based on meeting target maximum risk levels.

The second component of the programme consists of management standards for each practice. These standards include some that are common to all management – e.g. requirements for testing of sludge composition – and others that are specific to each management practice. For example, distributors of sludge to be used as fertilizer must label the product to identify its content and provide instructions for its proper use.

The EPA considered four regulatory options for setting pollutant limits for each use or management practice. These options differ primarily in the use of risk to the maximum exposed individual (MEI), aggregate incidence (or population risk), or a combination of the two, in setting allowable levels. In all options, wastes that meet the standards defining hazardous wastes under RCRA are subject to the RCRA hazardous-waste management standards. Therefore, the proposed sludge rules apply only to wastes that do not qualify as hazardous.

For some relatively low-risk practices, levels are set at the upper end (98th percentile) of concentrations found in current sludges. That is, for application to non-agricultural lands and for management in surface impoundments, most current sludges could continue to be managed as at present. For the higher-risk practices, or where there are significant uncertainties about potential risks, the proposed rule establishes levels based on a combination of MEI and population risks.

Role of benefits analyses in decision making
The proposed sludge rules present a number of issues that are similar to those faced by the Agency in developing the land disposal restrictions. The analysis of benefits performed for this rule exhibits many of the same limitations as those performed for those earlier rules. However, the Agency has made major strides in developing risk-assessment methodologies in the three years since the initial land disposal restrictions proposal. Many new techniques have been applied in designing and analysing the benefits of the sludge rules. The Agency recognizes that these risk-assessment methods may be controversial, and has solicited public comment on a variety of risk-assessment issues. Reaction to this rule will provide an interesting test of the Agency's ability to base regulations on explicit risk assessments, and will focus attention on a number of difficult scientific and policy issues related to risk assessment. The Agency has indicated that it may alter the proposed rule based on public comments and on additional study.

The benefits analysis performed for the sludge rule shares some limitations with earlier analyses done for various hazardous-waste regulations. Benefits are estimated primarily in terms of human health effects. Net benefits are not considered in determining target levels of protection.

The sludge rule RIA does, however, develop estimates of aggregate costs and aggregate health benefits for a portion of the facilities that will be affected by the rule. The RIA considers only publicly owned treatment works (POTWs). To develop aggregate estimates, the EPA used data on POTW sludge composition collected in a 1981 study of POTWs in approximately 40 cities. The Agency acknowledges that this study provides only limited information on baseline sludge characteristics. The original study was not designed to provide a profile of sludge quality, and a number of changes have occurred since 1981 that may have substantially altered the quality of sludges. The EPA has begun a new study of sewage sludge quality that will be used in developing a final rule.

Based on the limited 1981 sludge-quality data, the EPA characterized three types of sludge qualities. It then assigned one of the three sludge-quality assumptions to each POTW, based on estimates of the percentage of influent attributable to industrial sources. POTWs with higher portions of industrial wastes in their influent were assumed to generate the more contaminated sludges.

The assumptions about sludge quality and the distribution of different quality sludges among POTWs are necessary to develop aggregate costs and benefits, but are a major source of uncertainty in the RIA.

The Agency also lacked facility-specific data on current management practices or on factors that would influence a facility's compliance strategy. It was therefore forced to make a number of assumptions about these POTW characteristics to develop estimates of benefits and costs. Again, it is initiating a new survey on use and disposal practices and individual facility characteristics, as well as on sludge quality, to fill in these important data gaps.

The models and assumptions used to estimate benefits are to numerous and complex to describe here. The EPA considered release, fate and transport, exposure, and health effects for some 25 to 30 pathways and for numerous compounds. In general, the benefit analysis measured both maximum exposed individual (MEI) and population human health effects. Ecological benefits were discussed but not quantified.

The RIA estimated total costs for POTWs which were subject to the rule of US$157.7 million annually. The rule is projected to result in 9.5 fewer cancer cases annually (reduced from 12.3 cancer cases in the baseline), and 5,266 fewer cases of health effects due to lead exposure (compared with an estimated 5,998 cases in the baseline). The health effects associated with lead include hypertension, diminished learning capacity in children and prenatal birth effects.

These highly uncertain aggregate cost and benefit estimates did not play a major role in the design of the sludge rule. As with the land disposal restrictions rules, it is not clear that more reliable estimates of aggregate costs and benefits would have been given much greater weight, in light of the lack of consideration given to costs in the enabling legislation.

The extensive risk analysis performed to develop and analyse the sludge rule does appear to have played a useful role in influencing regulatory decision making. For example, the analysis of risks using both MEI and population risk estimates focused attention on cases in which regulation based solely on MEI risk appeared to be too stringent. The Agency decided to use a combined approach, setting more stringent MEI-based levels where the numbers of people likely to be exposed are large, and basing numerical limits on higher MEI risks when the numbers exposed via a particular pathway are expected to be small. More generally, however, it remains to be seen whether Congress and the public will view the risk-assessment methods used in this rule making as a reliable basis for designing a risk-based rule.

Municipal Solid Waste Landfill Rule

Purpose of the rule
The 1984 amendments to RCRA required the EPA to determine if existing standards for sanitary landfills are adequate to protect human health and the environment, and to revise existing standards for landfills that may receive certain hazardous wastes. A proposed revision to the standards for municipal landfills was published in 1988. The EPA is now reviewing public comments on the proposed rule and preparing a final version of the rule.

Policy options
The EPA has considered two general approaches to setting standards for municipal landfills. Under both approaches, the rule would be implemented largely by individual states, with EPA oversight. Under one approach, the EPA would establish minimum design and operating standards for different categories of landfills. The categories would be defined by landfill location characteristics that affect potential human exposure to contaminants in leachate from the landfill – net precipitation and time of groundwater plume travel to a specified point. The other approach defined performance standards which would be translated into specific design and operating standards for each landfill in the permitting process. These two alternatives represent different ways of implementing

the rule, which have implications for the costs imposed by the rule.

Role of benefits analyses in decision making
The RIA for the proposed Municipal Solid Waste Landfill Rule (MSWLF) used two approaches in evaluating the benefits of the rule. The first involved predicting human health effects from drinking-water exposure to contaminated landfill leachate. These health effects were not monetized. As an alternative measure of benefits, the value of lost drinking-water resources was also calculated. The extent of groundwater contamination was predicted, and the cost of replacing contaminated drinking-water supplies was calculated to value the lost resource. The RIA points out that the two approaches provide alternative measures of benefits and are not additive.

Much of the effort devoted to the benefits analysis for this rule involved development of methods to predict landfill releases, leachate characteristics, and fate and transport of toxic contaminants in groundwater. Many of the problems faced in the land disposal restrictions benefits analysis (described above) affected the benefits analysis for this rule as well. The MSWLF RIA was based on more comprehensive information on facility location characteristics than the land disposal restrictions RIA, because the EPA had conducted a survey of municipal landfills that included data on such factors as location of wells. However, the MSWLF benefits analysis still had to rely on numerous assumptions in the absence of complete facility characterizations, including estimates of leachate characteristics.

The MSWLF RIA was the first study of RCRA rules to devote serious attention to resource damages in addition to human health effects. The analysis assumed that groundwater would be unfit for human consumption when pollutant levels were predicted to exceed certain risk-based thresholds or taste/odour thresholds. The model predicting landfill failure and contaminant transport in groundwater provided estimates of the area of the groundwater plume contaminated above these levels. The analysis then valued the lost drinking water at replacement cost. Calculations were based on relatively simple assumptions about the source and cost of replacement drinking-water supplies. Costs were estimated for replacement of drinking water both for current users (characterized as the "use value") and for potential future users (defined as the "option value"). The resource damage estimates included only damages to drinking-water sources – potential damages to surface water were not considered.

Despite the more comprehensive estimates of benefits attempted in the MSWLF RIA, the rule has been found to impose costs well in excess of the estimated benefits. This is true both for the proposed rule and the alternative rules considered, including the minimum standards mandated by legislation. The low estimated cost-effectiveness has prompted extensive consideration of alternative regulatory approaches, including various combinations of design and performance standards. The cost-benefit analysis therefore has had some influence on the EPA's decision making for this rule. Nonetheless, the Agency is likely to promulgate a rule for which the estimated costs exceed estimated benefits by a substantial margin. This case study therefore presents the same dilemma discussed above with reference to the land disposal restrictions: either the methods currently used to assess benefits understate true benefits, despite the attempt to develop more comprehensive benefits estimates for the MSWLF rule, or, the public is demanding (and Congress is requiring) environmental controls more stringent than are justified by cost-benefit criteria.

Summary

A number of factors have been discussed above that affect the use of benefits estimates in environmental decision making in the United States. These comments are based in part on the case studies described above and in part on the authors' general experience with EPA rule making.

Not surprisingly, the cases discussed suggest that cost-benefit comparisons play the greatest role in decision making under the following circumstances:

● Benefits analyses play a greater role in decision making when the conclusions are very robust, and where ignoring uncertain benefits would not alter the policy conclusions. Where uncertainties in the estimates are great, and estimated net benefits might be either positive or negative given the uncertainties, formal benefits analyses are likely to be given less weight.
● Benefits analyses are more likely to influence decisions when the enabling legislation allows the flexibility to consider cost-benefit

comparisons as a criterion for rule making. Furthermore, if the analysis does not go against the political climate then it is likely to have more influence.

Monetized benefits estimates and benefit-cost comparisons are unlikely to play a significant role in environmental rule making unless the statutes authorizing such rules require, or at least allow consideration, of costs in setting standards. In addition, benefits analyses continue to be hindered by substantial limitations in the available data and risk-assessment methodologies.

Much of the discussion in the theoretical literature on benefits analysis focuses on how to value reductions in health risks and environmental damage achieved by regulation. Thus, the relative merits of hedonic studies, wage risk studies, contingent valuation techniques, and travel cost studies have been widely discussed. As described earlier, limited use has been made in the EPA's regulatory analyses of direct measures of willingness to pay – such as contingent valuation measures of the value placed on reduced risk from landfills. It may be that these techniques are simply viewed as too unreliable to provide useful guidance to policy makers. Instead, the EPA's analyses of benefits have generally involved predicting physical improvements in the environment and then attempting to value the outcomes. Often, the difficulties encountered in predicting health and environmental improvements prevent analysts from ever getting to problems of valuation.

In addition, controversy continues about the validity of calculating monetary values of human health risks by whatever means. The validity of discounting future benefits is particularly controversial, and decisions about whether or not to discount and at what rate can have substantial effects on the calculated net benefits of many rules, with benefits far in the future.

Beyond the issues of valuation, the EPA has encountered many difficult methodological issues in preparing physical measures of benefits. The land disposal restrictions and sludge rule cases illustrate the substantial data collection needed to support benefits analyses for many rules. In addition, these cases illustrate the need for better methods for predicting the relationship between the actions of the regulated community and resulting risks to human health and the environment. Ideally, more direct evidence on the relationship between human activities and actual contamination levels and health effects would be desirable. For example, a direct estimate of the relationship between gasoline-lead levels and blood-lead levels proved useful in estimating the benefits of the lead-in-gasoline rule. Unless more effort is made to collect data on direct measures of health and environmental effects, and to link these effects to specific causes, the EPA will have to continue developing modelling approaches to predict release, fate, transport, exposure and health effects for a variety of exposure pathways.

References

Mitchell, R. and Carson, R. (1989) *Using Surveys to Value Public Goods: The Contingent Valuation Method*, Resources for the Future: Washington, D.C.

US Environmental Protection Agency, Office of Air and Radiation (1988) *Regulatory Impact Analysis on the National Ambient Air Quality Standards for Sulfur Oxides (Sulfur Dioxide)*.

US Environmental Protection Agency, Office of Policy Analysis (1985) *Costs and Benefits of Reducing Lead in Gasoline – Final Regulatory Impact Analysis*.

US Environmental Protection Agency, Office of Policy Analysis (1989) *Summary of Ecological Risks, Assessment Methods, and Risk Management Decisions in Superfund and RCRA*.

US Environmental Protection Agency, Office of Policy Planning and Evaluation (1987) *EPA's Use of Benefit-Cost Analysis: 1981–1986*.

US Environmental Protection Agency, Office of Solid Waste (1986) *Regulatory Analysis of Restrictions on Land Disposal of certain Solvent Wastes*.

US Environmental Protection Agency, Office of Solid Waste (1988) *Regulatory Impact Analysis of Proposed Revisions to Subtitle D Criteria for Municipal Solid Waste Landfills*.

US Environmental Protection Agency, Office of Water, Economic Analysis Branch (1989) *Regulatory Impact Analysis of the Proposed Regulations for Sewage Sludge Use and Disposal*.

US General Accounting Office (1984) *Cost-Benefit Analysis Can Be Useful in Assessing Environmental Regulations, Despite Limitations*, Report to Congress by the Comptroller General, April 6.

Index

Printed in the United States
by Baker & Taylor Publisher Services